CROSSCURRENTS IN WORLD HISTORY

GENERAL EDITOR, NORMAN F. CANTOR

Abelard and Heloise

D. W. ROBERTSON, JR.

THE DIAL PRESS / NEW YORK / 1972

TO THE MEMORY OF

DURANT W. ROBERTSON (1886–1971)

*whose resourcefulness, courage, and inventiveness
led him from a rural hamlet in the South
to a high position in one of
the world's great corporations.*

Contents

[vii]

CONTENTS

Illustrations

(following page 112)

[ix]

Preface

*P*eter Abelard ranks as one of the most brilliant and original thinkers of the Middle Ages. When antecedents for the work of the great scholastics of the thirteenth and fourteenth centuries, men like St. Thomas Aquinas, Duns Scotus, or William of Ockham, are sought in the twelfth century, Abelard's name comes naturally to mind. Abelard is thought of as a rebel, a radical innovator, one of those few men whose insights enable them to open up new perspectives to be exploited fruitfully in the future.

St. Augustine had said in his great treatise *On Christian Doctrine* that "the science of disputation is of great value for solving all sorts of questions that appear in sacred literature," and it is this science, called "dialectic" in the twelfth century, that Abelard sought to master and to apply to the study of the Scriptures. He was beyond doubt the most distinguished logician of his day, but he was also a forceful and stubborn man, impatient with opposition and frequently tactless in his treatment of more conventional thinkers among his contemporaries. His contentiousness, however, did not imply any lack of faith. Far from wishing to attack the faith with reason, he strove to clarify it and to defend it. He once wrote to Heloise with unquestionable sincerity, "I do not wish to

[xi]

be a philosopher, if that means that I contradict St. Paul; I do not wish to be a disciple of Aristotle, if that means that I separate my-self from Christ." His efforts were those of a pioneer, and he did not create a "system" of the kind we associate with the *Summa Theologica* of St. Thomas.

Scholars of the nineteenth century, shocked by Abelard's juxta-position of conflicting Patristic opinions in his work *Sic et non* and by his emphasis on reason, tended to exaggerate his ration-alism. Taking note of his affair with Heloise and the strong oppo-sition of St. Bernard to Abelard's teachings, they thought of him as a free thinker, a kind of romantic rebel against the oppressive authoritarianism of the Church. Modern scholars, looking more closely at the culture of the twelfth century, have found Abelard less strange as a product of his time. Methods similar to those sug-gested in the *Sic et non* had been used earlier by students of canon law, and it is clear from Abelard's Preface that he had no desire to belittle Patristic authority but rather to sift and evaluate Patristic doctrines. St. Thomas was later to do this quite openly and to make a disciplined use of logic in formulating his own conclusions.

Many of Abelard's contemporaries admired his keenness of mind, and his lectures, famous for their clarity and vigor, attracted a multitude of students from all parts of Europe. But there were some who found his teachings dangerous, not because they were "pagan" or anti-religious in their implications, but because they seemed technically inconsistent with established principles. His method, the application of logic to revealed truth, also alarmed those who were rooted in the traditional methods of the past, which often involved "Scriptural collation," or the collection of relevant Scriptural quotations on a given point, rather than dispu-tation. Again, Abelard was fond of new terminology, and he liked to use old terms with new meanings. Both of these inclinations invited confusion and misunderstanding.

One term to which he gave a new meaning, which it has since retained, is the word *theology* itself. In the Latin tradition it had been used to describe pagan beliefs of the kinds described by Varro as "fabulous theology," or mythology, "civil theology," or beliefs associated with public cults, and "natural theology." But Abelard, to the disgust of some who knew him, did not hesitate to call one of his books *Christian Theology*, and another concerned with matters of the faith *An Introduction to Theology*. Neither St. Augustine nor St. Jerome would have called himself a "theologian," and it is difficult for most of us today to remember that technical studies by Latin Christian writers before Abelard were either studies in "divinity," or studies in "the Sacred page."

Abelard's fellow-masters were sometimes repulsed by his character, which did not make his innovations any easier to bear. In his youth especially he was extremely aggressive, vain, and disputatious. Any logician with a reputation attracted him as a natural enemy to be subdued. His spectacular success with students inspired envy and concern among others, and, at the same time, inflated his own self-esteem. It is true that he eventually came to recognize these weaknesses in himself, but too late to benefit his reputation, which was finally almost destroyed by the attacks of St. Bernard. The vigor of his mind, combined with a deeply serious sense of the importance of his own teachings, may have been responsible for his success, but it also provoked antagonism.

A few of Abelard's contemporaries were undoubtedly suspicious of him because of his sordid affair with Heloise, which injured his fame and impeded his advancement in the Church. But without the sobering effect of his castration and the influence of the mature Heloise, Abelard might have remained a relatively obscure figure, known chiefly as a great and influential master in the schools. Some of his voluminous writings were composed especially for Heloise after she had become Abbess of the Paraclete. Although it is risky to speculate concerning historical alternatives, it seems possible that Abelard might not have written very much at all, aside from treatises for the immediate use of his students, without her steadying influence and the availability of the Paraclete as a repository for his books. We should be willing to accord Heloise some credit for nourishing Abelard's literary ambitions and encouraging the production of his works.

Aside from *The Letters of Abelard and Heloise*, Abelard's works are seldom read today except by specialists, even though he was in part responsible for stimulating the development of what we call "theology," and for preparing the way for the great scholastic philosophers. But the legend of his affair with Heloise, after its inception in the late seventeenth century, has flourished in suc-ceeding centuries as one of the great love stories of all time. The legend still dominates the view of Abelard in the popular imagi-nation, and even colors, at times to the point of distortion, scholarly accounts of his career. He is thus a peculiarly fascinating figure because of his dual impact on European cultural history, first as a great teacher and philosopher, and then, many years after his death, as one of the world's great lovers.

There is something very attractive about the idea of a man who is at once a great philosopher and a great lover, and it is perhaps unfortunate that the philosopher and the lover must here be sep-arated by over five hundred years. There are, in effect, two "Abelards," each of whom has profoundly influenced subsequent generations. The second Abelard, moreover, has influenced the first Abelard, at least in reputation, producing a tangle of fact and fiction of a kind that makes history one of the most fascinating (and diverting) of all studies. Both Abelards are described in the pages that follow. There is first an account of Abelard's life. It is impossible to write a very full account without resorting to con-jecture, but I have tried carefully to distinguish conjecture from verifiable fact, so that the reader can identify my own attempts at elaboration. There follows a brief survey of the high points of the legend of Heloise, in which the second Abelard appears in a num-ber of different guises. In this legend both Abelard and Heloise shamelessly adapt themselves to current fashions, shifting to flatter succeeding stylistic tastes. Economic, social, and cultural changes have given them a remarkable plasticity. Even here there is room for differing interpretations, especially where the major documents are concerned, but I have thought it best to set forth my own views, without calling attention to the views of others, a procedure that would lead the reader into a maze of footnotes inappropriate in a book of this kind.

In Chapter XI especially I have quoted a great deal of English verse, mostly from Alexander Pope's *Eloisa to Abelard*. I am aware of the fact that because of certain inadequacies in our educational system most people do not read verse willingly. In fact, many often skip quoted verse passages in the hope that all they need to know will emerge from the surrounding context. I should like to assure the readers of this book, however, that the English verse quoted is far more worthy of careful attention than my own prose. Our earlier English poets of recognized stature always had something very definite to say, and they usually said it very well. I urge those unaccustomed to verse to read it in sentences, not line by line, and to forget anything they may have learned in school about the awesome mysteries (and consequent dullness) of "poetry." Good verse is like fine wine. It may seem unworthy of much acclaim to the uninitiated, but experience, if it is not encumbered by too much pedantic and irrelevant "instruction," lends it savor. A good wine, however, often tastes best in its own region. I hope that my efforts to place the verse in its cultural "region" will not encumber it, but make it more palatable, so that readers may wish to read all of Pope's poem, and not simply the passages quoted. The legend of Heloise has produced no finer work.

Certain acknowledgments are here in order. First, the quotations from Hugh of St. Victor in Chapter II are from pages 94–97 of *The Didascalicon of Hugh of St. Victor*, translated by Jerome Taylor and published by the Columbia University Press in 1961. In Chapter VIII *The Metalogicon of John of Salisbury*, translated by David D. McGarry, and originally published by the University of California Press in 1955, is quoted by permission of the Regents of the University of California. Finally, the quotations from Jean de Meun in Chapter IX are from the excellent translation by Charles R. Dahlberg, *The Romance of the Rose*, copyright © 1971 by the Princeton University Press, here reprinted by permission. I am grateful to these publishers for allowing me to use this material.

Quotations from the Bible in this book are from the Douay version, which is the English version closest to the text Abelard knew in Latin.

Other more general kinds of indebtedness will be apparent to alert readers. For example, I have used details, especially about twelfth-century Paris, from the excellent book by Urban T. Holmes, Jr., *Daily Living in the Twelfth Century*, which is the fruit of years of patient research. Perhaps some of the many students who have been privileged to hear Professor Holmes in person may, in reading the following pages, recognize my indebtedness to him with pleasant memories of a grand laugh and a contagious appetite for a detailed knowledge of medieval life. The list of useful books about Abelard, or Heloise, or both together, is too long to produce here. I might mention, however, that the second part of Charlotte Charrier's book on Heloise, which is unfortunately not available in English, is an indispensable guide to the legend.

It is customary at the close of a preface of this kind to include tributes of a more personal nature. My wife, Betty, has, in the course of my labors, both on this book and on others earlier, not only shielded me from those domestic difficulties so vividly described by Heloise, but has also patiently endured my own distracted airs, irritating refusals to engage in a more sociable life, and general intransigence. I do not know how to thank her.

PART I

Peter Abelard

CHAPTER I

Youth

Peter "Abelard," as he called himself, was the eldest son of Berengar of Le Pallet, probably lord of a small fief in the diocese of Nantes near the eastern border of Brittany. The name "Abelard" has been found spelled in thirty-seven different ways in medieval sources, and it is not, in any event, important, since if young Peter had followed in the footsteps of his father, he would have been known simply as Peter of Le Pallet. It is possible that "Abelard" meant something, as medieval names frequently did. For example, one prominent twelfth-century theologian was called "Peter the Eater." But if there is a pun in the name, we have lost its meaning. We know almost nothing of Abelard's family, and little about his first years beyond the fact that he was born in 1079. However, it is possible to learn something about conditions in Brittany during the late eleventh century and to supply a conjectural background.

When Abelard was born, Brittany was an independent country whose Duke, Hoël (1066–1084), had done much to quiet the feudal warfare that had disturbed the region during the earlier part of the century. He had been by inheritance Count of Cornuaille and Nantes, and when he succeeded his wife's father, Conan II, as Duke, he became Count of Rennes, Vannes, and Browerec, so that he held a great part of the duchy as his own domain. It is likely that Abelard's father Berengar assisted him in his various military enterprises, among them a campaign to aid Fulk Rechin of Anjou against Normandy in 1073–1074 and another against the rebellious Raoul de Gaël, who had returned to his Breton estates after having been expelled from the Earldom of East Anglia by King William of England. We read of a certain "Daniel of Le Pallet" among Duke Hoël's followers, a name that suggests a relationship with Abelard's family. Both Duke Hoël and his successor Alain Fergent (1084–1112) were on good terms with their Angevin neighbors to the east. Having lost his first wife, Constance, daughter of King William, Alain married Ermengarde, the daughter of the notorious Fulk Rechin of Anjou. She, however, was a pious, virtuous, and very able lady, who administered her duchy with great skill during Alain's absence on crusade between 1096 and 1101. And after his death she went to Jerusalem at the invitation of her brother, or half-brother, King Fulk, where she built a church over Jacob's Well. Meanwhile, the Bretons were traditionally on good terms with the great house of Blois. The Duchess Berte, the mother of Duke Hoël's wife, had been a beloved member of the family of Blois. At the time Abelard was born, therefore, Brittany was relatively peaceful and on good terms with its neighbors to the east, and thus it remained during his childhood.

In the normal course of events, young Peter as the first son of a feudal lord would have been heir to his father's domain. He would have been trained to serve in the hall, would have learned the intricacies of feudal administration, and by the time he was fourteen or fifteen, would have acquired proficiency in horsemanship and the use of arms. He could then look forward to attendance at the court of Alain and Ermengarde, following it about on its journeys around the duchy. But the relative peace of the country probably encouraged Berengar to pursue other aims for his son. His father, as Abelard tells us in his *History of My Calamities*, "had been educated a little in letters before he girded on the sword of knighthood. Whence he was afterward so filled with a love of learning that he decided to instruct any sons he might have in letters before they studied arms." This means that the Lord of Le Pallet had learned Latin in his boyhood. It is probable that his literary tastes were encouraged by Duke Hoël, who not only maintained a Breton harpist and a French minstrel in his court, but took a positive interest in books. In any event, Berengar was careful to see that his little son Peter was well instructed.

Abelard's family seems to have been relatively prosperous and to have had some influence among the noblemen of Blois and Anjou, as well as at the Royal Court in France. If the ancestral estate was typical, it consisted first of all of a fortified wooden tower set up on stilts or wooden columns over a courtyard on an artificial mound, or *motte*. A ditch and a thick hedge or palisade offered protection at the base of the *motte*, and there might be another further up. The lord's hall, where he ate and administered justice to his tenants, unless he had a seneschal to perform that duty, was on the first floor. Above was a *solar*, or chamber for the women and children of the household. Nearby were the outbuildings: the stables, a smithy, a granary, perhaps a winepress, *loges*, or open-roofed sheds, and huts for the servants. Chickens and other domestic fowl wandered about the workyard. A separate garden, enclosed by a palisade, contained fruit trees, herbs, flowers, and vegetables for the kitchen. This would have been a favorite place for the ladies to assemble on warm evenings. At some distance away, by the river, was a mill where the tenants came with their grain. And not far away was the village of small wooden huts with dirt floors occupied by the villeins, who, in late eleventh-century Brittany, were not serfs, but villein tenants not tied to the soil. In addition to working the lands they held from Berengar, they spent a certain number of days on Berengar's own lands and contributed certain donations of flesh, fowl, and produce to his household.

Dominating the village was the church, which in eleventh-century Brittany was likely to be occupied by a married priest whose father had been priest there before him. Hereditary priests were common at the time and caused little scandal, especially since a number of prominent bishops had been succeeded in office by their sons. On Sundays and feast days Berengar and his family would join the rest of the community at church, except on those great festivals when the lord and his lady were expected to attend upon the Duke. Berengar knew his tenants well, sharing the problems of the agricultural year with them, rejoicing with them at marriages, baptisms, or other celebrations, and mourning with them for their dead. The older men were especially well known to him, since he often relied on their memories when tenant boundaries or the customs of the fief were in question. Altogether, the community at Le Pallet had something of the atmosphere of a large family, joined to the more distinguished family of the Duke's court by Berengar's attendance there, perhaps with one or more brothers, uncles, and relatives from other parts of the duchy. Society generally was structured on a network of close personal relationships.

It is probable that young Peter was an exceptionally alert and questioning child with a generous share of self-confidence, energy, and initiative. He took to the instruction supplied by his father with enthusiasm. We do not know who gave him his first lessons, but we do know that the lords of Brittany frequently patronized *grammatici,* or clerks specializing in Latin studies. Abelard probably began by memorizing a psalm in Latin without understanding any of it, and then, on the basis of this text, had his first lessons in the intricacies of the Latin tongue. Early instruction included the elements of the faith: the Paternoster, or Lord's Prayer, the Apostles' Creed, the "Athanasian" Creed, selections from the Scriptures, the *Distichs* of Cato, and some instruction in the lives of the saints. If time permitted, the boy may have been introduced to Seneca, Cicero, Virgil, Lucan, Statius, and that favorite Latin poet of the period, Ovid. All this began when he was about seven, or even a little sooner.

Whoever his teacher may have been, he soon turned young Peter's aspirations away from Nantes, Rennes, and the court of Brittany toward the great cathedral cities of the east and north: Angers, Tours, Orléans, and Paris itself. The peace of the countryside and the general tranquility of the duchy probably made Nantes seem unattractive to a boy who wished to excel in some area where mastery was quickly rewarded. A sword without battles is a heavy ornament, and the tales of chivalry that Peter heard from his father probably sounded inspiring but remote. With his father's coopera- tion we can imagine his setting off for school as soon as he had mastered the elementary texts supplied by his tutor. Learning was the key to rapid advancement in the ecclesiastical hierarchy, espe- cially when there was an additional opportunity for aristocratic patronage. Thus the boy probably rode off one brisk September morning, attended by some trusted servants and perhaps by an older member of the family, all mounted on good horses with trap- pings newly furbished in the workyard below Berengar's hall, along narrow winding roads through forests and fields toward a cathedral town. We do not actually know where Peter received his early education, but probability favors Angers, whose school had ac- quired an excellent reputation.

The fame of the cathedral school of Angers was largely due to Marbod, who was *scholasticus*, or master, there from 1067 to 1081, when he was made Archdeacon, transferring his energies from the tutelage of boys to practical administrative affairs, although he undoubtedly continued to influence the school, which passed suc- cessively to two of his pupils, Geoffrey Babion and Ulger. The latter, who became master in 1107, was eventually made Bishop of Angers (1125). In 1096 Marbod became Bishop of Rennes, leav- ing Angers until shortly before his death in 1123, when he re- turned to retire in the Benedictine monastery of St. Aubin. Among his more famous pupils at Angers was a countryman of young Peter's, Robert of Arbrissel, who was to become a famous preacher and to found the Abbey of Fontevrault, which attracted many noble ladies, including the wife of our earliest troubadour, Duke William IX of Aquitaine. The abbey contained both men and women. They lived in strict separation, in spite of rumors about their behavior, but the entire establishment was ruled by an Ab- bess, a fact which made it unique among convents at the time. The idea of allowing a woman to rule men was later to provoke Abe- lard's disdain. Legend, or perhaps gossip, has it that Robert was the son of a priest who married a proud and noble lady who gave herself airs by calling herself "priestess." But this story may very well have arisen as a jocular expression of disapproval among those who were shocked by the unique organization of Fontevrault. The abbey actually enjoyed great success, and many distinguished persons, including Eleanor of Aquitaine, Henry II of England, and Richard the Lionhearted, were buried there. But Robert has left us no literary remains, and other scholars who studied at Angers before young Peter went there (if indeed he did) have more secure literary reputations.

One of the chief pursuits of the cathedral schools during the later eleventh century was the careful study of classical Latin poetry and the composition of Latin verses. In this respect Marbod himself excelled, although his poems have an obvious moral flavor. He was especially downright in his poetic warnings against women, for he thought a woman to be a kind of natural snare of the Devil. Marbod's Latin was not always classical in tone. He was in this respect much inferior to his contemporary Hildebert of Lavardin, whom he knew, and who was the finest Latin poet of the period. Marbod was a good teacher, however, and one of his more distinguished students was Baudry of Bourgueil, who has been hailed as a "true man of letters," if not the first of the kind in the Middle Ages. In the course of a busy ecclesiastical career Baudry composed not only a history of the conquest of Jerusalem, but a whole series of Latin poems, many of them light, and from the point of view of some of his contemporaries, "frivolous." He was especially attracted by the "levity" of Ovid as he called it, and he wrote deliberately to please the young. Love poems were not, therefore, beyond his capability, and he wrote imitations of Ovid's *Heroides*. In his expressed taste for a quiet rural life with a garden and flowery meadows nearby he almost seems to anticipate Philippe de Vitry and Petrarch in the fourteenth century.

Marbod's school would thus have been well known for its "grammatical" studies, or studies in eloquence based on classical models, at the time Peter decided to go there. But there was another kind of eloquence that was attracting the more alert minds of the late eleventh century: dialectic, or the art of constructing probable arguments. The most formidable proponent of dialectic at the time was Berengar of Tours, who was for a time Archdeacon of Angers. In his youth he studied under the great Fulbert of Chartres, whom he is said to have scandalized by belittling the liberal arts to maintain that the study of dialectic is superior to the study of *auctores*, or classical authors. He won notoriety through his espousal of an Augustinian or "spiritual" attitude toward the Eucharist, denying the material (but not the spiritual) presence of the flesh and blood of Christ in the sacrament. For this he was severely condemned, although the Church did not officially adopt the attitude he opposed until the Fourth Lateran Council of 1215. In some ways his career looks forward to that of Abelard himself, although he had no Heloise, and refused, in fact, to remain in the presence of women, whom he regarded as distractions unworthy of a philosopher. But in his general attitude he was a firm supporter of reason, enjoying quotations from St. Augustine such as the following observation from the treatise *On Music*, which he used in his tract against Lanfranc: "But I blush before that imbecility that seeks to fortify reason with authority, for nothing should be more excellent than the authority of reason and truth, which is of more worth than any man." A somewhat similar attitude, although never expressed quite so forcefully, was to be responsible both for Abelard's success and for his downfall.

Names like Marbod, Baudry, Geoffrey Babion, Ulger, and that of the notorious Berengar of Tours must have occupied young Peter's thoughts as he rode toward Angers, a pleasant city rising amid a fertile and productive countryside on the banks of the Maine. The unmistakable stamp of Angevin order on the surrounding fields and vineyards, and on the well-planned town with its dominating cathedral, parts of whose Romanesque walls are still in place, must have inspired the youth from the comparative remoteness of Brittany with a new sense of opportunity. Here was a new world, a gateway to a kind of fame his father's estates could not in themselves provide. Peter set about his studies with vigor. "As for me," he tells us, "the more I studied and the more easily I progressed, the more ardently I pursued the discipline of letters, and became so seduced by love of them that, abandoning the pomp of knightly glory, and leaving the inheritance and the rights of the first born to my brother, I gave up the court of Mars that I might be nourished in the bosom of Minerva." This decision, however, was probably not made until his father was convinced that the nourishment provided by Minerva would lead to a brighter future than the tutelage of Mars in the court of Alain Fergent could offer. Ultimately, father and son alike looked forward to the time when Peter would be a great abbot or a distinguished bishop. Even the title "Peter of Nantes" would probably have satisfied Berengar.

We know little about the actual circumstances of educational procedure at the early cathedral schools. The academic year was continuous, but it probably began formally on September 14, the Festival of the Exaltation of the Holy Cross. The students, who varied considerably in age and background, may have been divided at Angers into older and younger groups, although there was as yet no real "graded" system of classifying students. A boy simply took a course until he passed it satisfactorily. There is some slight evidence to indicate that Abelard studied under Ulger, but since Ulger did not become *scholasticus* at Angers until after Abelard had established a reputation of his own, it is reasonable to suppose that Ulger assisted Geoffrey Babion with the younger boys until he succeeded Geoffrey as master of the school. Lessons probably began after Lauds, early in the morning, and lasted all day with interruptions for the cathedral services. The students usually sat on rushes on a stone floor in an unheated room that was poorly lighted, especially in the morning, the late afternoon, and on cloudy days. At night they studied and prepared their lessons by the light of a candle. In the courses in the *trivium*—grammar, rhetoric, and logic—the morning hours were devoted to examining and correct-ing the work of the students. A considerable amount of memoriza-tion was required, for the most accessible texts are those one has in one's head, and the students were urged to imitate the texts they studied in their own Latin, a practice that encouraged a cer-tain amount of exhibitionism, especially with regard to vocabulary.

Discipline, both behavioral and intellectual, was enforced with a rod, regarded as a cure either for misbehavior or erroneous answers. This method undoubtedly discouraged those who had no real thirst for knowledge and eliminated boys with weak constitutions. But it did produce a few able scholars. In addition to the arts, the students read the Scriptures, which included, in the eleventh century, the writings of the Fathers. In his later years Abelard exhibited an excellent grounding in the Scriptures and the Fathers, especially Augustine and Jerome, and a firm command of the *auctores*, especially Ovid, Lucan, Seneca, and Cicero. All this knowledge did not arise spontaneously; it was undoubtedly acquired slowly and systematically, if not at Angers, then at some school not unlike it.

Like Berengar of Tours before him, Abelard became especially fascinated by dialectic. As he puts it in his *History of My Calamities*, "And since I preferred the art of dialectical exercise in arms among all the teachings of philosophy, I exchanged literal arms for these, and sought instead of the trophies of war those of disputation. Thus wandering about the provinces disputing wherever I heard this art to be thriving, I became an emulator of the Peripatetics." This activity earned him the epithet "the Peripatetic of Pallet," which was intended to be slighty humorous. St. Augustine had warned that although the science of disputation is useful, it may lead to an unfortunate "love of controversy," or even to "a certain puerile ostentation in deceiving an adversary." Just how deceptive young Peter was we do not know, but his military activities with probable arguments certainly exhibit "puerile ostentation," especially as he himself describes them. It may be that he was actually not quite so brash as he says he was, but it is certain that he was ambitious for fame and fortune. We can imagine him setting forth, after some years at Angers, with the blessings of Ulger, traveling inland again with a retinue of servants, this time toward Loches, where the famous Roscelin was teaching. Loches was an ancient seat of the House of Anjou located on the Indre beneath a high cliff, where work was beginning on a great stone donjon of the type that was to replace the wooden towers Peter had known in childhood. Roscelin had been condemned for some rather naive views concerning the Trinity, had recanted, and, after some time spent in exile, had returned to set up a school. Because of his reputed attitude toward the "universals," he is often celebrated as an early "nominalist."

The question of the "universals" that troubled so many masters of the late eleventh and early twelfth centuries had, originally, nothing to do with Platonic universals, or "ideas." Moreover, it had little direct bearing on matters of faith. It is true that there was a marked tinge of what might be loosely called "Platonism" in ordinary Christian thought. St. Paul's admonition that "the invisible things of God" are to be understood through "the things that are made" stimulated an interest among Christians in a world of the "intelligible" made up of things available to the understanding rather than directly to the senses. Although a "realm of the intelligible" was commonplace in much late antique pagan philosophy, this realm, in its Christian form, was not the product of a system of metaphysics. For example, St. Augustine regarded wisdom among human beings as a transient and imperfect reflection of an eternal and immutable Wisdom that he identified with Christ. In a similar way, most medieval Christians thought of the virtues as being not simply forms of behavior, or even concepts, but as realities outside themselves originating in God, which they themselves might reflect when they learned to love them for the sake of God. This attitude remained relatively unchanged throughout the Middle Ages, and is still evident, for example, in the writings of Petrarch, in spite of scholastic definitions based on Aristotle which made the virtues "habits of the soul." But the inclusion of revealed truths among unchanging realities did not in itself constitute a system of metaphysics. Spiritual realities were thought to underlie physical realities much in the same way that the "spirit that vivifies" lies beneath the "letter that kills" of the Old Testament.

The "universals" that concerned the early masters of medieval cathedral schools were simply the *genera* and *species* of Aristotelian logic, or, to put it simply, classes. For example, if we say, "Socrates is a man," we mean in effect, "Socrates is a particular individual belonging to the class (or 'universal') *man*." Or at least that is what we mean if we are using Aristotelian argument. There are other possibilities. For example, we might emphasize the word *man* to mean that Socrates is a truly outstanding individual, or, in theological discussion, we might mean simply that Socrates is a descendant of Adam. But if we use words like *man* very often to mean classes and we wish to be precise about them, it is natural that we should ask ourselves what such classes actually represent. Are classes things, convenient fictions, mere words, concepts, abstractions, metaphysical realities, or some combination of these, or something else entirely? This is not a completely idle question; a similar problem once occupied certain modern physicists in connection with their formulations concerning quantum theory. And it is true today that a great many people use words for classes without much reflection.

The masters of the early twelfth century had no clear answer to the problem of *genera* and *species* before them, either in Porphyry's *Isagoge*, an introductory treatise, or in the *Categories* and *Peri Hermeneias* of Aristotle available to them in the translations of Boethius. During Abelard's lifetime other works of Aristotle— the *Prior Analytics*, the *Posterior Analytics*, the *Topics*, and the *Sophistical Arguments*—were gradually being discovered, but the *Metaphysics* and the treatise *On the Soul* needed to complete the system were not known until later. There was, therefore, plenty of room for speculation and controversy. Traditionally, if a philosopher attributes a metaphysical reality to a class like *man*, he is called a "realist," and if he fails to do so he is called a "nominalist." It is still fashionable to speak of twelfth-century dialecticians in terms of nominalism or realism, with Roscelin standing almost alone in the nominalist position, although some authorities now place Abelard beside him. Historians of philosophy, searching for antecedents for St. Thomas, often reserve their accolades for thinkers who can be called "moderate realists," but this procedure invites a considerable over-simplification of the problem. The philosophers of the first half of the twelfth century produced an astonishing variety of theories about the nature of classes, and it is not always easy to fit these theories into any kind of scale between nominalism and realism, or even at times to say whether a given author is a nominalist or a realist. John of Salisbury, who remarks jokingly that there were as many theories as there were heads, gives us a little survey of contemporary opinion in Chapter 17 of the second book of his *Metalogicon*, adding his own observations and criticisms in Chapter 20. His conclusion indicates that he thought most of the controversy to be of small importance, and it is true that the argument subsided after about the middle of the twelfth century.

Roscelin shocked Anselm of Bec by saying that the classes in logical discourse are mere audible words (*voces*), and he was probably still maintaining this view when Abelard came to study under him. We should understand that this rather restricted view of logical terms, which probably originated in a distinction suggested by Boethius between "words" and "things," does not mean that Roscelin did not believe in revealed truth, or that he neglected "the invisible things of God," or that he was in any modern sense a rationalist. He simply thought that classes are not in themselves things, but are rather verbal devices for saying something about something else. Young Peter, as might be expected, disagreed with his master, contending that *genera* and *species* should not be called *voces*, or audible words, but *sermones*.

What did Abelard mean by *sermones*? It used to be fashionable to translate *sermones* as "word concepts," and to call Abelard a "conceptualist." But this view has been severely criticized, for Abelard did not elaborate a system of concepts in connection with his logic. It might be better to translate *sermones* as "elements in meaningful discourse," the meanings of which are established by human convention. It is clear that Abelard did not elaborate any metaphysical implications that *genera* and *species* might be said to suggest. He was not sufficiently impressed by the work of the school of Chartres, where Platonic philosophy was cultivated on the basis of a knowledge of the *Timaeus*, to develop their implications along Platonic lines. Bernard of Chartres held that the classes

represent exemplary forms based on eternal forms in the mind of
God, but Abelard seems to have been primarily interested in their
purely verbal significance. It is possible to look upon his *sermones*
as being not much more than an elaboration of Roscelin's *voces*,
designed to give them more contextual relevance in discourse. John
of Salisbury, who had a more thorough knowledge of Aristotle
than was available to Abelard, did not show any sympathy for
Abelard's doctrine of *sermones*. But we should not belittle Abelard
because he lacked the library facilities, so to speak, that were
available to later writers.

Roscelin undoubtedly stimulated the interest, and the opposition,
of his eager young pupil, and he probably watched his departure
with relief. He was later to exhibit marked animosity toward him,
a fact that strongly hints at the sharpness of Abelard's weapons.
Exactly where else our young Peripatetic went seeking out opponents to overcome we do not know. It is not unlikely, however,
that he traveled up the Loire to Tours, where the canons of the
Cathedral of St. Martin were still praying regularly for the soul
of Berengar. Abelard was later to address a letter to them. Perhaps
he went on to Orléans, which was becoming a center for the study
of the Latin classics, and he may have proceeded as far as Troyes,
where he made some acquaintances who were to help him later on.
All this would have required considerable time, but would have
enormously enriched his experience, introducing him to a wide
variety of opinions, texts, and lecturing techniques. Moreover, he
probably met a number of prominent noblemen because of his
connection with the court of Brittany, and it would be interesting
to have his remarks about them. It is a shame that he tells us no
more about his travels in his *History*, but simply says, "Eventually
I came to Paris, where the discipline of dialectic used to flourish
especially, approaching as my master William of Champeaux, who
was both in fact and reputation foremost among dialecticians."
Here at last was the master of them all, but young Peter was quite
ready to unsheathe his sword once more.

We can imagine him approaching the city that had become the
heart of the Kingdom of France along the road from Orléans, ob-

[15]

taining his first glimpse of it as he looked down on the valley of the Seine from the left bank. The slope toward the river was still largely taken up with fields and vineyards, but a large building about four hundred feet long and three hundred feet wide would have caught his eye on the left side of the road. This was the Palais de Hautefeuille, a Roman edifice still containing some pagan altars and columns. We do not know its original purpose, but in the twelfth century some said it was the original home of Ganelon, whose treason, immortalized in the story of Roland, was easily associated with paganism. It became the meeting place of the mer-chants of the city. Farther down amid some fields and outbuildings on the left stood a trapezoidal building called the Thermes. Again, it was of Roman origin and uncertain purpose. On the right of the road a cluster of small streets and houses below some larger structures marked Ste. Geneviève, a house of Augustinian canons below which were houses largely occupied by students. Farther down the road the rue de Garlande led off to the right toward a marketplace, and some distance beyond that near the little river Bièrre stood a hermitage, which, under the inspiration of Abelard's master William of Champeaux, was soon to be converted into one of the greatest theological schools in Europe, St. Victor.

A little farther down before the Petit Pont stood a gate tower, the Petit Chastelet, where travelers over the bridge were inspected by the royal officers. Before it to the right ran the rue de la Boucherie, where many students had rooms. On the left of the Orléans road this street was the rue de la Huchette, leading to the Pré-aux-clercs, a field where students liked to disport themselves along the river, and beyond it was the great Benedictine Abbey of St.-Germain-des-Prés with its own village. As he passed through the Petit Chastelet Abelard found the bridge lined with small houses, one of which would be occupied by a famous master later in the century. From the spaces between the houses he could see the traffic on the river. Across the bridge on the island was the city proper, bisected by the street called the rue de la Juiverie for about half its length and the rue de la Lanterne for its other half. On the left were some streets occupied by prosperous merchants, and beyond them on the end of the island was the Royal Palace with its gardens. On the right in the middle of the island was the Synagogue. Behind it were some crowded narrow lanes and beyond them near the bank of the river was the Cathedral of Notre Dame. When Peter reached the city in the early years of the twelfth century, the great Cathedral we know today had not yet been built. The building he knew was erected against the old Roman wall that surrounded the island, set in ten or twelve feet from the shore. It had a long, low nave with two rows of columns of black and white marble topped with acanthus capitals. There was a decorated tile floor, and the ceiling beams were gilded. We should probably find the decoration a little garish if we could see it today, but the intention was undoubtedly to create an air of richness. Adjoining the Cathedral was the cloister that Abelard was to come to know very well, for it was here that he heard lectures by William of Champeaux and later delivered lectures himself.

If he wished to explore further before settling down, he could have crossed to the right bank over the Grant Pont guarded at the end by the Grant Chastelet. On the right, after he crossed the river, was the busy commercial section of the city surrounded by a palisade, and toward its center on the riverbank was the open marketplace called the Grève. The road stretching beyond the Grant Pont, the Chaussée St. Lazare, was one of two routes to the Abbey of St. Denis, which was not far away. The crowded un-paved streets of the city were covered with black mud, which clung to the shoes of pedestrians and on a wet day splattered menacingly from the hooves of passing horses and the wheels of carts. But young Peter was well mounted, so that he had little to fear from this source. Being relatively wealthy for a student, he probably found a house for himself and his servants not far from the Cathedral.

The ground floor, built for a workshop, would serve as a court-yard. The young master himself occupied the first-floor chamber containing a bed, some chests, a pole upon which to hang clothes, a writing table with a candle, some benches, and a board that could be set up on trestles for meals. The servants would sleep together on the upper floor. There may have been a garden of sorts at the rear. Paris was even then known for its good food, and the hot pies sold by vendors in the streets were famous. Young Peter, a knight of dialectic, was unmoved by these amenities; indeed, if we are to believe his later statements, he paid no attention either to the servant girls in the neighborhood who cast admiring glances on the handsome youth from Brittany, nor to the prostitutes who assisted in the education of the students. He eschewed idle pursuits, perhaps emulating the abstemiousness of Berengar of Tours. As a nobleman, he would have paid his respects soon to members of the Court of France, among whom his father may well have had friends. We do not know what other students thought of him at first, but his early success indicates that he had an attractive manner, perhaps with an air of assurance that some found pleasing. He is also credited with a keen sense of humor and an engaging ability to use jokes to vivify serious discourse.

William of Champeaux was a man of impressive administrative talent as well as a competent theologian. He had studied under Anselm of Laon, with whom he maintained close relations, and when Abelard first met him he was a canon of the Cathedral and the *scholasticus*, or master, of the school. Abelard tells us that William welcomed him among his students at first, "but later," as he puts it, "I became most burdensome, for I sought to refute his teachings, frequently attacked him by reasoning against him, and sometimes seemed to be superior to him in disputation." He does not tell us what these early disagreements were about, but they must have concerned technical problems of logic. Young Peter was skeptical concerning accepted opinions on this subject and quick to detect the weaknesses of commonly accepted views. William, on the other hand, not being a highly original thinker in the disciplines of the *trivium*, probably wished to select what he regarded as the best traditional opinions without too much question. In a position of responsibility, he represented academic caution, a restraint that can produce a kind of reliability on the one hand, but also a certain stuffiness on the other. Peter had no such responsibilities, but instead a ready wit and a quick tongue.

William's older and more advanced students, who had learned to accept his views, soon began to resent young Abelard's intransigence and to envy his facility. The situation grew steadily worse, generating so much antagonism that Abelard was forced to leave the school. However, this eventuality would not have arisen if young Peter had not had many followers himself among the younger students. Instead of returning home in discouragement, he set out to establish a school of his own, confident that many students would follow him. Thus, "a mere boy," as he says, he selected for this purpose "the then prominent stronghold of Melun, a royal residence." The selection of this location, which was indeed a favorite residence of the Capetian kings, indicates that he had strong support at court. As a matter of fact, Abelard says that William attempted to forestall his plans, but that "because there were among the powerful in the land some jealous of him, by relying on their help and his obvious envy which brought many to my side, I gained what I wished." He does not tell us who his friends at court were, but in evaluating his early career we should not forget that he came from an aristocratic family of some influence and that his success was not altogether due to personal merits. This fact may well have alienated some of his clerical associates who lacked similar connections.

Melun itself was an ancient Roman town, located between twenty and thirty miles southeast of Paris on an island in the Seine. By Abelard's time it had grown to include an area on the adjacent right bank of the stream, which rose in a slope overlooking the original town. There, amid influences more noble than clerical, Abelard proved to be astonishingly successful. "From the time of the establishment of this school my reputation in dialectic began to spread so wide that the fame not only of my fellowstudents [at Paris], but that of my master itself, having been greatly diminished, was extinguished altogether." William's fame was not, of course, "extinguished," and Abelard is here exaggerating his own prowess, but he attracted a substantial number of students to his lectures. The fact that he was successful at all is singular. John of Salisbury tells us that Abelard's method in lecturing on a text was to make it seem as easy as possible, following the advice of St. Augustine, who said that one ought to explain anything so as to make it readily understandable. Although John attributes the superficiality of Abelard's discussion of the universals to the application of this principle, we may surmise that Abelard actually sought simplicity rather than superficiality, and that his efforts in this direction were much appreciated by students, who, in all ages, are subjected to a great deal of unnecessary obfuscation on the part of teachers who do not themselves understand what they are saying. Abelard's success at Melun was undoubtedly the result of the comparative reasonableness and straightforwardness of his discourse.

Encouraged by his success, Abelard decided to move closer to Paris, and took his students downriver to Corbeil, a town located at the junction of the Seine and the Essorme that had recently become a royal fief. There, unfortunately, he became ill and was forced to return home to Le Pallet, probably in 1105. The rigors of teaching in the early twelfth century approached those described for us by George Buchanan in his sixteenth-century poem "Of the Wretched Condition of the Teachers of Humane Letters at Paris." The academic day was a long one, demanding constant alertness during the morning hours when the work and recitations of the students were corrected, and spontaneity and ingenuity in the afternoon when expository lectures had to be delivered on the assigned texts. The lectures would cover systematically both the literal interpretation and the doctrinal content of the text. And the exposition was interspersed with *quaestiones*, or systematic discourses on particular points. Abelard was especially fond of these, since they enabled him to utilize the resources of dialectic at length. Jocular examples are especially effective in the illustration of points of logic, and Abelard had a reputation, which he undoubtedly sought to maintain, for jocularity.

In the twelfth century, moreover, as Abelard's own career as a student testifies, the master might be subjected to rather severe questioning or criticism from the students. The rooms for teaching were often damp and dark. Discipline could be a trying problem, especially on those days when the master was not feeling well or had not adequately prepared his lectures. He was responsible, more-over, for the behavior of his students at all times, in the streets and in their rooms, as well as in the classroom. Many of the problems both of lecturing and maintaining discipline could undoubtedly be met with various kinds of subterfuges or routine procedures of a dilatory character by the experienced and well-established teacher. But Abelard was a novice. His success depended on his ability to attract students, and he lacked the experience to substitute stock explanations for spontaneous thought. He would have spent many hours straining his eyes by candlelight at night in order to keep his students supplied with fresh material, and it is likely that on many occasions he was himself little advanced beyond some of them in preparation and background. It is not, therefore, surprising that he proved to be physically unequal to the task he had set for himself.

Abelard's abandonment of his school meant a temporary end to his rivalry with William of Champeaux, although he implies that certain students may have followed him to Brittany: "Since I was removed from France a little for several years, I was sought eagerly by those who wished instruction in dialectic." We may well doubt that this seeking extended to much more than queries about his whereabouts. However that may be, recovery from his malady, which in all likelihood was a series of complications arising from nervous and physical exhaustion, probably required only a few weeks in the relatively tranquil atmosphere of his father's estate. The generous meals in the hall, the solicitude of his mother, the routine of agricultural life, and the physical exhilaration of hunt-ing, a favorite pastime of the aristocratic classes, would have soon put flesh on his bones and color in his cheeks. Why, then, did he remain at home for several years? It may be that he actually thought of himself as having been defeated by William, but it was much more probable that he was distracted by other concerns.

The neighboring county of Anjou suffered a great deal of turbu-lence in the late eleventh and early twelfth centuries. Fulk Rechin, who was a morally reprehensible and indolent ruler who did not keep his vassals under orderly control, had a son by his second wife, Ermengarde of Bourbon, one Geoffrey Martel. When his third wife, Bertrada de Montfort, with whom he was completely infatuated, bore him a son, Fulk the Young, he transferred some of the affection he had bestowed on Bertrada to him, and, perhaps with Bertrada's connivance, neglected Geoffrey. Meanwhile, in 1092 King Philip of France seized Bertrada, who was apparently very fetching, and openly proclaimed her as his wife even though he already had one wife still living. The ecclesiastical hierarchy was, of course, furious, and Bishop Yvo of Chartres actually spent some time in prison because of his objections. As Abbot Suger put it, "Ravished by concupiscence for his ravished woman, he devoted himself to satisfying his pleasure," gradually leaving the care of his kingdom to his son, later Louis the Fat. Back in Anjou Geoffrey Martel, who was not a man to relinquish his rights without a struggle, openly attacked his father for the favoritism shown young Fulk and, because of his father's weakness, was able to gain considerable power in the administration of Anjou.

In 1105 Henry I of England asked Geoffrey Martel and Alain Fergent of Brittany to assist him in conquering Normandy. Both responded favorably. But in May 1106 during a local siege at Condé against a rebellious and felonious baron named Normand, Geoffrey Martel was traitorously slain by a bowman. Rumor had it that Bertrada was ultimately responsible for the murder, but no real proof was forthcoming. But Alain Fergent assisted the Count of Anjou at Condé, where they were finally successful. In the following summer both Bretons and Angevins assisted Henry at Tinchebrai, where Henry's brother Robert Curthose was captured, so that Normandy passed to English hands. Fortunately, Fulk the Young, now undisputed heir of Anjou, proved to be a very different man from his father. He was fierce and able in warfare and pious and just in his personal life. For our purposes, however, the point of all this is that during Abelard's sojourn in Brittany, Alain Fergent and his court were engaged in feudal warfare.

This military activity suggests that Abelard may have been asked to look after his father's estates while Berengar and his second son were off campaigning. In view of his almost insatiable thirst for knowledge and fame as a philosopher, it is difficult to imagine Abelard whiling away his time in the Breton countryside unless he had some special reason for doing so. Meanwhile, he probably formed new associations in Nantes and Rennes, both among the clergy and among noble acquaintances of his father. During these years he matured a great deal. He had achieved re-markable success as a scholar and unusual fame as a teacher for a man of his age. When he returned to Paris he would be a more formidable if less brash contestant for philosophical distinction. But brashness was a Breton trait, not easily subdued by age, and Abe-lard, still fortified by noble connections and comparative wealth, was not yet ready to face the world with an air of humility. If anything, he felt renewed determination. This time he would not fail.

CHAPTER II

Fame

When Abelard returned to Paris, in 1108 or 1109, William of Champeaux had been made Archdeacon of Paris and had then abandoned the secular habit to become a regular canon of St. Augustine, taking religious vows. His administrative ability asserted itself in the founding of the Abbey of St. Victor, located, as we have seen, on the left bank of the Seine a little upriver from the Cathedral. Both the abbey and the school that it sponsored flourished, a fact that aroused Abelard's unconcealed envy: "William . . . changing his original habit, entered the order of the regular clergy, with the intention, as was said, that the more religious he might be believed to be, the more readily he might be promoted to the status of a major prelate, as indeed was to happen when he was made Bishop of Châlons." The elevation to the bishopric did not occur, however, until 1113. Meanwhile Abelard, who would clearly have enjoyed elevation to a bishopric himself, sat once more at William's lectures, seeking an opportunity to discredit him.

The opportunity arose soon enough, for William, like Abelard himself, had reacted against the teaching of Roscelin concerning the universals, taking what has been called an "extreme realist" position. According to Abelard, William taught that "the same thing exists essentially in all the individuals of a class, and that there is no diversity of essence among them, but only in the variety of their accidents." That is, when we say, "Socrates is a man," what we mean by *man* exists essentially in Plato, Alcibiades, and in other men as well as in Socrates, so that they all have the same essence. Abelard tells us that he forced his master to alter the word "essentially" in the original statement and to substitute for it the term *indifferenter*, now usually said to mean "in a similar way." But current explanations of the content of this encounter are not very convincing, and it is possible that Abelard's term may have had some other force. The incident itself was nevertheless important because of its effect on Abelard's reputation. William of Champeaux was a very distinguished master. If Abelard succeeded not merely in irritating him but in changing one of his doctrines, he could justly claim a notable achievement.

Many of William's students apparently agreed with Abelard, for he tells us in his *History* that after his criticism William's "lectures fell into such negligence that they could hardly be called lectures in dialectic." Although Abelard says nothing about it, he was probably lecturing, perhaps in a nearby church, at the same time that he was attending William's lectures. For he goes on to say that "from this incident my prestige and authority received such force that those who had vehemently supported that master of mine, and had vigorously attacked my own teaching, flocked to my school." Wherever this school may have been, the master in dialectic at the Cathedral, whom William had installed to replace him when he left for St. Victor, was so impressed that he gave up his chair in order that Abelard might lecture there.

But William had not yet finished with his young rival. Instead of attacking Abelard directly, William, with typical administrative "strategy," attacked his predecessor, whom he had himself installed, accusing him of the basest crimes. Achieving success in this, he replaced his former student with another, thus displacing Abelard. We should understand that a probable third, and silent, party to this maneuver was the Bishop of Paris, who was ultimately responsible for the conduct of the school at the Cathedral. He probably felt that a man of well-established reputation like William should be given greater credence and trust than Abelard. In view of subsequent events, we must admit that his judgment was sound, however unjust William's behavior may have been. Taking advantage of court favor once more, Abelard removed himself and his students to Melun, where they remained for a time.

Abelard was unwilling to rest at peace with his enemies. He was an ambitious man, anxious to gain entry by any possible means into the cloister of the Cathedral at Paris, where his voice would have an authority it could not claim elsewhere. The increasing success of the French kings in winning the loyalty of their chief vassals and in enlarging their own domains lent a growing prestige to the city, which was becoming the center of European learning. In the next century the Cathedral school would become the University of Paris. Because of his brilliance as a lecturer, Abelard could attract a following of interested students without much institutional support, using a church or a monastic center as a base of operations. But for the kind of prestige he cherished nothing could replace the Cathedral. Thus, when William left the city temporarily, Abelard moved closer, setting up, as he says, "an encampment for my school at Mont Ste. Geneviève outside the city limits, so that I could lay siege, as it were, to him who occupied my place." He was still at this time handling his dialectic as though it constituted arms and armor to promote his own success. The Abbey of Ste. Geneviève was outside the jurisdiction of the Bishop of Paris, so that Abelard could lecture there with impunity so long as the canons did not object, casting missiles of brilliant logical formulations on his enemy below in the Cathedral close.

But William soon returned to St. Victor, and there began a kind of warfare between the two masters in which their students participated with enthusiasm. We can imagine young men in their teens moving from one to the other, disputing with one another about their relative merits, even on holidays, when most of them sought recreation on the Pré-aux-clercs. When William wished to assist his new protégé at the Cathedral, however, by attacking Abelard, he only succeeded in ruining him. For his own lectures on

Priscian were judged better than those in the city, so that students came to him instead of going to hear his former student. Thus the *trivium* at Paris moved to the left bank, leaving the Cathedral to carry on studies in other subjects, although there were apparently no very famous masters there of any kind. Unfortunately, we have no record of this debate, of the strategies of the participants, or of the activities of the students, some of whom must have been prompted by one master to ask embarrassing questions of the other. It all ended rather inconclusively, in spite of Abelard's ambiguous claim to victory, for William was made Bishop of Châlons and Abelard returned home to Le Pallet, all in the year 1113, leaving the left bank in comparative quiet.

Abelard's homecoming must have been something of a disappointment. He was now thirty-four, which meant in the twelfth century that he was a man of middle age. He was without ecclesiastical preferment, although his success in teaching must have proved moderately lucrative, so that he was by no means impoverished, and he had influenced a number of young men who were later to achieve some prominence. His mother, Lucia, he says, asked for him, since she wished to enter a religious house, as her husband, Berengar, had already done before her. This was not an unusual course for elder members of noble families to take. In the previous year Duke Alain Fergent had entered the monastery of Redon, turning over the duchy to his son Conan. There were no "homes for the aged" in the twelfth century, and when a man or woman could no longer manage the ordinary affairs of life comfortably, a monastery provided a quiet refuge made doubly attractive by the opportunity it offered for devotion. With reference to this last point, it should be emphasized that medieval people often took a very real interest in the care of the soul, seeking what they regarded as spiritual nourishment with genuine enthusiasm. It is possible that Abelard was asked to assist in making the necessary arrangements both for the care of his mother and for the continued administration of the family estate under the direction of his brother. He would also have wished to pay his respects to the new Duke. Again, he does not tell us how long he remained in Brittany, but when he returned to France he was determined to learn something more of divinity. Perhaps his mother had wished him to do this, since dialectic was, in spite of its popularity in the schools, merely an instrument, a tool by means of which one may say something about something else in a reasonable way. As John of Salisbury was to point out later, when dialectic turns upon itself, it easily becomes sterile. Abelard probably came to realize also that without exegetical knowledge he could not advance very far in the hierarchy of the Church. As events proved, his age and experience had neither dulled his wits nor dampened his impatience in the face of what he regarded as stupidity.

At the time the most famous master of Scriptural studies was Anselm of Laon. Anselm had probably studied under the great St. Anselm at Bec, he had taught brilliantly at Paris, where William of Champeaux was among his students, and he had later returned to Laon, where he had taught some of the most distinguished ecclesiastics of the time, not only in France, but in Germany and Italy as well. His fame rested partly on some glosses on the Scriptural text, mostly of Patristic origin, which look forward to the famous *Ordinary Gloss*, produced later in the twelfth century, that was to become a standard work of reference. He also collected *sententiae*, or series of acceptable theological principles, again often interspersed with Patristic quotations, that could be used to form a body of doctrine introductory to the Scriptures themselves. These look forward to the *Four Books of Sentences* of Peter the Lombard, produced at Paris a few years after Abelard's death, which was still the standard introduction to theological study in the Renaissance. "Theology" was not a separate science in its own right in the twelfth century, framed in an artificial metaphysical structure, but a series of principles to be used as an introduction to the study of the Bible. Anselm and his followers helped to provide two of the basic tools for theological study: a series of accepted doctrines arranged in an orderly way, and a series of accepted glosses on the text of the Bible that provided a guide to preliminary interpretation. In view of the distinction of Anselm's disciples and their ecclesiastical success, the school at Laon was a logical place for Abelard to further his ambitions.

The journey to Laon was a long one, probably taking Abelard

and his servants up the Loire to Orléans, thence to Paris, and up what was left of the ancient Roman road toward Soissons and, beyond it, Laon. The city itself, which had once been a royal seat, was located on a plateau that rose with steep slopes from the surrounding countryside. It was a windy eminence, noted for the longevity of its inhabitants. At the time of Abelard's arrival both the city and its Cathedral were recovering from severe civil strife, vividly, if not always accurately described for us in the autobiography of Guibert de Nogent.

Guibert saw the world in garish hues and was very fond of what might be called very pious wild tales. The real troubles began with the election of one Gaudri as Bishop in 1106 under the influence of the King of England, who was at Rouen. The clergy of Laon, led by Anselm, who was Dean and Chancellor of the Cathedral as well as *scholasticus*, objected, but the election was confirmed by the Pope. In 1110 Gaudri formed a conspiracy to murder one of the leading noblemen of the city, the distinguished crusader Gerard of Quierzy, who was guardian of the Benedictine convent of St. John and a very pious man. But he had a sharp tongue that he had not hesitated to employ against Gaudri. The city meanwhile had been divided into two parties: the merchants, who wished to have what they regarded as their ancient liberties restored, and the nobles, who wished things to remain as they were. The bishop had sided with the nobles, while Gerard favored the merchants. Gaudri set off for Rome, leaving behind a group of conspirators, including two archdeacons at the Cathedral, to accomplish the murder. On January 7, 1110, a group of these men found Gerard alone in the nave of the Cathedral and there murdered him. The royal Provost and his men pursued the offenders, but were unable to capture them and resorted to the punishment of looting and burning their houses. The nobles, loyal to the bishop, openly associated with the conspirators, but the King, approving the action of his officers, seized the bishop's temporalities and closed the gates of the city to him.

With consummate audacity, Gaudri excommunicated the men who had pursued the conspirators. He was forced, however, to excommunicate the conspirators as well, an action that was far from pleasing to his followers among the noblemen of the town. Unable to reconcile himself with the King of France, he sought refuge with the King of England. In Laon itself anarchy reigned for a time. Murder, arson, and outrageous theft flourished in the streets. To restore order, all the people of Laon, including the noblemen, agreed to form a commune which gave the citizens civil liberties, the right to organize their own judicial bodies, and the right to substitute an annual tax for feudal obligations. The word *commune* in this context has none of the radical overtones it later acquired; there was no "political theory" involved in its establish- ment. What was desired was simply an organized government that could keep order. In order to maintain it, however, it was necessary for the citizens to make a payment to the King for their privileges.

Because of this last requirement, the commune did not endure for very long, at least for this time. Gaudri managed to return to the city, organize the noblemen, and offer King Louis a larger payment than the burghers had been able to collect for their rights, so that the commune was dissolved in 1112. Incidentally, we should not hasten to condemn the King for avarice and short-sightedness. It is unlikely that he had any theoretical interests in political struc- tures at all; on the other hand, the welfare of the royal treasury was something in which he had a very legitimate interest.

But the dissolution of the commune angered the merchants, who at once formed a conspiracy to murder their bishop. This was personal vengeance, and no more; men had not yet learned to condone murder in the name of political ideology. When the opportunity arose, they entered the Bishop's Palace, overwhelmed its defenders, and found Gaudri in hiding. They dragged him forth to the cloister where they smashed his head and cut off his legs, leaving the dismembered corpse to lie in the dirt. On the next day Anselm obtained permission to remove it for burial. The burghers, meanwhile, sought out all the noblemen they could find, cutting down men, women, and children indiscriminately. Fire broke out in the Bishop's Palace, spread to the Cathedral, and leaped to the nearby Abbey, whipped by the winds of Laon. On the next day Thomas of Marle, a nobleman with a reputation for banditry that is perhaps exaggerated, offered the burghers his protection. Many of them, fearing the vengeance of the King, followed him out of the city, leaving it to be looted at will by peasants from the countryside. Order was gradually restored by the King. Since the Cathedral was severely damaged, a party of clergymen and laymen set out on pilgrimage to raise money for its repair, and by the middle of 1114 it was back in service again. But its structure had been weakened, so that later in the century it was rebuilt in the new Gothic style under the supervision of Walter of Mortagne, one of Anselm's students and a critic of Abelard's, who eventually became Bishop of Laon.

Anselm was thus not only an old man, burdened by the duties of his administrative offices as well as by those of his teaching, when Abelard arrived; he had recently experienced a series of events sufficiently harrowing to have unnerved a much younger man. He was obviously not in vigorous health, for he was to die a short time later—in 1117. We can readily understand that his lectures must have reflected his past achievements rather than any new and spontaneous insights looking forward to fresh developments, and that he would have regarded over-inquisitive students with impatience. In his later years, in fact, he had gained a reputation for severity as well as for rigorous orthodoxy. But Abelard was not prepared to make any concessions because of mitigating circumstances, and was unwilling, as usual, to adjust his own attitudes in such a way that he might subject himself to unpleasantness for the sake of tranquility and orderly procedure. Youthful brashness had given way to a settled impatience and an intolerance of anything he regarded as being inferior. "I went to this old man," he wrote, "who had achieved fame from long practice rather than from reasoning or memory. For if anyone uncertain approached him on any question, he went away more uncertain. He was wonderful in the eyes of his listeners, but a nobody in the sight of his questioners. He had a miraculous command of words, but was contemptible in sense, and empty of reason."

This criticism implies something more specific than it seems to indicate at first glance. Abelard, who had been trained in dialectic, expected to be able to raise questions regarding principles set forth in Scriptural interpretation and to have them settled with disciplined logical arguments, or with "reason." Anselm, who had been trained in a different atmosphere, probably responded to his questions by quoting a passage or two from Patristic sources, adducing at the same time a number of accepted Scriptural principles. The latter procedure had long been thought satisfactory, and continued to be employed throughout the Middle Ages, but it would hardly have pleased Abelard, who wished to reduce explanations to a strictly logical form. His fondness for dialectic looks forward to the elaborate *quaestiones* favored by the later scholastics.

We should not hastily condemn Anselm, for the systematic collection and sifting of Patristic opinion on given texts was a scholarly task of great magnitude, and it was still being carried on by the masters of the mid-century like Peter the Lombard, whose influential commentaries on the Psalms and the Pauline Epistles are little more than ordered collections of Patristic discussions. It is true that Anselm devoted part of his afternoon sessions to *collationes*, or comparisons of *sententiae* or conclusions from the Fathers. But these comparisons were probably elaborated by adducing orthodox principles with further Patristic or Scriptural support.

The result was that Abelard became bored and inattentive, attracting criticism from his fellow-students, who, less ambitious than he, and more docile, were respectful of the aged master. At this time Abelard was an elder among them, for they were for the most part probably not more than seventeen years old, while he was in his thirties. There then took place an incident that was to win Abelard lasting, if indirect, ill fame. His own account of it from his *History of My Calamities* is worth quoting in full.

Meanwhile, it happened one day after certain collations of sententiae that we students were joking among ourselves. One of the others with malice aforethought asked me what my opinion was concerning the reading of the sacred Scriptures, since I had not yet studied except in the field of natural philosophy. I responded that I thought this kind of pursuit, in which the salvation of the soul is studied, to be most bene-ficial, but that I was much astonished that literate persons able to understand the expositions of the Fathers should not find their writings or glosses sufficient so that no further guidance was necessary.

At first this sounds as though Abelard were returning to the tech-niques of the ordinary monastic schools, where the Bible was studied in the light of Patristic commentary alone. Undoubtedly the rather sarcastic statement was intended as an invitation for further criticism, which it did, indeed, provoke.

> Many of those who were there laughed at me and asked me whether I could explain the Scriptures in this way and would presume to try. I replied that if they wished I was ready.
> "Certainly," they said, "we agree. Let there be found and brought to you an expositor of some obscure Scriptural text and we shall test what you have promised."
> All agreed on the most obscure prophesy of Ezechiel. Tak-ing the expositor, I at once invited them to a lecture on the next day. Giving me unsought advice, they said that such a task should not be hastened, but that I, being inexpert, should take more time studying to investigate and to make firm my exposition.

Abelard's reply to this is characteristic. It describes perhaps better than any other single statement the nature of his lecturing tech-nique and the secret of its success: "I responded indignantly that it was not my custom to become perfect by practice but to rely on ingenuity, adding that I would either call it off entirely or they would not object to coming to my lecture at a time of my own choice."

There is nothing more fascinating than to watch an expert in some subject "thinking on his feet," offering new ideas spontane-ously as his mind plays over various possibilities. Abelard's natural facility, fortified by his training in dialectic, enabled him to lecture in this way, for he could seize upon questions raised by the text, state them clearly, analyze them reasonably, and reach a probable conclusion. We do not know what "expositor" he had to guide him. Ezechiel is one of the most difficult of all Scriptural books, and there were not many commentaries available, chiefly one by St. Jerome and some homilies by St. Gregory the Great. Whatever source or sources he used, however, we can be certain that he interspersed his exposition with *quaestiones* and their solutions. The commentary on Ezechiel does not survive, but this technique is the distinctive feature of Abelard's later commentary on Romans, which reflects his lecturing habits. The students must have been astonished at the result. "Few came to the first day of my lectures," Abelard says, "because it seemed ridiculous to all of them that I who had been hardly expert at all in the reading of the Scriptures up to that time, should approach them so hastily. But all who attended the lecture were so pleased by it that they extolled it with unique praise and compelled me to continue my exposition in the manner of my first lecture. When this was known, those who had not attended flocked eagerly to my second and third lectures, and all were anxious to have the gloss I had made on the first day transcribed."

Thus the master in dialectic began to acquire fame as an exegete. But he was an exegete of a new kind, who carried his exposition a step further than the conventions established by Anselm and his school. It is unlikely that Anselm understood or appreciated what Abelard was doing. From his point of view the younger man was simply going off on a rather dubious side-track, and doing so on the basis of very little experience. There was probably not, at the time, any such thing as a license for teaching. Such licenses were used later when educational procedures became more systematic. But Anselm was nevertheless successful in forbidding Abelard to teach, using an argument, as Abelard tells us, to the effect that if Abelard "as a beginner in that study [*i.e.*, exegesis] should write something in error, that error would be attributed to Anselm himself." Although Abelard called this "envious calumny," suggesting that it was urged by two of Anselm's students, Alberic of Rheims and Lotulf the Lombard, it is true that in the twelfth century a very close personal tie usually existed between master and student, so that if Abelard taught at Laon everyone would assume that he did so under the sponsorship of Anselm. With bitterness and disap-pointment, therefore, Abelard once more set out for Paris, fortified a little, perhaps, by the indignation with which his own students regarded Anselm's prohibition.

At about the same time Abelard arrived in Paris, a certain Hugh arrived at the doors of St. Victor, where he presented to the first abbot, Gilduin, some relics of St. Victor he had obtained in Mar-seilles. The gift helped to provide a warm welcome, and Hugh entered the order. After taking his vows, he began to teach the *trivium* and was soon made master of the school. He became one of the most influential Biblical scholars of the Latin Middle Ages, winning for himself the title "the Second Augustine."

Hugh was not, like Abelard, a brilliant teacher, but he was a far more profound and learned scholar, whose books became standard texts. Among them was *The Didascalicon*, a guide to the arts and their study which was widely used in the universities of medieval Europe when they eventually replaced the cathedral schools as centers of learning. One chapter of this book, which was completed shortly after 1125, is devoted to the subject of humility, concerning which Hugh says at the outset, "Now the beginning of discipline [*i.e.*, study] is humility. Although the lessons of humility are many, the three which follow are of especial importance for the student: first, that he hold no knowledge and no writing in contempt; second, that he blush to learn from no man; and third, that when he has attained learning himself, he not look down upon everyone else." When he comes to elaborate the third point, Hugh undoubtedly refers to Abelard generally and specifically to the incident at Laon: "So it is that in our days certain peddlers of trifles come fuming forth; glorying in I know not what, they accuse our forefathers of simplicity and suppose that wisdom, having been born in themselves, with themselves will die. They say that the divine utterances [*i.e.*, the Scriptures] have such a simple way of speaking that no one has to study them under masters, but can sufficiently penetrate to the hidden treasures of Truth by his own mental acumen. They wrinkle their noses and purse their lips at lecturers in divinity. . . ." Thus did Abelard, unnamed but unmistakable, serve as a bad example to generations of students, affording Anselm a kind of ultimate triumph over his renegade pupil.

There are, of course, two ways to look at Abelard's success with his students and his contempt for the masters of the past. He may have been a very brilliant but essentially naive product of the Breton borderland so overwhelmed by his own insights that he was blind to the impression he was creating. On the other hand, it is possible to attribute to him a terrible vanity based in part on genuine achievement and on an awareness of the weaknesses of established attitudes and procedures. As we shall see, he was himself in later life inclined to take the second view. Vanity in the twelfth century was considered to be a much more serious weakness than it is today, and men were generally much more sensitive to its dangers. It is certainly true that he demonstrated little tact, especially in his conflict with Anselm, and that if he had gone about introducing his innovations more systematically and with greater humility his own writings might have had much greater influence. He set out originally dressed in armor, as it were, and bearing arms, not for the sake of truth but for his own glory, and it required many years marked by intense suffering for him to learn that he who lives by the sword shall die by the sword.

But just as twelfth-century society was held together by personal relationships, so also it derived its dynamism from personal rivalries. And Abelard was soon to antagonize some very powerful rivals indeed, much more influential than Alberic of Rheims and Lotulf the Lombard. At about the time of his return to Paris, one Bernard was installed at Clairvaux by Abelard's old master and enemy William of Champeaux, and while Abelard grew in fame at Paris, Bernard was beginning to attract enormous audiences to hear his sermons and to admire his saintly character in the valley of the Aube. Stories concerning Abelard undoubtedly reached Bernard, and there is no reason to think that he liked what he heard.

At Paris, probably again with the assistance of his friends at court, Abelard was made a canon of the Cathedral and readmitted to the chair he had lost through the stratagems of William of Champeaux. He at once resumed his lectures on Ezechiel, but at the same time, he continued to lecture on the subject he loved best, dialectic. Students flocked from all over Europe to hear him, and his fame and influence rose steadily until about the year 1118. At the same time, he became very wealthy, probably acquiring a substantial little *familia* of servants, a stable of well-fed horses, and a wardrobe that set him off from his fellow-canons and lent him an air of distinction. This success must have irritated the canons of St. Victor across the river, angered his old masters Roscelin and William of Champeaux, to whom he professed no indebtedness, and outraged Lotulf the Lombard and Alberic of Rheims. But it must have gratified Abelard's friends at court and pleased the members of his family in Brittany, who could now anticipate his elevation to high office with confidence. But disaster came from an unexpected quarter that had nothing to do either with Abelard's professional competence or with his theological opinions. As he might have put it, he encountered Eve.

CHAPTER III

Heloise

*W*ealth and a steady routine of teaching gave Abelard
something he had never fully enjoyed before: leisure.
Now, installed in the highest teaching position he
could hope to attain, confident in his own methods, and secure
with a large store of learning available to his memory, he could,
and probably did develop a system of routine procedures that made
long hours of study by candlelight superfluous. Those flashes of
wit and insight that characterized his lectures now sprang forth
without much premeditation. Since he still sought advancement
in the hierarchy rather than fame in later generations he spent
little time in writing beyond that required for his students. He
was, in fact, flourishing both mentally and physically with energy
to spare and no real outlet for it in his daily routine. It is not
surprising that he forgot the implications of a saying by one of
his favorite authors, Ovid: *If you destroy idleness, Cupid's bows
are broken.*

Conversely, if you enjoy idleness, the little god will begin his
hunt. Hunt he did, and his arrow soon found the eye of Abelard.
A standard medieval remedy for the arrows of Cupid was hard
study, but Abelard was beginning to enjoy freedom from this
remedy. As he himself says in his *History*, "Just at the time I

[39]

excelled all the world in philosophy, I relaxed the reins of libido, which I had previously grasped most continently." These "reins" constitute a standard medieval figure, becoming the reins in the hand of Temperance as she is depicted in Gothic and Renaissance art. Once the "horse" is loosed, restraint becomes very difficult. This horse is not goaded by sentiment, but by what Abelard explicity calls "lechery."

Lechery is something that has vanished, along with most other vices, from the face of the earth, not because men are no longer lecherous, but because we have learned first to excuse the vice, the iniquity of which was emphasized out of all reasonable proportion during the later nineteenth century, and then to glorify it as the expression of a natural human potential, and to cherish it as a remedy for the inherent isolation of the individual "personality." Popular corruptions of the teachings of Freud have lent it an additional sanctity. We are, moreover, prone to project our own views on the subject hopefully on the unsuspecting past. A recent play about Heloise and Abelard contains a nude love scene in which the sexual activity of the lovers is made an object of devotion approved by a chorus of monks and nuns. We shall have occasion to examine the historical development of the attitude implied here in later chapters. Meanwhile, it will suffice to say that attitudes during the twelfth century were quite different. "Sin" was then not something exotic, pagan, or productive of redeeming social values, but simply irrational conduct. And lechery was regarded as one of the greatest enemies of manliness or virility. When an ecclesiastic wished to say something degrading about a nobleman or another ecclesiastic, he accused him of lechery, not out of what we would call "prudery," but to cast doubt on his manliness and competence. The survival of this practice in the pages of medieval chronicles, mostly written by ecclesiastics, has given the noblemen of medieval Europe rather lurid reputations.

The social consequences of lechery among noblemen when it actually prevailed could be especially devastating. Abelard was himself quite familiar with the fact that Anjou had fallen into a condition of near anarchy because of the idleness and lechery of

Fulk Rechin. And the example of Philip of France, who became so besotted with Bertrada de Montfort that he lost control over his realm, was fresh in everyone's memory. This does not mean that noblemen were expected to be continent, but that they were discouraged from devoting so much attention to their own self-satisfaction that they became inefficient. Modern men are often unaware of the fact that strong sexual passion for a specific woman is actually a form of self-love. One does not, that is, love the woman but the peculiar satisfactions she affords. Today, sentiment, sentimentality, or "sincerity" are often used to obscure the actual situation, but neither classical nor medieval men were quite so naive. Lechery was thought of as being even worse among philosophers and divines, since it provided a compelling distraction from study. It is true that at the time Abelard approached Heloise a few bishops had wives, that married priests or priests with concubines were commonplace, and that many monks and nuns were notoriously lecherous, and, moreover, that these deviations were regarded with a certain complacency except by reformers. But it is also true that greater restraint was expected the more advanced one became in the social or ecclesiastical hierarchy. A physician might prescribe warm young wenches for an ailing bishop without alarming anybody, but if the bishop clearly neglected his duties in order to cultivate the wenches, he might find his contemporaries intolerant. Abelard was a proud man, keenly ambitious for advancement. A reputation for lecherous self-indulgence would hardly help him.

Nevertheless, he allowed Cupid to influence him at a time when he was almost forty years old, and he decided, on the basis of careful reasoning, that a young girl he knew of named Heloise would be a most suitable vehicle for the satisfaction of his desires. We know very little about Heloise except what he tells us in his *History*: "There was in this City of Paris a certain young girl named Heloise, the niece of a certain canon named Fulbert, who, the more he loved her, the more he exerted himself affectionately to promote, in so far as he was able, her knowledge of letters. And she, who was not least in beauty of countenance, was supreme in her literary learning. The astonishing learning of Heloise as a girl was mentioned years later by Peter the Venerable, Abbot of Cluny, so that we have other testimony beside Abelard's to the fact. She was especially well trained in grammar, or Latin literature, and had read the classical authors popular at the time. This fact has led certain modern authorities to seek in her a kind of "enlightened paganism" in part responsible for her attitude toward sexual activity. But no careful readers of Cicero and Seneca, or even of Virgil and Ovid, will consider pagans any more "free" in this respect than Christians, at least not medieval Christians. It is true that Ovid was considered a libertine in the nineteenth century, but this view rests merely on the fact that he describes sexual acts quite openly, not on what he actually says or implies about them. However, Abelard said nothing about Heloise's attitudes toward sexual love. He did say that since he was so famous and "outstanding in the attractions of youth and beauty" no woman could deny him. But Heloise would be especially easy because he "cherished a love of letters." That is, his learning, as well as his "beauty" and somewhat dubious "youth" would serve as bait. Abelard was probably quite elegant sartorially by the standards of his time, especially since he was not required to wear a habit as a canon, but could go about dressed as he pleased. Moreover, he envisaged a mutual exchange of amorous correspondence, in which he and Heloise could write "more audaciously" than they could speak, and thus "maintain pleasant colloquies." Unfortunately, if any amorous correspondence passed between the two during his courtship, we do not have it. But it is important to observe that Abelard regarded the learning of Heloise not as something in itself admirable but as a convenient aid to seduction.

Having made up his mind that this girl of about sixteen or seventeen would be the most suitable object for his affection, Abelard sought an occasion to implement his decision. Pretending that his "household and domestic cares" were interfering with his studies and becoming too expensive, he asked to rent a room in Fulbert's house "at whatever rent he sought fit to ask." This offer of high rent should have aroused the old canon's suspicions, since it is not altogether consistent with the excuse concerning expenses. But, as Abelard says, Fulbert was "extremely avaricious" and "anxious at the same time that his niece become more proficient in her literary studies." That is, he was so overcome by greed and vanity concerning his niece that he readily accepted Abelard's offer. We need not be especially surprised at Fulbert's greed. As a canon of the cathedral he would have received a small stipend along with certain grants of bread and wine. Abelard does not tell us whether he held a benefice, but even this would have left him in constant worry about the maintenance of a large household. It is possible that he had inherited some property, or income from property, in connection with the care of his brother's daughter. He had sent her as a small girl to a nunnery at Argenteuil to be educated, and, since she had been unusually apt, had probably exerted himself to supply her with books, which were expensive, and with a series of tutors. He may have had in mind the possibility of marrying her to a wealthy merchant of the City. In this respect she would not have had much appeal to a nobleman, who would be naturally inclined if not obliged to seek feudal benefits with a wife.

Abelard thus provided a solution to two of Fulbert's problems, money and a tutor for Heloise. Abelard says, "He committed her to my care so that whenever I returned from school, whether by day or by night, I should devote myself to teaching her and should chastise her energetically if I found her idle." Poor Heloise! She was at the time little more than a child, and even if her new mentor had not had ulterior aims, these freedoms would have made her life miserable. Abelard was astonished by Fulbert's simplicity, "no less dumbfounded indeed than if he had entrusted a tender lamb to a hungry wolf. For when he gave her to me not only to be taught but also to be severely disciplined, what else had he done but unwittingly give license and occasion to my desires, so that what I could not get by flattery, I could at the least more easily obtain by blows?" Heloise would naturally have been frightened by his advances, and, as he admits in one of his letters addressed to her later, blows were sometimes necessary to make her compliant. The rod, a tool of the schoolmaster, thus became part of the armament of the lover. We can picture Heloise, overawed by the physical maturity and the prestige of her lover, frightened by threats and afraid to complain to her uncle.

The beatings first administered in "correction" became a disguise for the lovers after Heloise, who learned to enjoy amorous pleasures, became cooperative. "Under the cloak of study," Abelard wrote, "we freely practiced love, and the secret retreats that the study of letters required were just what love wished." Fulbert probably provided a small chamber furnished with a writing desk, books, benches, and perhaps a convenient cushion or two. "My hands more eagerly sought her breasts than the books before us, my eyes more readily turned to her in love than toward reading what was written; and in order that we should arouse less suspicion, I sometimes beat her in love rather than in anger, not for wrath but for pleasure that surpassed all ointments in sweetness." The lovers were both novices at their amorous sport and had much to discover about its ramifications, some things evidently surprising and delightful to both of them. Having no experience, even conversationally, with the subject, they engaged in unrestrained explorations. "No step of love is omitted by the lover, and, if he can think of anything unusual, he adds that too. And since we were inexpert in joys of this kind, we went about them with more ardor and were less restrained by fastidiousness." Heloise learned to seek the services of her tutor with enthusiasm, while Seneca, Virgil, Lucan, Statius, and even poor Ovid lay neglected in their dusty parchment covers on a nearby bench. The ready intelligence and self-confidence that made Abelard a formidable knight of Minerva would have soon made him expert in the arms of Venus.

But love and study do not mix well, and Abelard's single-minded concentration on his newly acquired art soon affected his teaching. "It was most tedious," he wrote, "for me to go to my school and remain there, especially when I devoted my nights to amorous vigils and saved my days for study." The commentary on Ezechiel probably deteriorated into a hit-or-miss affair, characterized by desperate stratagems and long-winded circumlocutions. "My teaching became so negligent and tepid that I did nothing from ingenuity, but taught everything by habit. Under the circumstances even the lectures on dialectic must have suffered, for the syllogism is a dry thing when a man is thinking of warm lips, smooth female rotundities, soft inner thighs, and skillful hands. Abelard's students, of course, noticed the decline in his effectiveness and deplored it. He calls attention to "the sorrow, the sighs, and the laments" of the young men who "sensed this occupation, or rather perturbation, of my mind." Abelard's condition illustrates well, in fact, the medieval contention that love of this kind makes a man unfit for anything else.

Our philosopher did have one accomplishment. He wrote songs. Or at least he says he did, claiming that many of them were still being sung years later "chiefly by those who are detained in a similar style of life." This statement has given rise to a flurry of interest among literary historians, who have eagerly searched the love poetry of the twelfth century, both in Latin and in the vernacular, for Abelard's songs to Heloise. But no such songs have been found, although they are also mentioned in a letter attributed to Heloise written many years later. Some have suggested that they must have been influenced by the rise of "courtly love," so that they resembled the productions of the early troubadours. However, the courtship of Heloise as Abelard describes it has nothing whatsoever in common with what scholars, rather vaguely, call "courtly love," if, in fact, it is at all possible to determine what they mean by it. As for the troubadours, Abelard knew something about the first of them, Duke William IX of Aquitaine. But it is very difficult indeed to imagine Duke William, a warrior and a crusader who had much experience with women, approaching any woman in the manner in which Abelard approached Heloise. Abelard's behavior would have seemed to him childish. Moreover, the Duke would not have been very highly regarded in Breton circles, for after the siege of Condé, where Geoffrey Martel was murdered, Fulk the Young went to Paris to appeal to the King. Duke William was designated to escort him home, but held him prisoner instead, demanding certain Angevin castles in return. The blackmail worked, but it did not endear the Duke to his northern neighbors. Abelard's songs, if they existed at all, were probably amorous complaints without any of the wit that enlivens most early troubadour poetry.

The lovers succeeded in concealing their activities for "several months." By that time custom had cemented their relationship into a strong mutual affection. Those who are inexperienced in amorous play and who live in a society that discourages it are likely to cling tenaciously to the source of their first pleasurable experiences. Abelard may have been an unscrupulous seducer, but he was no gay deceiver. His conscience bothered him, as well it might, and he was far from being completely without qualms in his attitude toward his victim or toward her uncle. Cathedral canons in the twelfth century formed a rather intimate community bound by personal ties to each other and to the hierarchy of the institution whose functioning was the product of their joint effort. Moreover, Abelard must have been deeply concerned about his own reputation, since ambition for ecclesiastical preferment still moved him. How could he become an abbot or a bishop if he were known as the betrayer of a fellow-canon and the seducer of an innocent girl? The echoes of his conduct at Laon were still reverberating across the river at St. Victor as well as among Anselm's students, who were scattered across Europe in influential positions. We can therefore understand his deep concern. Discovery came at last. Fulbert must have come home unexpectedly and interrupted the lovers at their favorite study.

Abelard is quite vehement about the result: "O how much sorrow struck the uncle when he knew it! How much sorrow the lovers suffered in separation! How confused I was for shame! With what contrition concerning the affliction of the girl I suffered! With what sorrow she burned for my shame! Neither of us was concerned except for what might happen to the other." The tutor was forced, of course, to leave Fulbert's house and to resume those "household cares" he had abandoned. But after a steady diet of sexual pleasure for several months, separation was almost unbearable. Heloise had lost her famous philosopher and her well-dressed and handsome lover at the same time, and Abelard had been forced to part with pleasures he had left untasted for over half a lifetime and had experienced, with all his accumulated energy, for the first time. "Love," he says, "burned more fiercely" after the separation, "while shame over the past rendered passion more shameless." He adds, by way of explanation, but not without irony, "The poetic fable of Mars and Venus caught in a trap was re-enacted in us." One must read the fable to see the point about shame and to discover the irony. Here is the version in Ovid's *Art of Love*:

A story is told, well known everywhere, of Mars and Venus caught by the guile of Mulciber [i.e., Vulcan]. Father Mars, disturbed by insane love of Venus, was turned from a terrible warlord into a lover. Nor was Venus, than whom no goddess is softer, bashful or difficult at the prayers of Gradivus [i.e., Mars]. . . . But they used to conceal their copulation well, and their crime was full of modest shame. On the evidence of the Sun—who could deceive the Sun?—Vulcan became aware of the acts of his wife. What a bad example you set, O Sun! Ask a reward from her, and if you keep quiet, you too can have what she can give. Mulciber arranges a hidden snare above and around the bed. He feigns a journey to Lemnos; the lovers come for their assignation; entangled in the snares they lie naked. He [i.e., Mulciber] summons the gods; the captives provide a spectacle; the tears of Venus could hardly be restrained. They cannot cover their faces or even hide their obscene parts with their hands. Then someone laughing says, "If your chains seem onerous to you, O Mars, transfer them to me!" He [i.e., Mulciber] hardly releases the captive bodies at your prayers, Neptune. Mars hastens to Thrace, she to Paphos. After this deed of yours, Vulcan, what they concealed before they do more freely.

Thus, Abelard implies, it was with Heloise and himself. A terrible warrior of the schools became a lover. When his affair with Heloise was concealed, they acted in shame, but after Fulbert discovered it, they behaved shamelessly. Mars, of course, did not enhance his reputation by this behavior; in fact, in the Middle

Ages he was regarded as a bad example, illustrating the danger of cultivating Venus.

Not long after the lovers were separated, Heloise wrote to Abelard "full of exultation" to announce her pregnancy. Although Abelard probably did not share her exultation, he was sufficiently moved to take advantage of Fulbert's absence from home one night to steal Heloise away. They set out in all probability with two or three servants, well mounted, but with Heloise disguised as a nun so that she might more easily pass through the Petit Chastelet under the eyes of the royal guards. They would have ridden up the Orléans road and southward toward the Loire, hastening toward Le Pallet, where Abelard put Heloise in the care of his sister to await the birth of the child. Abelard returned at once to Paris to resume his duties. Fulbert was outraged once more, but hesitant to attack Abelard while his niece was in the hands of his family. To make sure that he would not be seized and held as a hostage, however, Abelard always went accompanied by an armed guard. This state of affairs could hardly last very long. Abelard saw Fulbert frequently at the Cathedral and elsewhere in Paris, the story of the affair was on everyone's lips, frequently exaggerated, and Abelard was in constant fear of the opinions of the court, where there must have been much unseemly laughter, of the canons of the Cathedral, of the scholars of St. Victor, and of the students, who doubtless enjoyed the scandal. His conscience also disturbed him. Finally, he approached Fulbert directly, reminding him somewhat inappropriately of "how women had cast down many of the best men in ruin since the beginning of the human race," and offering to marry Heloise. Fulbert agreed to the marriage and the contract was sealed with kisses between them, which were, in the twelfth century, commonly administered for this purpose.

A great deal has been written about the niceties of canon law involved in this arrangement, and we do not know how Abelard intended to reconcile his marital status with his ecclesiastical ambitions. He was, at the time, a canon, and married canons, who were not necessarily priests, were common. For that matter, if

Abelard had been sufficiently unscrupulous, he might have managed to keep a wife and go on to higher ecclesiastical positions. Efforts of the Church to discourage marriage among beneficed priests were still meeting with strong local resistance. But increasing pressure and the vigorous spirit of reform that was sweeping across Europe in the first half of the century would have made the prospects discouraging. Neither Abelard nor Heloise showed any concern for canon law. They were worried instead about his status as a philosopher. As we shall see, there are certain features of Abelard's account of his own career that are historically suspect, and we cannot be sure that he always recorded events with a scrupulous eye to literal truth. Considering the length of *The History of My Calamities* and the span of time it covers, he devotes a surprising amount of space in it to the views of Heloise on the subject of marriage.

When Abelard returned to Le Pallet to bring Heloise home for her wedding, he must have faced another difficult situation. Their child, Astrolabe, had been born. We hear very little more about him, although Abelard wrote an admonitory poem full of moral instruction for him shortly before his death, and later Heloise wrote to Peter the Venerable of Cluny seeking a benefice for her son, who had become a priest. Abelard's family must have regarded both the child and the proposed marriage with some disfavor. It is easy to imagine some of the older men commenting among themselves on the dubiousness of Berengar's decision to send his son to school. Bastards were not in themselves an unusual feature of aristocratic life. In fact, even minor noblemen could and did sometimes produce them in astonishing numbers without resorting to rape, being accused of "paganism," having their religion questioned, or in fact being criticized very much at all if they did not allow the process of begetting to interfere with their military and administrative efficiency. There may have been other bastards at Le Pallet. But they were more appropriate for men of military rather than ecclesiastical distinction. As for the marriage, it would be of no benefit whatsoever to the estate and would not help Abelard's career.

The most troublesome person Abelard encountered, however, if we are to believe him, was Heloise herself. She did not want to marry Abelard, not, as she explained, because she did not love him, but because she did. Her argument, reported very fully by Abelard, points out that Fulbert would never be satisfied with the solution proposed and that marriage would detract from Abelard's fame, injuring the Church and shaming the philosophers. But these considerations lead to an attack on marriage generally reminiscent of the arguments in St. Jerome's treatise *Against Jovinian*, which is indeed used directly. St. Jerome's treatise has been widely misunderstood. It is not an attack either on women or on marriage actually, but simply an elaboration of the Pauline doctrine that although marriage is good, chastity for those who can manage it is better. The comparison leads the old saint, who was a master of classical rhetoric, to dwell on the disadvantages of marriage in order to make continence seem more attractive. Heloise plays a delightful trick on her audience: she elaborates arguments concerning the disadvantages of marriage, but fails to carry through to its logical application to Abelard the argument in favor of continence. The result is a remarkable piece of medieval humor, probably reflecting Abelard's wit rather than any actual conversation on the part of the historical Heloise, and it may serve as an illustration of the kind of jocularity with which our philosopher enlivened his lectures in dialectic. But the reasoning is learned, full of citations no longer familiar, and the humor has been lost to most readers since the Middle Ages.

Heloise launches her little sermon on "the infamy and difficulties of marriage" by quoting St. Paul (1 Cor. 7:27–28), "Art thou loosed from a wife? Seek not a wife. But if you take a wife thou hast not sinned. Nevertheless such [who take a wife] shall have tribulation of the flesh." He also said (verse 32), "But I would have you to be without solicitude." She asserts that the same view is held by the philosophers, calling attention to what is said by Theophrastus in the "Golden Book" quoted at length by St. Jerome, and to a remark by Cicero to the effect that "he could not devote himself to a wife and to philosophy at the same time."

Having established her authority among both divines and philosophers, Heloise launches into a bill of particulars concerning the
disadvantages of marriage for the scholar: "How is it fitting for
scholars to associate with wet-nurses, to place writing-desks among
cradles, books or writing-tablets with distaffs, styluses or pens
with spindles? Who is there intent on sacred or philosophical
meditations who could sustain the crying of children, the silliness
of nurses comforting them, the tumult among the men and women
of the household? Who would be able to tolerate the constant
dirty messes of the little ones?" Indeed, the concentration necessary for really devoted scholarship is difficult in such surroundings,
which is probably one reason that so few of our young "doctors"
are scholars, although it is true that they are discouraged more
effectively in other ways. But it is doubtful that little Heloise
actually said anything like this, much less what follows. The
wealthy, she asserts, may tolerate these things because their houses
have many rooms and they do not have to worry about expenses.
But wealthy men, who are "implicated in daily concerns," do not
study philosophy. This observation leads her to a description of
the Life of the Philosopher.

The "distinguished philosophers of the past," she says, "above
all condemned the world," by which she means the amenities and
pleasures of life, "not merely relinquishing temporal concerns but
fleeing from them, cutting themselves off from all pleasures so that
they might rest in the embrace of philosophy alone." The "embrace
of philosophy," we might interject, is hardly the same thing as "the
embrace of Heloise." But to continue, Heloise quotes Seneca in support of this view. He said that "once you interrupt" the study of
philosophy "it disappears. Other concerns are to be resisted, nor
are they to be simply regulated, but banished." As a mistress, that
is, philosophy demands either exclusive attention or she will not
be compliant at all. Heloise compares philosophers with good
monks, who give up everything for the love of God, a comparison,
incidentally, that was heartily endorsed by Abelard in one of the
sermons he later wrote for her after she became an abbess. She
points out that among all peoples—pagans, Christians, or Jews—a

few men have been of outstanding merit, "separating themselves from the people by a certain uniqueness of continence or absti-nence." It is not simply "the pursuit of knowledge" that charac-terizes the philosopher, she affirms, quoting St. Augustine for support, but "a laudable mode of life" marked by "sobriety and continence." Her little sermon concludes in a burst of rhetoric: "But if laymen and pagans lived in this way, restrained by no profession of religion, what is it proper for you, a clerk and a canon, to do, lest you prefer wicked delights to divine offices, lest this Charybdis swallow you precipitously, lest you imprudently and irrevocably immerse yourself in these obscenities? If you care nothing for clerical prerogatives, at least defend the dignity of a philosopher. If you condemn reverence for God, at least let the love of virtue temper your impudence. Remember that Socrates was married, and remember also that foul incident by which he first atoned for that falling away from philosophy, so that after-ward others might be made more cautious by his example. Jerome did not pass it over when he wrote concerning Socrates in the first book of *Against Jovinian*: 'One time when he had withstood an infinite number of invectives cast at him by Xanthippe from the upper floor, and had been doused with dirty water, his response, as he wiped his head, was no more than this: "I knew that a shower would follow such thunder!" ' "

Abelard would probably have liked to have his audience imagine him listening to this as he sat with Heloise in the hall at Le Pallet, perhaps after dinner as the servants were clearing away the table, while his brother and sister, intent on the next steps in their routine of domestic affairs, paused for a moment to listen open-mouthed to the outburst from their young guest. The thunder they had heard could only be followed by another condemnation of Abelard's conduct, for had he not "loosed the reins of libido" and abandoned the continence proper to a divine and a philosopher? Had he not neglected his studies and his students, endangered his career, and, in short, abandoned altogether that life of continence that marks the true philosopher? Even his efforts to "do the right thing," as it were, by proposing the honorable solution of marriage were here

greeted with scorn. He must have felt, indeed, that an "infinite
number of invectives" had been cast at him, at least by implication,
from an entirely unexpected quarter. Would these, he must have
wondered, be followed by a shower of dirty water?

The only logical conclusion he could expect would be a final
denunciation of his conduct and an injunction that he forget
Heloise altogether, devoting himself, as Seneca had recommended,
to complete self-restraint in uninterrupted study, and satisfying
himself only with those solaces to be obtained in the embrace of
philosophy as so many distinguished pagans, Christians, and Jews
had done before him. We can imagine him thinking to himself,
ruefully, that the nun's habit Heloise had worn as a disguise had
somehow penetrated the surface and become a part of her mentality, in spite of the infant Astrolabe. But the "dirty water" came
finally in another form. For Heloise, completely abandoning logic
with a somewhat alarming feminine flair, is made to say that it
would be "more pleasing" to her and "more virtuous" for him if
she became his mistress rather than his wife. "Then love alone
would keep me for her, and no force of nuptial bond would restrain me, and that if we were separated at times, we should find
the pleasure of our meetings greater because they would be less
frequent." Abelard was to have, in effect, the freedom from
"solicitude" recommended by St. Paul, the uninterrupted devotion
to philosophy recommended by Cicero and Seneca, the superior
life of continence setting off monks and philosophers from the rest
of humanity, and greater pleasure in carnal copulation with Heloise
at the same time. It is small wonder that generations of scholars
since the late seventeenth century, not really much in love with
St. Paul, Jerome, Augustine, Cicero, and Seneca, and certainly not
attracted by the austerities of the philosophical life, have found
Heloise extremely attractive. Here is that miracle of having one's
cake and eating it too unfolding before our very eyes. But medieval
audiences, whose expectations were somewhat less sanguine, must
have envisaged Heloise's "virtuous" Abelard with that amusement
which is always the just reward of the hypocrite.

Heloise concludes by saying that if the marriage is carried out, "the sorrow of our perdition will be no less than the love that preceded it." But Abelard could only wipe his head without saying anything at all. The situation in Paris was impossible as it was, and the business of making Heloise his mistress would hardly have improved it. In fact, that is what got them into trouble in the first place. They would simply be following further in the footsteps of Mars and Venus, doing shamelessly what they had done shame-fully before, a course that would neither placate Fulbert nor endear Abelard to his students, who would laugh at him, nor to those ecclesiastical authorities upon whom the prospects of his promotion in the hierarchy depended. Marriage seemed the only solution, even if Heloise showed distinct promise of becoming a very able Xanthippe. As for Heloise, it is obvious that Abelard does not here present her in a very good light, but makes her instead ridic-ulous. We should not consider the historical Heloise as the source of the false reasoning Abelard attributes to her, although she may very well have made a simple offer to be his concubine. As we shall see, however, the amusing verbal antics attributed to her would not have proved offensive to Heloise after she became Abbess of the Paraclete in later years when Abelard's *History* came to her attention. Time and circumstances, for reasons we shall consider, would have made them a kind of compliment.

In any event, Abelard paid no attention to any objections Heloise may have had to their marriage. Leaving little Astrolabe with Abelard's sister, the couple returned to Paris secretly. There "having kept secret vigils at night in a certain famous church," they were married at dawn one day, doubtless immediately after Lauds, in the company of Fulbert and some friends of Heloise. Abelard, of course, wished to keep the marriage secret, as Chaucer would say, "for shame of his degree," or out of fear of what his associates would think about it in a man of his status. Fulbert, on the other hand, wished to make the marriage known for fear of what people of all kinds might say about Heloise. Fame, that fickle bestower of rewards and punishments to the vain, was at stake in both instances. During the centuries that followed, incidentally, the Church did all it could to discourage secret marriages, and by the

time of Rabelais they were considered to be notoriously reprehensible. A secret wife is just about as dangerous as a mistress. When
Fulbert would say that his niece was married to the great Abelard,
Heloise, as Abelard tells us, would deny it vehemently, cursing
her poor uncle. Finally, Abelard could stand the strain no longer,
and, dressing Heloise in a nun's habit, he took her to the convent
at Argenteuil where she might seem to be a nun without taking the
vows of a nun. There he visited her secretly from time to time,
meeting her at least once alone in the refectory, which was dedicated to the Holy Mother of God, and there making love to her.
Here a man forty years old, a famous exegete and philosopher, was
compelled to visit his wife in the refectory of a nunnery, lifting her
nun's habit for those amorous caresses both knew so well. When
Abelard contemplated this activity, he must have been a little
ashamed of his noble birth, not to mention being worried a little
about the Blessed Virgin. She was a fountain of mercy to all good
men in the twelfth century, but it would hardly do to excite her
risibilities.

When Fulbert learned that Heloise was at Argenteuil, he did
not learn at the same time of Abelard's carefully concealed visits.
He and his friends, Abelard tells us, "thought that I had deceived
them greatly, believing that I had made her a nun in order to get
rid of her easily." He who devises worldly stratagems runs the risk
of being caught by them in unexpected ways, and the stratagem of
the lovers proved to be exceptionally risky. They did not get caught
in the refectory, but Fulbert's wrath at the idea of his niece being
cast aside was uncontrollable. He conferred with his friends, who
recommended decisive action. As Abelard describes it, "One night
when I was asleep in a private chamber of my lodgings they bribed
a servant of mine to let them enter, and they punished me with
that most savage and shameful revenge that filled all the world
with astonishment. That is, they cut off those parts of my body
with which I had done the deed they deplored." Another servant,
more faithful, must have raised the hue and cry in the streets,
arousing the neighbors, for two of Abelard's assailants were captured, and, in accordance with the crude but effective justice of the

time, "deprived of their eyes and genitals." The creation of a pair of sturdy beggars by this means, however, was of small comfort to the philosopher. Heloise had lost her treasured solaces forever. But the lovers had lost something else: Abelard's fame.

Ever since he was a mere boy setting out to conquer the world with dialectic, Abelard had been seeking fame. He had struggled bitterly with William of Champeaux, one of the most influential scholars of the day, to win fame. He had, at some risk, subverted some of the students of old Anselm of Laon to win fame. He had worked hard, long, and successfully to obtain a mastership at Paris, to win fame. Heloise had objected to their marriage to preserve his fame, and after they were married had vigorously denied that the marriage existed, just to preserve his fame. Now that fame was gone, vanishing at the stroke of a knife in the night. "When day dawned," Abelard tells us, "the whole city congregated about me, and it is difficult if not impossible to describe the extent to which they were stupefied with astonishment, or how great was their lamentation, or how much they irritated me with their clamor, or how greatly they disturbed me with their complaints. The clerks especially and particularly my own students tortured me with their intolerable laments and wailings, and I suffered much more from their compassion than from my wounds, feeling the embarrassment more keenly than the injury, afflicted by the shame more than by the pain." We can imagine the people jostling in the narrow street, eagerly questioning one another while seeking to avoid the drainage ditch in the middle of the thoroughfare, anxious to learn more of the disaster and its causes. Abelard's fellow-canons and his own students who entered the house to console him were probably questioned eagerly by the throng as they emerged, and it would have been easy for Abelard to hear snatches of the queries, the conjectures, and the expressions of astonishment through the windows.

At the time Abelard was a very vain man, or at least this is the impression he creates. He did not think immediately of Heloise, now isolated both from her uncle and from him, nor of Astrolabe, nor even of the delights of which he had suddenly been deprived.

He thought only of his shame and loss of reputation. "There ran through my mind thoughts of how much fame I had acquired, and of how easily and quickly this fame had been brought low, if indeed it was not extinguished, and of the just judgment of God in that I had been afflicted in that part of my body with which I had sinned." Thoughts of justice only brought his mind back to thoughts of infamy, however, and he imagined himself a public spectacle. "I frequently thought of how just my betrayal had been by him whom I had previously betrayed, of how my rivals would praise such equity, of how great and lasting a sorrow these wounds would bring to my family, and to my friends when they came to know of what had happened, of how rapidly the whole world would come to know of my singular infamy, or of what I should do and what attitude I should take when every finger was pointed at me in public, insulted by every tongue, a monstrous spectacle for all." The shame of eunuchry was heighted by memories of fulminations against it under the Old Law, and there echoed in Abelard's mind the words of Deuteronomy 23:1, "An eunuch, whose testicles are broken or cut away, or yard cut off, shall not enter into the church of the Lord." Even animals in that miserable condition were considered unfit for sacrifice. The colorful embroidered *cotes* and fur-lined mantles that hung from the pole in his room, and the fine linens in his chest, in fact all that sartorial splendor that set Abelard off as a man apart must have seemed depressingly and ironically useless to him as he sat brooding in his chamber. There he was, a disgraced creature, alone in spite of the painful sympathy of his students.

Eventually Abelard did think of Heloise. What could he do with her? She was his wife, but he could no longer function as a husband. Suicide was rigorously condemned both by Cicero and by Christian law. That course would only confirm his reputation as a betrayer, for the great exemplar of suicide was Judas, who had hanged himself after the betrayal of Christ. Abelard would hardly have wished to join the family of Ganelon, that exemplar of treason whose ancient home, they said, lay across the river. To leave Heloise once more to the mercies of Fulbert would have been

cruel, and to take her home to Le Pallet would only create a problem for his family, since she could hardly be expected to lapse
into a docile routine there, refraining from contact with men.
There seemed only one course open, and Abelard took it. He sent
orders to Argenteuil that Heloise was to take the veil.

The sorrow of Heloise at the news of Abelard's misfortune must
have been intense. She too would have been bitterly disappointed
at the loss of his fame, but even more bitter to her was the thought
that the man she considered to be the greatest philosopher of the
day was now lost to her forever. She accepted his order to take the
veil, blaming herself, somewhat irrationally but with a certain self-
satisfaction, for his disgrace. When her friends sought to restrain
her, "thinking the yoke of monastic rule intolerable for one of
her youth," she replied by quoting the words of Cornelia, wife of
Pompey the Great, when his downfall seemed imminent and she
considered her marriage to him to be the cause. At least these are
the words attributed to the lady in Lucan's *Pharsalia*:

> O greatest husband!
> O my unworthy marriage bed! Did Fortune have power
> Over such a mighty head for this? Why did I wed thee
> If I was to be the cause of thy misery? Now take the penalties.
> But I gladly atone for them.

The great commander of the armies of dialectic had fallen, had
taken his "penalties" for the marriage, and Heloise, like Cornelia,
was willing to atone for her crime in marrying him. Abelard was
doubtless aware, when he wrote his *History,* of a certain exaggeration in these words he attributes to his wife. He was, after all, no
Pompey, and the real cause of his troubles was his own weakness
rather than the decision of Heloise to submit to marriage. That is,
Heloise is made to display a great deal of injured vanity herself
in her reasons for taking vows, and vanity, we might add, is a far
different thing from the devotion that ought to motivate a prospec-
tive nun. Medieval readers, who were not sentimental, must have
read the defiant quotation from Lucan with an amused smile. But
we may again doubt that the actual Heloise, as distinct from the

character in Abelard's *History,* went quite so far. And again there are reasons why a display of vanity at this point would prove to be ultimately complimentary to the Abbess of the Paraclete, enhancing the remarkable extent of her reform. Abelard, however, assures us that having spoken the above words, Heloise "hastened to the altar and speedily before the bishop took the blessed veil, and bound herself to the religious life before everyone."

Abelard himself hastened to do the same thing, not out of "devotion," as he says, but out of "shame." His friends had urged this course upon him. One of them, a certain Fulk of Deuil, wrote him a letter showing that through pride, avarice, and lechery Abelard had subjected himself to Fortune, or to that apparently fortuitous alternation between prosperity and adversity that eventually cuts down all those who set their hearts on the transitory goods of this world. Now, after his mutilation, Fulk points out, he can become a good monk, free of the vices that harmed him. Fulk stresses Abelard's subjection to the blandishments of fame. He had also heard that Abelard loved women inordinately and that his fondness for prostitutes made him avaricious. But he assures his friend of the practical advantages of his new state. He can spend the night in the houses of married women without arousing the suspicions of their husbands, he can pass unharmed by choirs of virgins in the splendor of their youth, and he need have no fear of sodomy or other difficulties. He acknowledges the laments of the city over Abelard's wound, but urges him not to appeal to Rome for vengeance, for it is impossible, he says, to get anything from Rome without money. Finally, he urges his friend to take no vengeance on Fulbert but to love his enemies. This jolly epistle, if it was sent to Abelard at the time, must have been far from consoling. But there were probably others who urged him more seriously to enter the regular life of the monastery. The habit of a monk was a kind of denial of worldly concern, and Abelard was now well suited for it. Having been made a eunuch by the hands of men, he might now become, in the words of the Gospel, a eunuch for the sake of God.

Arrangements for him to enter a monastery were probably made by friends at court, for he took his vows at the Abbey of St. Denis, which, at the time, was almost an instrument of the French royal house and an important administrative center. It had been founded by King Dagobert in honor of St. Dionysius, or St. Denis, the patron saint of France, and it had long been the traditional final resting-place of French kings. The abbey was conveniently located, not far from Paris, and probably seemed to Abelard and to his friends an excellent place to begin his monastic career. Once there, he was urged to resume his teaching, both by the abbot and by numerous students, so that, as he says, "What I had before done for the love of fame or for money I should seek to do for the love of God." Having administered previously to the wealthy, he should now, they said, devote himself to the education of the poor, becoming "not a philosopher of the world, but a true philosopher of God." Doubtless all this seemed reasonable at the time, but Abelard was still ambitious, and not far away, at Argenteuil, Heloise was probably hoping that her former husband would now rise to fame once more within the confines of the cloistered life. As for herself, she had a long "atonement" before her, and, in actual fact as distinct from the later picture we get in the *Letters,* she probably devoted herself energetically, with only occasional uncomfortable lapses, to the settled routine of her new career. In terms of Abelard's *History,* both could now look forward to that life of continence and sobriety that distinguishes philosophers of all ages—pagan, Christian, and Jewish—from the vulgar multitudes. Poor Heloise could, that is, enjoy the ideals she had praised so vociferously in her little sermon on marriage.

CHAPTER IV

The Fugitive

*I*n the year 1120, when Abelard was beginning to display his usual energetic intransigence at St. Denis, other events were taking place elsewhere that boded further ill for his future. A certain Norbert, born into the illustrious family of Gennep at Xanten, after a youthful life as a pleasure-seeking courtier, had been suddenly converted, become a priest, and set out on an apostolic pilgrimage. His success was astonishing as he progressed through the countryside preaching on the theme of peace, and seeking to quell the feudal wars of the local magnates through whose territories he passed. Huge crowds, comparable in size to those attracted by Bernard of Clairvaux, welcomed him. He was joined by Hugh of Fosses, who gave up his possessions in order to become his disciple. The pair passed through Rheims shortly before the great council there in 1119, and proceeding until they reached the Abbey of St. Thierry, they met the new Bishop of Laon, Bartholomew of Vir. Returning to Rheims with the bishop, they attended the council, which, among other things, passed stringent measures to reform the clergy, including a new injunction against married priests that was greeted with riotous dissent by the clergy of Normandy. Norbert sought approval for his preaching from Pope Calixtus, but the pope and the bishop wished him to make something more of himself than an itinerant preacher, and urged him to come with them to Laon after the council.

At Laon Norbert was placed in charge of a college of canons, which he set out to reform by adding much more stringent regulations than those usually governing Augustinian regulars. This effort was not successful, but Norbert decided to set up a house in the forests of Prémontré, and there, in 1120, the first cells of the new Premonstratensian Order were erected. Norbert was strongly influenced by his friend Bernard of Clairvaux in the formation of his new rule. Among his first "White Canons," as the Premonstratensians were called, were some students from the Cathedral school at Laon, who doubtless brought with them stories of Abelard and his treatment of the late Master Anselm, stories now revived by rumors of Abelard's downfall at Paris, which probably became more lurid each time they passed from one ecclesiastic to another. In the following year a house of Cistercians was established at Foigny, also in the diocese of Laon. Bernard and Norbert were both avid clerical reformers and popular preachers. It is not unlikely that in the course of time Abelard often served as a bad example in their popular sermons. The astonishing success of both the Premonstratensians and the Cistercians during the next few years must have appalled poor Abelard, who was now forced to seek advancement as a regular himself.

Ironically, Abelard was little pleased with St. Denis. Although he had just recovered, rather precipitously, from a life of extreme laxity, he could not bear the laxity of his brothers in the monastery, whom he proceeded, illadvisedly, to castigate. As he puts it, "This abbey of mine to which I had brought myself was at the time devoted to a most secular and wicked way of life. The abbot himself surpassed his monks in evil life and notoriety, just as he surpassed them in rank. By frequently and vehemently reprimanding their intolerable filthiness both in private and in public I made myself immoderately burdensome and odious to all of them." It is true that before the reforms instituted by Suger, who became abbot in 1121, the abbey was both morally and structurally in a state of decay. Bernard perhaps exaggerated a little when he called it a "workshop of Vulcan," but Abelard had some reason to complain even if the complaint sounded odd coming from him.

He had, however, abandoned neither his vanity nor his ambition, and the monks soon set him apart in a cell of his own where he could teach. In this enterprise, no longer distracted by Heloise, he succeeded very well indeed. "Such a multitude of students gathered there," he says, "that neither did the place suffice to house them, nor did the neighborhood suffice to feed them." We can imagine the irritation of the monks when students flocked to the abbey, an irritation perhaps tempered a little by pride. Abelard began once more to accumulate wealth, since students in such numbers hardly represented "the poor" he had originally set out to educate, and, at the same time, his self-confidence was largely restored.

The substance of Abelard's teaching has some bearing on subsequent events, so that it is important to know a little about it in a very general way. In the first place, he did not give up the study of the *trivium*, or the "secular arts" as he calls them, in which, he says, he was "better grounded," and which had the greatest appeal to the students. He used them, he says, "as a kind of hook to attract those lured by a philosophical flavor to the study of true philosophy." This is the traditional procedure of what is usually called "Christian humanism." Abelard cites Origen, his favorite Patristic author, as a precedent, but he might well have mentioned Lactantius, Augustine, Boethius, and many others. The peculiar distinction of Abelard's method was that the particular "secular art" he knew best was dialectic, and the use of dialectic for this purpose was at the time still fairly new, although it was to become commonplace in the next century. Again, the grammatical scholars of his day were busy interpreting passages in works like *The Consolation of Philosophy* of Boethius or Plato's *Timaeus* "by integument," as they said, or by discerning beneath the figurative surface language of such works, foreshadowings or allegories of Christian truth. At about the time Abelard entered St. Denis, William of Conches, who became famous for this method, began

[63]

teaching at Chartres. He soon produced a commentary on *The Consolation of Philosophy* in which he treated Plato's "World Soul" as an "integument" for the Holy Spirit. This is not the same thing as saying that the "World Soul" *is* the Holy Spirit, but simply that it suggests the idea and may be a convenient figure for it. Abelard was to adopt a similar doctrine for a time. He also used other figurative materials from the realm of "grammar." Both the dialectic and the grammar when used in this way were highly relished by students, but they were, at the same time, resented by more conventional exegetes. Although figurative materials from the *auctores* had long been used, especially by St. Augustine and his followers, they were peculiarly offensive to the literal-minded or to men with serious reforming zeal. Abelard taught exegesis, or "theology," as well as the arts, but he made the latter more relevant in new ways to the former. The appeal of this method to the students may be judged from the remark, "My scholars in both kinds of studies began to multiply, and all other schools to dwindle enormously."

The chief aim of the new techniques was clarity. As we have seen, Abelard had a special facility for making obscure or complex ideas readily understandable. With characteristic boldness he attacked one of the most difficult problems of all, the mystery of the Trinity, producing a treatise *On the Divine Unity and Trinity* that he was to elaborate later in versions of his *Theology*. His aim was not to express any new or unorthodox teachings on the subject, but to make accepted doctrines as they might be found in the Fathers, especially in St. Augustine and Boethius, both of whom wrote treatises on the Trinity, more understandable to his own contemporaries. He expresses this aim very well himself. His students, he wrote, "had asked for human and philosophical reasons, earnestly demanding those things that might be understood rather than those things that might merely be spoken, saying that any explanation that cannot be understood consists only of so many superfluous words, that nothing can be believed unless it is first comprehended, and that it is ridiculous to preach something that can be understood neither by the teacher nor by the taught, for the

Lord Himself condemned the blind who would be leaders of the blind [Matthew 15:14]." It is not difficult to see here a reflection of the basic attitudes of Berengar of Tours, and neither is it difficult to see that these attitudes might produce troubles for Abelard just as they had for Berengar. The Trinity, moreover, was a delicate subject about which ecclesiastical authorities were extremely sensitive, as Roscelin had discovered, and any new tampering with it would have been especially suspect coming from Abelard.

Abelard's success at St. Denis apparently irritated his old rivals at Laon even before his treatise appeared. Alberic of Rheims and Lotulf the Lombard, who became firm friends of Bernard of Clairvaux, were now installed at Rheims, where they directed a school of some distinction, and together they began a campaign to discredit Abelard, "objecting," Abelard says, "behind my back that since I had become a monk I had no business lingering over secular studies, and that I had presumed to become a master of sacred studies without having been taught by a master myself." There was some substance, as we have seen, to the latter charge, although the former had little to recommend it, since *auctores* had been studied in monasteries for centuries. Bernard of Clairvaux, whose training was monastic, was well versed in the *trivium* as well as in Scriptural study. But the allegation that Abelard was teaching sacred studies without having been trained in them was more just, and the masters of Rheims had some success in uniting "bishops, archbishops, abbots, and whatever persons of note they could find" to prevent him from teaching. The new treatise on the Trinity offered a specific piece of evidence that could be used against him.

Among Abelard's enemies was his old master Roscelin, who is said to have complained to the Bishop of Paris about the orthodoxy of Abelard's new book. Some correspondence passed between Abelard and Roscelin at about this time. We have only Roscelin's reply to a letter Abelard wrote to the canons of St. Martin of Tours, among whom Roscelin was then established. Disregarding its theological content, we can readily see from it how much the affair with Heloise had damaged Abelard's reputation. Roscelin points out that having been admitted to Fulbert's house, and having been entrusted with the care of Heloise, Abelard taught her to fornicate rather than to dispute, which was undoubtedly true. But he also thought that Abelard should not have resumed his teaching, "lest," as he said indelicately, "just as your tail, with which you were wont to punch indifferently when you could, was cut off by virtue of your uncleanness, so also your tongue, with which you punch, as it were, should be cut off as well." He accused Abelard further of paying his whore for past favors with money gained from teaching. We may hope that Abelard was, in fact, contributing to the comfort of his former wife. But the tone of Roscelin's letter, although he did not, like Fulk of Deuil, attribute to Abelard a taste for prostitutes, indicates that a book on the Trinity by the former master at the Cathedral at Paris was likely to be regarded with grave suspicion whether there was any theological basis for that suspicion or not.

It is not surprising, therefore, that the masters of Rheims, Alberic and Lotulf, were able to persuade their archbishop and the Papal Legate Cono of Praeneste to summon Abelard to a council held in 1121 at Soissons, not far from Laon. It seems likely that Bishop Bartholomew, patron of Norbert, may have attended this council, although Abelard says nothing about it, mentioning only Geoffrey of Lèves, Bishop of Chartres, but stating that there were other bishops there. He describes the proceedings of the council, at least insofar as they affected him, in great detail. Alberic and Lotulf apparently prepared for Abelard's arrival by preaching to the assembled clergy and the good men of Soissons, asserting that Abelard had written of "three gods" instead of one, although this was malicious slander probably based on rumor alone. The aroused populace "almost stoned" Abelard when he arrived. Today we find it difficult to understand why the theology of the Trinity could be used to arouse popular emotion, but the issues that arouse mass fervor vary widely from time to time and from place to place, seldom having any real relevance to the actual situation in which people find themselves. This is just as true today as it was in the twelfth century. It must have been with mixed feelings that Abelard journeyed once more to the neighborhood of Laon, and we can imagine that this reception was especially unnerving, in spite of the company of some of his closest disciples, who went with him. Soissons was a pleasant town set amidst some forested hills on the left bank of the Aisne. Across the river was the wealthy Abbey of St. Médard, which boasted lordship over numerous villages and manors and whose abbots could command many vassals in time of war. Here Abelard was eventually to go, if only for a few days.

When he arrived in Soissons, Abelard took a copy of his little book to the Papal Legate, saying that if he had written anything contrary to the faith he was prepared for correction and satisfaction. But the Legate refused to read it, demanding that he take it to his accusers. In his account of this event in his *History* Abelard indulges in a typical literary flourish, which is worth brief examination since it reveals the ironic indirection characteristic of medieval literary style. He says, "But he [*i.e.,* the Legate, Cono] immediately commanded me to take the book to the archbishop and my rivals, so that they who had accused me concerning it might judge me, and that these words might be fulfilled concerning me: 'Our enemies themselves are judges.'" The quotation is from Deuteronomy 32:31, but it omits the first half of the verse, which runs, "For our God is not as their gods." That is, when his readers, most of whom would have had an intimate knowledge of the Bible, suddenly remembered the verse, they would have recognized the implication that it was Abelard's accusers, actually, who were making "three gods" of the Trinity, not Abelard himself. He proceeds to illustrate this fact, or alleged fact, in his narrative.

The little story he tells first bears repeating, not because the issues at stake are especially exciting today, but to illustrate the kind of intense feeling that they were arousing among his contemporaries. He tells us that his rivals put off the examination of his book at the council, which occupied itself with other matters, because they could find nothing in it to condemn. Meanwhile, he went about the city preaching his doctrines to good effect, so that, he says, "All who heard me commended the clarity of my language and what I had to say." Abelard's physical disability had apparently left his energy unimpaired and had not dimmed his skill at public oratory, much to the irritation of his enemies. He describes an effort by Alberic to trip him up.

One day Alberic, seeking to test me, approached me with some of his disciples, and, after some flattering remarks, said that he was astonished to find in my book that although God begat God, and there is only one God, I denied that God begat Himself.

To which I at once replied, "If you wish, I shall give reasons for this position."

"We do not care," he said, "for human reasoning, or for the testimony of the senses in such matters, but only for the words of authority."

He had read the book, which he had brought with him. I turned to the place I remembered but to which he had paid little attention because he was seeking only things he might use against me. As God willed, I soon found what I sought. It was a doctrine entitled, "Augustine, *On the Trinity*, Book I." The quotation was this: "He who thinks God of his own powers to have generated Himself errs more in this belief, because not only does God not do this, but neither does any creature, spiritual or corporal. For there is no thing whatsoever that generates itself."

When Alberic's disciples, who were with him, heard this, they were stupefied. He, however, in order to protect himself said, "It is to be understood properly."

I rejoined that this was not news to me, but that the objection was not relevant at present since he had requested the words alone rather than the sense. If he wished to listen to reason and sense, however, I said that I was ready to show him how, in accordance with his teaching, he had lapsed into the heresy of saying that the Father was His own Son. When he heard this, he became like a madman, resorting to threats and saying that in this conflict neither my reasons nor my authorities would be tolerated. And then he retreated.

It is evident that neither participant in this little encounter was dominated by the spirit of charity.

However, we are likely to sympathize spontaneously with Abelard's clear readiness to employ reason and to deprecate the authoritarianism of Alberic. But this represents a simplification of the issue. Abelard did base his contention that God did not beget Himself on an authority—the authority of St. Augustine, which is very formidable indeed. When Alberic pointed out that Augustine was to be understood properly, Abelard then offered to employ "reason and sense" not only to explain the authority, but to demonstrate Alberic's heresy. This does not represent a denial of authority, but an offer to "give reasons," or to employ logic, to make both the authority and Abelard's own teaching comprehensible. In short, Abelard does not here advocate sheer "rationalism," but exactly the kind of combination of authority and logic that was to be employed systematically by the great scholastics of the next century, like St. Thomas Aquinas.

Alberic as Abelard portrays him does not appear in a very good light, and his angry retreat represents an obvious capitulation. Although Abelard probably exaggerated Alberic's stupidity in this little narrative, Alberic's reaction is not atypical of the reactions of many of Abelard's contemporaries to his use of dialectic. But these contemporaries were not always stupid, and they had, in their own time, a legitimate point of view. St. Augustine had made a careful distinction between two kinds of reason: a "higher" reason whose function is *sapientia* or "wisdom," the knowledge of things human and divine; and a "lower" reason, whose function is *scientia* or "science," the knowledge of things perceived through the senses. Traditionally, the realm of the "intelligible" was approached through the "higher" reason, although analogies might be employed from the visible world on the ground that "invisible things" are to be understood through "the things that are made." Thus for St. Augustine matters of the faith were reasonable and there was no conflict possible between faith on the one hand and reason on the other. When Abelard discussed the nature of the Trinity on the basis of "human reasoning, or the testimony of the senses," he was, in effect, employing the "lower reason" to deal with things that were the province of the "higher reason," or at least this was the impression he created among some of his con-temporaries.

In our own world, dominated by a scientific outlook, wherein the realm of "the intelligible" has disappeared, "wisdom" is very difficult to understand. But we should try to realize, first, that at the time of St. Augustine, when a realm of intelligible realities was commonplace even among pagan philosophers, "wisdom" was readily comprehensible to most educated persons, and, second, that in Abelard's time there were still many who felt that the province of revealed truth should be explained in its own terms. As all careful students of St. Augustine are aware, it is possible to en-gage in very disciplined and fruitful thought without resorting to Aristotelian logic. Many humanists throughout the Middle Ages thought that such logic was, in fact, a bar to understanding. Neither Petrarch nor Erasmus had any respect for it. And we ourselves should keep our historical distance. There is a wide gap between Aristotelian logic and the inductive procedures of modern science. Abelard's "reason" looks forward to St. Thomas, but not to the modern world. In its own day it was new, exciting, and extremely provocative. But the issues it raised were peculiarly issues of the twelfth century.

The council dragged on without paying any attention to Abelard until the morning before the final session, when the Legate, the archbishop, Abelard's accusers, and others assembled in a prelimi-nary meeting to determine what they were to do about his case in a formal way. There the distinguished Geoffrey of Lèves, who had succeeded Yvo as Bishop of Chartres, delivered a long speech in Abelard's defense. He pointed out that Abelard had many fol-lowers and a wide reputation, so that if he were condemned out of hand his fame would only be increased. He suggested that he be asked to appear before the session to answer questions. No one, evidently, was anxious to engage in any disputes with Abelard about the Trinity, so that this suggestion was rejected. Then Geoffrey proposed, quite reasonably, that Abelard be dismissed for the time being and that his abbot, Adam of St. Denis, who was present, later call a larger and more learned assembly to consider the debatable teachings. To this the Legate agreed, and Abelard was granted permission to return to St. Denis to await further developments.

But Alberic and Lotulf were not satisfied. As all academics are aware, when reason fails and justice obviously smiles on the opposition, it is often possible to achieve one's ends through administrative chicanery. They therefore went to the archbishop, pointing out that it would be "shameful" to have the case transferred elsewhere and "dangerous" to allow Abelard to escape. On these grounds they and the archbishop persuaded the Legate to condemn Abelard's book outright, to burn it publicly, and to confine Abelard perpetually in a strange monastery. Abelard, they said, had lectured from his book publicly and had permitted it to be transcribed without papal or ecclesiastical authority. His condemnation would afford an example to others not to make the same mistake. This appeal to the vanity and thirst for power of the administrators worked, and the Legate decided to act accordingly. Bishop Geoffrey, having heard of these "machinations," as Abelard justly calls them, advised the poor victim to bear what was coming quietly and patiently, assuring him that the violence of the opposition would ultimately benefit him, and that the sentence of imprisonment would soon be lifted.

Having almost escaped, Abelard was thus forced to appear before the council and to throw his treasured little book into the fire with his own hand. The act was greeted in silence until someone remarked that he had read in the burning book a statement to the effect that the Father alone is omnipotent. The Legate, Bishop Cono, who was not a very astute man, arose and announced that any child knows better, since everyone is aware that there are three Omnipotents. To the astonishment of many of those present he thus evoked the "three gods" that Abelard had been accused of advocating in the first place. A certain Thierry, the master of a school, who was among those present, arose laughing and quoted a line from the Athanasian Creed—"And nevertheless there are

not three Omnipotents but one Omnipotent." He then gave the
assembly a little lecture on the folly and immorality of condemning
Abelard without allowing him to defend himself. The archbishop
then arose, probably in great embarrassment, to correct the statement of the Legate and to suggest that Abelard expound his faith
before all, so that he might be judged. Abelard was very anxious
to do just this. He far outstripped any of his adversaries both in
quickness of mind and in Patristic learning. His fondness for
reading the Fathers "in the original," so to speak, rather than in
the snippets that appeared in glosses and books of *sententiae* gave
him an enormous advantage over many of his contemporaries.
We can imagine him smiling to himself as he prepared to arise
and confront his enemies, and we can also, perhaps, sense the
nervous excitement of his disciples as they looked forward to his
triumph, seeking to anticipate the strategies he would use and the
arguments he would advance.

But if Abelard was more brilliant than his opponents, he could
not compare with them in the techniques of what we today call
"politics." For just as he was arising from his seat, they interjected
that it would be sufficient for him to recite the Athanasian Creed.
To make sure, moreover, that he would not make any mistakes,
they would supply a written text so that he could read it. Both
the Legate and the archbishop had by this time probably had
their fill of disputation, even though Abelard had not said a word.
Moreover, it is probable that the vast majority of those assembled
were blissfully ignorant of the theology of the Trinity, knowing
only that Abelard had engaged in various kinds of disreputable
activity in the past and would probably do so again if the opportunity arose. Alberic and Lotulf prevailed, so that Abelard, weeping bitterly, was forced to read the Athanasian Creed, and was
then hauled away across the river to the Abbey of St. Médard to
be imprisoned, doubtless in a small procession where he could be
jeered by the citizens in the streets.

At St. Médard Abelard made a good impression at once. The
prior, Goswin, who had once attended some of Abelard's lectures
at Paris, praised him for his profound learning and his enormous

eloquence, and Abelard himself indicates that the monks there looked forward to his permanent residence among them and sought eagerly to console him. He was, however, extremely gloomy, falling into despair. As he puts it, "I compared those things I had previously suffered in the flesh with those I suffered now, and thought of myself as the most miserable of men. I found what I had formerly suffered as of little moment as compared with my present injury, and lamented the injury to my reputation much more than the injury to my body. For I had been brought to the latter by a certain unchastity, but I had been led to this very obvious violence by a sincere intention and love of truth, which compelled me to write." He could not understand why God had permitted him to be punished when he was innocent. The burning of his book and the official condemnation would together constitute a blot on his record that would make his further advancement very difficult indeed. We find him at this point still deeply concerned about his fame and almost faithless where Divine Providence was concerned.

This situation was not much ameliorated when he was released after a few days from his imprisonment. Bishop Geoffrey had probably not been silent about the spectacle he had witnessed, and it seems likely that Abelard's friends at court may have intervened on his behalf. He tells us that his enemies at the council went so far as to deny their part in his condemnation and asserts further that even the Legate began to talk about "the envy of the French" in connection with it. All this would seem to indicate either that the account of the council in the *History* is exaggerated, as it may well be, or that pressure was being applied elsewhere, since administrative officials do not ordinarily hasten to correct their errors of their own accord. Abelard returned to St. Denis, where he may have written his *Grammar*, now lost, probably as a manual for his students. But his own thoughtlessness soon engendered another crisis. One day he happened to be reading the commentary of St. Bede on the Acts of the Apostles, a work that won widespread acclaim in the Middle Ages and was considered to be a standard authority. In it Bede asserts that Dionysius the Areopagite was actually Bishop of Corinth. The St. Dionysius for whom the Abbey of St. Denis was named was thought to have been the Areopagite of Acts 17:34, who, hearing St. Paul, "did believe." He was also said to have been Bishop of Athens and the author of certain treatises, actually composed in Syria around 500 A.D., and, finally, he was supposed to have been the Apostle to the Gauls buried on the spot where the abbey was founded. This legend was contained in an official biography by Abbot Hilduin (d. 840), who translated the Greek works of the Syrian Dionysius for Louis the Pious. A new and better translation was supplied later in the ninth century by John the Scot, who worked at St. Denis under the patronage of Charles the Bald.

When Abelard discovered that Bede's account did not harmonize with the official legend, he was apparently amused, but instead of keeping this amusement to himself, as he should, he "jokingly" remarked to some of the monks nearby that Bede did not agree with their official history. The matter might have rested there, but the brethren failed to see the joke and angrily called Bede "a most mendacious writer." This was enough to arouse Abelard's indigna‑ tion, for, as John of Salisbury tells us, he had a great respect for those in the past who had labored hard and assiduously in such a manner that their successors might benefit from their work, a commendable attitude that is not quite the same thing as unthink‑ ing faith in authority. When he was asked, therefore, which authority he preferred, Bede or Hilduin, he replied that to him Bede, "whose writings were esteemed by the whole Latin Church," as indeed they were, seemed to him preferable. The monks then accused him of slandering the Kingdom of France, although he assured them that he did not care whether St. Denis was the Areo‑ pagite or not, so long as he was a good man.

Modern scholars, distorting these events, have hailed Abelard as a champion of modern "scientific philology," setting himself up in opposition to blind authoritarianism. But to characterize the casual reading of Bede as "scientific philology" is to make that discipline even more insignificant than it ordinarily seems to be. Actually, the whole affair was in itself trivial, especially since Abelard was later to write a defense of the traditional account of St. Dionysius, but the offended monks ran to Abbot Adam, who, taking advantage of this opportunity to get rid of Abelard in a decisive way, held a chapter meeting in which it was agreed that he was to be held in captivity until he could be turned over to the King for judgment.

Still smarting from the proceedings at Soissons, Abelard had little faith in administrative clemency, so that, feeling that the whole world was against him, he fled to the territory of Count Thibaut of Blois, where, he says, he had "previously spent some time in a cell." He says further that Count Thibaut knew him slightly, but we do not know when Abelard had previously visited Provins, which was his destination, or how he came to be known to the count. Thibaut was the son of the ill-fated crusader Stephen of Blois and the devout Adèle, daughter of William the Conqueror and sister to Henry I of England. Count Thibaut frequently came into conflict with the King of France, since his family ties with the English court were very strong. In November, 1120, he suffered a serious emotional shock when the famous, or infamous, White Ship, carrying across the channel much of the English royal household, including young William, heir to the throne, sank in a storm. Although the ship was a masterpiece of naval architecture as it was then understood, the mariners were apparently drunk. The disaster saddened Adèle, so that she soon entered a nunnery, and Thibaut began to show increasing interest in acts of piety and devotion.

Abelard thus approached him at a fairly auspicious time. Moreover, he had known the prior of St. Ayoul in Provins, who, he says, was "delighted to see me and looked after me with all diligence." Again, it is a shame that he does not tell us more about his acquaintance with Thibaut or his friendship with the prior, but it is evident, with regard to the first, that he continued to exert a certain amount of influence in aristocratic circles.

But he had not been in the friendly atmosphere of Provins very long when Abbot Adam appeared to discuss certain affairs of his with the count. Wishing to take advantage of this contingency, Abelard and his friend the prior asked Thibaut to intercede with the abbot in Abelard's favor, asking absolution for him and per-

mission to resume the monastic life wherever he could find a convenient location. It is possible that at this time Thibaut granted
Abelard the land that was later to be the site of the Paraclete,
although we do not actually know who was responsible for the
grant or when it was made. But after holding a council, the abbot
refused Abelard's request, threatening him with excommunication
if he did not return to St. Denis, and his friend the prior of St.
Ayoul with a similar punishment if he continued to harbor him.
What Thibaut thought about this we do not know. Perhaps the
abbot had not fared well in his negotiations with him and wished
to express his displeasure. Abelard says that Adam and his brethren behaved in this way because "they thought it a great glory to
them that I had turned to them in my conversion, as if holding
all other abbeys in contempt, so that now it would be a disgrace
to them if I should transfer to another abbey and leave them."
But this sounds like diplomacy of the usual administrative type,
and it is likely that Adam really wanted revenge. He did not get
it, for a few days after he departed from Provins he died.

It was now necessary to make some arrangement with Adam's
successor, Abbot Suger, who was one of the ablest administrators
of the century, famous today for having introduced some of the
earliest significant elements of the Gothic style when he rebuilt the
Abbey Church of St. Denis. He was just as interested as Abelard
was in reforming the life of the monks, but he wished to do it for
the greater glory of France and the royal house, not simply to
correct a laxity of demeanor that was common to a great many
well-established houses of regulars in Europe. Abelard probably
seemed to him a troublesome figure of dubious reputation, so that
when he appeared before him in company with the Bishop of
Meaux, one Burchard, to make the same request he had made of
Adam, Suger was inclined to deny it. However, Abelard was able
to interest the royal seneschal, Stephen of Garlande, in his cause,
and the Royal Council apparently granted that Abelard might go
his own way, establishing himself wherever he wished so long as
he did not subject himself to another abbot.

Thus it was that some time in 1122 Abelard managed to establish himself in "a solitary place in the area of Troyes," actually

near Nogent-sur-Seine, where with the permission of the Bishop of Troyes he erected an oratory of mud and thatch in the name of the Holy Trinity. At first he was there alone as a simple hermit, with only one clerk for company, but soon students learned of his whereabouts and began to congregate about him for instruction. "When," he says, "students knew I was there, they began to assemble from everywhere. Having left cities and towns, they dwelt in solitude; having abandoned spacious houses, they made for themselves little huts. Instead of soft beds, they made straw pallets, and instead of tables, they piled up turfs." Eventually, he says, the students erected "structures of stone and wood" to replace the huts. Thus Abelard resumed his teaching, far from the cloister of St. Denis and the amenities of Paris.

At this point in Abelard's *History* there are two long discourses that appear to be digressions, one on the austere and dedicated life of his students, who are said to have abandoned the delights of the world and its manifold temptations for the sake of study, which is rather optimistic, and another on the new name he introduced for his establishment, the "Paraclete." We shall have occasion to return to these later. Meanwhile, the first one on the life of the students probably misrepresents the actual situation.

Abelard was an intensely devoted scholar, a brilliant teacher, and a philosopher and theologian capable of great insight and profundity. But he was no administrator. As he later demonstrated when he wrote a rule for Heloise, he could develop organizational procedures in theory, but he never showed any aptness whatsoever for their practical application. The crowds of students who flocked to hear him at the Paraclete may have at first willingly suffered hardships, as he said they did, but as the school grew and it was necessary to make extensive arrangements for food and lodging for them, the task of keeping order must have strained Abelard's capabilities. His lectures were highly successful, and their fame spread, but rumors of student misbehavior and the antagonism of those who did not approve of his conduct, methods, and doctrines combined finally to make it necessary for him to abandon his new foundation altogether.

The rumors concerning student misbehavior are reported by one

Hilary, known today as the author of Latin plays on Lazarus, Daniel, and St. Nicholas, who attended Abelard's school, liked it, and, after its dissolution, wrote a poem lamenting its passing. Abelard says nothing about these rumors, but tells us instead that his school fell before the stratagems of his former rivals, who, when its fame reached them, "excited against me certain new apostles, to whom the world generally gave credence, one of whom prided himself on having reformed the life of regular canons, the other that of monks." The first of these is clearly Norbert, whom Abelard was later to attack violently in one of his sermons for Heloise. The second is Bernard of Clairvaux.

Bernard of Clairvaux—St. Bernard (1090–1153)—was to become the most powerful ecclesiastic of the twelfth century. He was the son of a crusader, but like Abelard preferred not to take up a military career. As a boy, orphaned at an early age, he studied at Châtillon-sur-Seine, entering the Abbey of Cîteaux in 1112, bringing with him thirty followers. Cîteaux had been established as a reformed Benedictine house by Robert of Molesme, who instituted there a very strict and literal observance of the Benedictine Rule, involving a reduction in the time devoted to the celebration of the canonical offices and a return to manual labor, which, under the circumstances, meant agricultural labor. Young Bernard and his friends stimulated a truly remarkable growth of the institution, which had not been prospering under its third abbot, Stephan Harding. Within three years after Bernard's arrival, four sister houses—La Ferté, Pontigny, Clairvaux, and Morimond—had been founded, and at one of these, Clairvaux, Bernard became abbot. His preaching attracted enormous audiences, and under his inspiration the new order spread rapidly. By 1134 there were over thirty Cistercian houses, as they were called, and by the end of the century there were over five hundred. At the time Abelard abandoned his school at the Paraclete Bernard had become one of the most prominent ecclesiastics in France, a man frequently consulted on a wide variety of issues both by noblemen and by the higher clergy. His later career continued to be spectacular. He drew up the Rule for the Knights Templars, successfully supported the claims of

Pope Innocent II against his rival Anacletus II, had the satisfaction of seeing one of his own monks, Eugenius III, elected Pope, preached the Crusade with such success in 1146 that King Louis VII and Queen Eleanor took up the Cross, and, shortly afterward, persuaded the Emperor Conrad III to do likewise.

In the second decade of the twelfth century Bernard was not an enemy to be lightly opposed, and he became even more formidable later, as Abelard was to learn. In a treatise on Baptism directed to Hugh of St. Victor at about the time Abelard abandoned his school, or shortly thereafter, Bernard attacked certain doctrines that Abelard had advanced. Although the popular sermons of Bernard and Norbert do not survive, it is reasonable to assume that both reformers attacked Abelard in their preaching, con-demning him both for his conduct with Heloise as they understood it and for his teaching. At least Abelard implies that they did so: "These men running through the world preaching and impudently defaming me as much as they could, made me for a time contempt-ible before ecclesiastical as well as secular authorities, and dis-seminated so many evil rumors about my faith and my works that even my foremost friends turned away from me, and even those who retained a little of the former love they had maintained for me pretended in every way that they could not favor me for fear of them. God is my witness that whenever I knew of an assem-blage of ecclesiastics about to be called together I thought it would be for the purpose of condemning me more thoroughly."

It is likely that Count Thibaut, who was deeply impressed by Norbert's preaching and by his sanctity, withdrew his support, and that Abelard's friends at court were embarrassed by the extremely effective preaching of Bernard. Ecclesiastical authorities were un-derstandably reluctant to assist him. First there had been the affair with Heloise, then the condemnation at Soissons, then the scandal at St. Denis, and finally the attacks of Bernard, who found Abe-lard's teachings suspect and his conduct reprehensible. Poor Abe-lard had nowhere to go. "Frequently," he lamented, "I fell into such despair that I was inclined to flee Christian territory to the lands of the pagans and there on the basis of an agreement made for tribute quietly lead a Christian life, for I thought they would accord me more welcome the less Christian they suspected me to be because of the charges brought against me, and would on account of them believe me to be more easily inclined to their religion." The ironic smile in this complaint reveals that in spite of his enemies Abelard had not altogether lost his self-confidence.

He had one friend left. Back in Brittany Duke Conan, who seems to have been keeping an eye on his philosopher all along, arranged to obtain him an abbacy. The Duke was busy putting down some bandits who eventually fortified themselves in the church of the Abbey of Redon, but he had time to give thought to the brother of his vassal of Le Pallet, who may have been with him on campaign. The abbey he had in mind for Abelard was St. Gildas de Ruis, which had recently lost its abbot. Duke Conan obtained Suger's consent to appoint Abelard as the new pastor, and the monks, submitting to the will of their Duke, elected him without difficulty. Now at last Abelard would be an abbot, driven westward, he says, by "the envy of the French," although he might well have considered his own part in stimulating French animosity. The monastery had an evil reputation for irregularity, but Abelard found the prospect better than the persecution he was suffering. He might well have been less sanguine had he known that four years later Ermengarde of Brittany would accept the veil from St. Bernard, and that Cistercian houses would soon spring up in the duchy just as they were springing up all across Europe. This would mean that the most intelligent and most sincere candidates for the regular life in Brittany, especially among noblemen, would become Cistercians, and that St. Gildas would have to accept novices of inferior status.

Abelard's love for Heloise had, in effect, led him from the cloister at Paris to a remote Breton shore. But she would lead him back to France when he learned to love her for attributes less tangible than those with which he had ensnared himself in Fulbert's house.

CHAPTER V

The Exile

The ancient Abbey of St. Gildas de Ruis had been restored and brought to a state of prosperity in the early eleventh century by a certain St. Felix (d. 1038). It was located in a fertile coastal region noted for its grain, wine, fruit, and fish, on the extremity of the peninsula of Ruis, which is almost an island. Nearby was the ducal residence of Sucinio, established in the second decade of the twelfth century. Although the monastery had achieved local fame in the eleventh century, it had decayed considerably by the time Abelard reached it in 1125, and it is likely that Duke Conan had hopes that under his leadership it would flourish once more and become a credit to the duchy. Although he remained there for about ten years, Abelard apparently made little headway with his monks; as we have seen, his talents did not lie in the realm of administration. Heloise was to fare much better than Abelard did in this respect.

The gloomy picture Abelard gives us of his abbey is somewhat exaggerated. "The land," he says, "was barbarous, the local language was unknown to me, the wicked and unmanageable habits of the monks there were well known to almost everybody, and the people of that region were inhumane and disordered." It is true that the land was devoted to agriculture and that the people, probably including the monks, were predominantly Breton-speaking peasants without much refinement. Ruis was a ducal fief, probably administered by a local official who exacted all he could from the countryside. Abelard says that "a certain tyrant in that region had so subjected the abbey to himself, seizing the occasion of the disorder in the house for his purpose, that he had reduced the adjacent lands to his own use and burdened the monks with greater exactions than he would have imposed on Jewish tributaries." Unable to care for themselves as an organized group, the monks had to rely on their own individual resources. And when Abelard came, they expected him to furnish them with the necessities of life. They had, as Abelard tells us, not only themselves to support, but also their concubines, sons, and daughters. "They took delight in worrying me about their needs, and, at the same time, stole and carried away what they could, so that, lacking anything to administer to them, I should be forced either to abandon discipline or abandon the abbey altogether." This perplexing situation must have seemed formidable, and there was not much Abelard could do about it without help from the Duke. After the affair with Heloise and her offer to become Abelard's concubine, we can perhaps appreciate the irony of Abelard's dilemma in trying to control monks who were supporting concubines and their children. Here Abelard remained for four years without much to console him. His skill at dialectic was useless to him, and there was no one to listen to his expositions of the Scriptures. He had few books except those he had brought with him or those he could borrow at some pains from other monasteries. He saw Duke Conan occasionally when he visited Sucinio, and it is possible that he was able through the Duke to ameliorate the exactions of the local "tyrant." Members of his family may have visited him from time to time. At least he managed to survive, and he could hardly have done so if the situation had remained as he describes it. He apparently did not succeed in dampening the animosity of most of his monks, which was a natural by-product of their habitual greed and general laxity, although some of them must have assisted him in his painful efforts to bring order to the house. Meanwhile, he was worried about the fate of his oratory at the Paraclete, now almost abandoned, since, he says, "The extreme poverty of the place hardly sufficed to supply the necessities for one man." He was anxious that the Holy Offices continue to be celebrated there. Bernard had his burgeoning Cistercian houses, and Norbert's Premonstratensians were spreading almost as rapidly. Poor Abelard had nothing except a dangerous abbacy in which he felt himself powerless, and the faint light that still flickered in the wilderness near Nogent-sur-Seine.

In 1129, however, when all hope seemed lost, something happened that was at first discouraging but soon turned to Abelard's advantage. At St. Denis Suger had been busy enriching his abbey in various ways. He not only obtained royal grants, but he also made a thorough investigation of the abbey's ancient claims to lands and feudal rights. In the course of these studies he discovered the basis for a claim to the property of the nunnery at Argenteuil, where Heloise, having been there ten years, was now prioress. Suger decided to act in this instance as he had in others and demanded that the nuns be dispersed and that the property be turned over to the abbey. With reference to the nuns, he alleged that they were guilty of misconduct, to the scandal of the surrounding community. In a medieval context this may be taken simply as a general accusation of poor administration, but Suger was usually scrupulous in his dealings, and it may well be that Heloise was having disciplinary troubles not unlike those experienced by Abelard at St. Gildas, but less extreme. Older houses of regulars were commonly lax, a fact that accounts in part for the enormous success of the reformers, men like St. Bruno of the Carthusians, Norbert, and Bernard. But only two or three straying nuns at Argenteuil would have been sufficient to cause talk locally and to incur a general censure that may have been undeserved. Suger's claim was upheld at a synod attended by Geoffrey of Lèves, who had defended Abelard at Soissons, so that it is unlikely that Suger acted out of personal prejudice.

When Abelard heard of this turn of events he hastened to his oratory. We can imagine him, now decorously attired in his

monastic habit, accompanied by a few trusted monks, riding
rapidly across the countryside through Rennes, Le Mans, Chartres,
and on to Nogent. Meanwhile, he sent messengers to Heloise and
her followers begging them to take refuge in his oratory. We have
no evidence of any relationship between Abelard and Heloise after
his departure from St. Denis prior to this time, but he had probably followed her career with interest and may well have contributed to her material welfare when he was able to do so. There
was ample room at the Paraclete for a few nuns to establish the
beginnings of a convent. Heloise agreed to the new arrangement,
and Abelard granted to the nuns and their successors the lands of
the Paraclete in perpetuity. The grant required the consent of the
Bishop of Troyes and the confirmation of Pope Innocent II, which
was forthcoming in 1131. All this meant extensive negotiations,
involving Count Thibaut as well as the ecclesiastical authorities.
It seems evident that the latter regarded Heloise as a reliable nun
of good reputation. The scandals at Argenteuil had not been
attributed to her, and she was thought of as being "sufficient" to
preside over a congregation of regulars once more. This fact is of
some importance, since it indicates that she had adapted herself
well to the cloistered life. Her early training in the arts now served
her in good stead, since she was sufficiently literate and, at the
same time, her experience enabled her to understand the personal
problems of her charges and to carry on the complex work of
administration required of her.

Abelard was highly pleased by the comparatively rapid growth
of his new venture. "At first," he says, the nuns at the Paraclete
"sustained an impoverished life, and were for a time most desolate,
but the Divine Mercy they awaited and most devoutly served soon
consoled them, exhibiting to them the True Paraclete [or God
"the Comforter"], and causing the surrounding population to be
merciful and propitious toward them." Once the nunnery had
been established, both the local bishop and the secular lords would
have had an interest in its success. King Louis exempted the Paraclete from all customs in 1134, and in the same year the Bishop
of Melun granted the nuns certain tithes or portions of income

received by churches. Two years later further tithes were granted them by the Archbishop of Sens. Among the lay benefactors were Count Thibaut and his successor, Henry the Liberal, husband of the famous Countess Marie, daughter of Eleanor of Aquitaine. Abelard says that "earthly goods were multiplied for them more in one year than they would have been for me in a hundred. For since the feminine sex is weaker, the more readily their especially miserable poverty moves human affections, and the more pleasing their virtue is to both God and man. God allowed such grace to fall over that sister of mine, who was over the other nuns, that bishops loved her like a daughter, abbots like a sister, and laymen like a mother; and all were astonished equally by her religion, prudence, and the incomparable gentleness of her patience." This statement may be somewhat optimistic where it concerns the material welfare of the convent, but the praise of Heloise for her virtue is supported elsewhere. The echoes of Xanthippe in her makeup, if they were ever actually there, now vanished completely. Bernard of Clairvaux visited the Paraclete in 1131, where he was welcomed "like an angel." He found nothing to criticize on this occasion except a minor point in the liturgy, concerning which Abelard wrote him a letter of explanation and defense. On this and subsequent visits Bernard encouraged Heloise, who had probably not yet learned of Abelard's strong bias against him. We may be sure that if the convent had not been above reproach, Bernard, who had a sharp eye for weaknesses among regulars and little love for Abelard, would not have hesitated to denounce it.

Abelard's enthusiasm for his new establishment was not based on any romantic attachment to Heloise, although he probably still felt a great deal of affection for her and a sense of obligation to promote her welfare. The new nunnery gave him, at last, something useful to do. He could make little progress with his monks at St. Gildas, but he could help Heloise in a great many ways. The nunnery could use such things as liturgical pieces, collections of sermons, a special rule to set it off from other convents, and, above all, a suitable account of its foundation to provide an exemplary narrative for its nuns and to establish its basic traditions. During the Middle Ages almost every organization had its own special cult to foster its *pietas*, or respectful attitude toward its own peculiar traditions. Just as Aeneas maintained his *pietas* in spite of temptations and lapses, fostering what we might call the "patriotism" of the Romans, so also the French developed a *pietas* based on such exemplary figures as St. Denis, Charlemagne, and Roland; the British had their Arthur, or, in Abelard's time, were soon to have him; and organizations of all kinds, whether of merchants, tradesmen, noblemen, or ecclesiastics, sought to gather their best ideals in exemplary form and to emulate them in their current activities. Today, we are likely to regard such attitudes as narrow and prejudiced, pretending as we do a cult of humanity as a whole, but Abelard was undoubtedly anxious to furnish those special traditions and practices for the Paraclete that were, in his day, practically a necessity. He would, of course, constitute a part of those traditions himself.

There was a further consideration, however, that he does not mention or even hint at but that must have been very much in his mind. During the twelfth century a book prepared for students, for example, a book like Abelard's treatise condemned at Soissons, might circulate very rapidly. On the other hand, if it was not cherished for some reason by an institution of some kind it might soon disappear. Thus the work of the masters of St. Victor found a permanent place in the library there, cathedrals would keep the works of the masters of their schools, and monasteries preserved the productions of their own monks. Abelard could not look for-ward to any lasting repository for anything he might write at St. Gildas, since the future of the institution seemed dim, most of the monks were Breton-speaking Celts, and he had no reason to think that his name would be long remembered there. The Paraclete offered much better prospects. Altogether, therefore, the new establishment gave Abelard an opportunity for useful work of permanent value and provided at the same time a repository for anything he might produce in the realms of philosophy or theology. These considerations undoubtedly deepened his interest in Heloise, to whom he could now look as a kind of personal savior and not merely as a reminder of past misfortune. His efforts now would not only help her, but would also help him. Her continued virtue and good reputation had become a matter of supreme importance to her former seducer. The practical situation in which he found himself suggested strongly that he learn to love Heloise in a new way, and he did not hesitate to do so. We should not assume, however, that since the practical considerations existed, Abelard's love was not "sincere." As we shall see, he eventually came to see his predicament as a manifestation of God's grace consistent with the Order of Providence.

Once the Paraclete was again well established, Abelard also had a place to retreat from the persecution of his own monks. Many persons in the neighborhood of Nogent blamed him for not aiding the nuns in their poverty or assisting them by preaching. There-fore, he says, he "began to return to them frequently, in order to serve them in every way possible." During the early 1130s he often visited Heloise, taking with him works for the benefit of the nuns such as the *Hymns and Sequences* which contained some spiritual direction for the community in its introduction. The liturgical pieces are of good quality, although they are by no means as attractive as the similar works composed by a fellow-Breton, Adam, who arrived at St. Victor in 1130, and there composed some of the finest liturgical poetry ever inspired by the Christian Church. Abelard could not be expected to do everything superbly, but he could be depended upon to do what he set out to do well. His method of composition was, like his lectures, characterized by spontaneity rather than by great care.

At this point in the *History* there appears another long "digres-sion," first on the suitability of eunuchs as servants for women, and then generally on the ample precedent that exists for holy men to engage in the spiritual instruction of members of the opposite sex. These matters are introduced ostensibly because, although some maintained that Abelard was devoting insufficient attention to the nuns, others asserted that he was drawn to them, as he says, "by a certain concupiscence of the flesh, as if I could hardly suffer or suffer not at all absence from my first mistress." In addition to the fact that he was about fifty years old, Abelard had been a eunuch for a number of years, so that the charge was, to say the least, absurd. The digression has, however, a significance unrelated to any whisperings of this kind, which we shall consider later. Meanwhile, it does contain incidentally some material of another kind that is significant in relation to Abelard's change in attitude, especially his attitude toward fame.

During his youth Abelard had eagerly pursued fame for the sake of his own personal aggrandizement. The loss of this fame when Fulbert enjoyed his revenge hurt him, as we have seen, more than his wound. And he was thrown into despair at Soissons, he says, because of the injury to his fame, this time in spite of the fact that his intentions were good and he was without any real guilt. Referring to the scandalous whispers arising from his visits to Heloise, he says, "But what I endured much less from the wound, I was now made to suffer a longer time through detraction, and I was tormented more by the diminution of my fame than by that of my body." Now, however, there is a difference. His loss of fame before had been an injury to his vanity; his loss of fame now was no longer an injury to his vanity but a deterrent from good works. He goes on to explain and elaborate by quoting Proverbs 22:1 and a passage from St. Augustine: "For it is written, 'A good name is better than great riches.' And, as St. Augustine says in a certain sermon *On the Life and Manners of Clerks*, 'He who trusting to his conscience neglects his fame is hard-hearted.' And, as he says earlier in the same work, 'Let us provide, as the Apostle says, "good things not only in the sight of God, but also in the sight of all men." On our account our conscience is sufficient for us. In our concern for others, our fame should not be polluted but should flourish in us. Conscience and fame are two things. Your conscience is for you; your fame is for the benefit of your neighbor.' " In other words, an evil reputation renders a man powerless to do good, just as castration renders him powerless in other ways. Abelard would now exert himself to restore his fame, not for his own vanity, but for the sake of Heloise and her nuns.

This new attitude, which marks a turning point in Abelard's

spiritual development and a definite step toward conversion, did not quite prevent him from engaging in a certain amount of detraction himself. He never attained that warm and optimistic tolerance that characterized Peter the Venerable of Cluny, but that was a rare quality that we can hardly attribute to Bernard of Clairvaux either. In the course of his discussion of the suitability of male instructors for women he points out that "the weaker sex needs the stronger to such a degree that the Apostle always decrees that the man should excel the woman as the head," a decree, incidentally, that the Apostle shared with Aristotle, who used the same figure. This consideration leads to the observation that nuns require a rule different from that used by monks, and, further, to an attack on institutions in which abbesses dominate the clergy: "And in many places, the natural order having been confounded, we see these abbesses and nuns dominate the clergy themselves, to whom the people are subject, and in this way they can lead them to evil desires more easily the more they exercise power over them and severely plague them with that yoke." This is a thinly veiled attack on the order of Fontevrault, which generated a great deal of animosity in certain circles. For example, Abelard's old master, or presumed master, Ulger, now Bishop of Angers, engaged in a violent quarrel with Abbess Petronilla of Fontevrault in 1136. Ulger was so vituperative that Bernard of Clairvaux intervened lest he cause scandal. Abelard's veiled attack should probably be attributed in part to jealousy, for Fontevrault was flourishing.

Among the works composed for Heloise while Abelard was at St. Gildas should be included the series of sermons he sent to the Paraclete. These are not great sermons; they do not deserve a place beside those of St. Augustine, or St. Caesarius of Arles, or St. Bernard. In part their quality may have been impaired by the inadequate library facilities at St. Gildas, but they also show signs of haste. In the prefatory epistle Abelard refers to the hymns and sequences already delivered. It is possible that one or two of the sermons may have been written earlier and were simply included in the collection in appropriate places. On the whole, these sermons, written especially with their problems in mind, would have been of far more benefit to the nuns than a collection of Patristic sermons of a kind that they might have used otherwise. Moreover, they could hear the words of the founder of their order.

One or two points in the sermons are of special interest. There is, for example, the attack on Norbert, referred to earlier, in the sermon *On St. John the Baptist*. Abelard accuses Norbert of having been sufficiently presumptuous to have sought to raise the dead. He and a disciple of his, Abelard alleges, lay prostrate in prayer before a corpse. When the corpse failed to respond, according to the story, Norbert arose and castigated the large audience before him, accusing them of interfering with the preachers and spoiling their miracle by demonstrating infidelity. "Oh, what a frivolous and inexcusable excuse!" Abelard exclaims. We should probably attribute this story, which was undoubtedly false, to Abelard's anger because of Norbert's sermons against him, and to jealousy of Norbert's thriving Premonstratensians. Stories of this kind, some of them much more outrageous, were circulated by the ene-mies of Bernard of Clairvaux too, as readers of Walter Map are aware, and it is unlikely that any highly successful reformer es-caped them entirely. Certainly Abelard himself, who became known as a "lover of women," suffered from slander of this kind.

The same sermon contains an extended passage that makes the comparison between philosophers and monks adduced in the little sermon on marriage attributed to Heloise, but without any conclu-sion to the effect that either should have mistresses for greater virtue and pleasure. Here the philosopher is said to be like a wild ass, whose lonely and unburdened life is much better than that of the severely burdened domestic ass. Just as the wild ass leads a better life, so also the life of the continent man is better. Abelard undoubtedly hoped that his nuns, unlike the monks of St. Gildas, would remain continent as they should, and also that they would devote themselves to study under the direction of the learned Heloise and thus set themselves apart from nuns of other orders. He was later to elaborate the desirability of continence in his *Christian Theology*, using some of the same authorities presumably adduced by Heloise, but again avoiding her very odd conclusion.

He says no more about learning in these sermons, but he once wrote Heloise a long letter, not included in *The Letters of Abelard and Heloise*, urging that she and her nuns study the original languages of the Scriptures. Whether she had any success in this pursuit we do not know, but the letter does illustrate once more Abelard's desire to take special advantage of the capabilities of Heloise in order to make his order truly distinguished.

Continence is recommended once more, or, rather, the lack of it is severely condemned, in a sermon *On the Feast of St. Stephen.* Abelard observes that "in all religious convents avarice seems more tolerable than the wickedness of lechery, especially among devout women." Today the medieval insistence on continence seems severe, but there was nothing peculiar then about Abelard's rigorous attitude. It was thought that just as a knight must undergo very severe hardships for his lord, suffering cold and heat and even giving up life itself if necessary, so a monk or nun should be willing to forego the more extravagant pleasures of eating and drinking, and sexual pleasures altogether, for the sake of devotion. Some monks and nuns undoubtedly had difficulties remaining continent. Even some of the saints, as everyone knows, had experienced such difficulties. Nevertheless, sexual temptations were probably not so strong then as they are today, when sexual stimulants confront us constantly in popular entertainment, advertising, fiction, and even in our educational system and in our churches. When such stimulants are lacking and men are constantly occupied with necessary business, they can more easily remain continent without difficulty. Freud would have been puzzled by medieval people, who were on the whole neither very squeamish about sex nor likely to glorify it. Preoccupation with sex and sexual indulgence were then usually attributed to youth and idleness, and their appearance among "idle youth" surprised no one.

In this same sermon on St. Stephen, Abelard also considers once more the problems arising when men preside over nuns. Such men, he says, should be especially concerned to remove all libido with the sword of continence, citing the example of "that greatest of Christian philosophers Origen" who actually, if ill-advisedly, castrated himself so that he might have free access to women in order to instruct them. Abelard makes no attempt to defend Origen's action, which was universally condemned by the Church, but if there was a "psychological" effect of Abelard's own castration, it appears only in the fact that he seems to have taken a certain pride in a condition that made him especially fitted to preside over the Paraclete. He did not mull over the loss of sexual pleasures, nor did he lose his intellectual aggressiveness. He does show a special admiration for Origen, but this admiration was shared by other men of his time, including Bernard of Clairvaux. He obviously thought that his own eunuchry would elicit a certain admiration from the nuns of the Paraclete, who would be happy to think that their founder, at the time he established their order, was incapable of falling once more into that vice that had led to his downfall.

While he was supplying books for his nuns, Abelard implies that his visits to them were interdicted altogether by slander. Persecuted on all sides, he says, he could find no place to rest, but was rather like Cain "a fugitive and a vagabond" carried from one place to another "incessantly tormented by combats without, fears within, or rather by combats and fears alike." His monks tried to poison him, first by tampering with his food, and then by placing poison in the chalice he used at Mass. On one occasion, he says, he visited "the count," by whom he means Duke Conan, at Nantes when the Duke was ill. There, in a house belonging to his brother, a monk he had brought with him poisoned his food, thinking he would be less vigilant there. When Abelard passed up the dish for lack of appetite, a fellow-monk who ate the food was killed. At St. Gildas his unruly charges set thieves upon him to kill him.

But these efforts were not so successful in injuring him physically as was what he calls "the Hand of the Lord." For one day he happened to fall from his horse, breaking "the channel" of his neck. This fracture, he says, "afflicted me far more than my earlier injury." Recovery must have been slow, painful, and never quite complete, if, that is, we can take the event literally. The difficulty here lies in the fact that it was said that Norbert, having led a wild youth, was riding one day between Xanten and Freden when he fell from his horse. Like St. Paul traveling toward Damascus, he was astonished by the incident and immediately converted. Abelard's fall occurs just prior to the statement of his own acceptance of Providence in his *History*, and it is possible, whether the fall occurred or not in actual fact, that he had both St. Paul and Norbert in mind. It may be significant also that in Gothic iconography the vice of pride was often shown as a man falling from a horse. Since Abelard does say that his own fall was Providential, it certainly had a significance for him beyond its literal implications, although this fact does not preclude the possibility that it was an "historical" event. It is often difficult to determine whether events as Abelard describes them are actual events or simply a part of the thematic configuration of his so-called autobiography.

When Abelard expelled some of the worst offenders among his monks from his abbey, they only returned to oppress him. The situation assumed such critical proportions that he was forced to call upon Duke Conan and a Papal Legate for assistance. In the presence of an assembly led by the Duke on the one hand and the Legate on the other, the expelled monks were forced to abjure the abbey. But when Abelard returned to his congregation, he found that even those among the monks he had trusted were also recalcitrant, threatening him with a sword, "so that," as he says, "I barely escaped them under the protection of a lord of the country." Although we may assume that the outbreaks against him were sporadic, and that the administration of the duchy was ready to assist him in any way possible, his years at St. Gildas must have been extremely difficult, relieved only by his efforts on behalf of the growing establishment of nuns at the Paraclete, three-fourths of the way across what is now France. Since he did not leave St. Gildas until around 1135, these efforts must have occupied a great deal of his time for some four years. As we have seen, the nuns needed a rule and an account of the establishment of their order. Abelard supplied these things in a form that seems somewhat curious to us today, but that was not quite so strange in the early twelfth century: a series of "letters." These are the

Letters of Abelard and Heloise, which became, through various accidents of history, his most famous work, although its fame bears no relation to its actual character, as we shall discover.

At this point, however, it is important to realize that the "conversion" of Abelard, outwardly associated with his castration and his entry into the regular life at St. Denis, did not take place in a spiritual sense until he had suffered for some years at St. Gildas. Indeed, the last pages of the *History,* in which he describes himself as being still in Brittany, are devoted to this spiritual conversion. When he entered St. Denis, he did so, as he says, not out of devotion but out of shame. But repentance brought about by worldly shame is false repentance, as Abelard himself explains in the eighteenth and nineteenth chapters of his *Ethics.* True contrition arises only because of the realization that one has failed in his love for God. Although this principle has been attributed to Abelard himself, it is actually Patristic, and it was sufficiently familiar in the sixteenth century to appear in the pages of Shakespeare, whose Duke in *Measure for Measure,* disguised as a friar, admonishes Juliet

> lest you do repent
> As that the sin hath brought you to this shame,
> Which sorrow is always toward ourselves, not Heaven,
> Showing we would not spare Heaven as we love it,
> But as we stand in fear.

Juliet replies obediently,

> I do repent me, as it is an evil,
> And take the shame with joy.

As a contrast we may consider Othello, whose false repentance culminates in suicide, the final act of despair.

After Abelard entered St. Denis, he gloried once more in the fame that brought students flocking to hear him, and after the Council of Soissons, he fell into a state of despair because his intentions had been good and he was firmly convinced of the validity of his written arguments. Despair is an aspect of what was called the irremissible "Sin Against the Holy Spirit" and is hardly characteristic of spiritual conversion. In fact, we should place the low point in Abelard's spiritual development here, not during the period of his preoccupation with the physical solaces of Heloise. In medieval terms lechery is a serious vice, or a serious inclination to irrational conduct. It is doubly serious, however, because it may lead to despair, which is even worse, since despair may lead to a denial of God's grace and to a consequent impeni- tence. The principle is well illustrated on a stone capital in the Romanesque Church of the Madeleine at Vézelay, where St. Bernard's sermon inspired King Louis to become a crusader. On one side of the capital are two figures. One, a nude woman tearing at her breast while a serpent gnaws at her crotch, represents the discomforts of lechery. The other, a tailed grotesque plunging a sword into its body stands for the wrathful despair to which lechery may lead.

The beginnings of a recovery are evident when Abelard decided to call his oratory the "Paraclete," since through that act he deli- berately called upon the Holy Spirit, or God "the Comforter," for assistance. But his initial experience at St. Gildas served only to depress him further, and it was not until Heloise had become established at the Paraclete that he was able to find life purposeful and to devote himself to useful work. The change of heart is evi- dent in his altered attitude toward fame, once a source of personal glory, but now an adjunct to good works. There is a sense in which Heloise, simply by being virtuous and efficient, was the inspiration for Abelard's salvation. This fact is not stated openly in the His- tory, but it is nevertheless made abundantly evident by implication. The actual conversion, which represents a realization that persecu- tion is natural to the Christian life and the further realization that suffering is a part of the Providential design, is described in what must have been, in the twelfth century, very moving language. Abelard begins by quoting John 15:20, "If they have persecuted me, they will also persecute you," developing this theme with a series of Scriptural passages and a quotation from St. Jerome. Today we do not often realize that a Christian was expected to bear the Cross, as it were, and, in one way or another, to find himself transfixed upon it. God the Comforter is not readily available to those who have insufficient courage to bear the nails patiently.

Having quoted his authorities, Abelard continues, "Prepared by this evidence and by these examples, let us endure our troubles more securely the more injuriously they befall. Let us not doubt that they are profitable if not for our merit at least for our testing." The theme is as old as the first work of Christian literature, the *Octavius* of Minucius Felix, a dialogue between a Christian and a pagan in which the pagan expresses puzzlement because the Christian God allows His subjects to be tormented. The Christian replies that God tests those who love Him, purifying them with adversity, just as gold is purified by fire. Abelard has now learned to endure adversity and to trust in Providence: "And since all things are governed by Divine Providence, let every one of the faithful in every affliction be consoled by this, that the Supreme Goodness of God never permits anything inordinate, and that whatever happens perversely, He brings to the best conclusion." This is one of the great themes of *The Consolation of Philosophy* of Boethius, which inspired hundreds of literary and artistic works throughout the Middle Ages and the Renaissance. It was to be stated forcibly in English for almost the last time in *The Essay on Man* by Alexander Pope, who put it very bluntly: "Whatever is, is right."

After further Scriptural quotations, Abelard concludes by warning that "anyone who is wrathful because of his own trouble, doubting that it is brought about by Divine dispensation, recedes from justice, subjecting himself to his own will rather than to that of God and rejecting the message of 'Thy will be done' with secret desires, thus placing his own will before that of God."

With this admonition Abelard's *History* comes to a close. It indicates that he had at last turned resolutely away from that kind of worldly fame he set out to conquer with the arms of dialectic in his youth. He would go on working, writing books on both theology and philosophy, and he would not lose entirely a certain Breton self-assurance. But from this point onward he would seek the salvation of Heloise and the glory of God rather than wealth, ecclesiastical rank, or empty fame. The composition of the *History* itself, which we shall now examine, required a great deal of personal humility. At the time he was about fifty-five he had been converted not by preaching but by a gradual process of understanding, assisted by the example of Heloise, who had grown from a vain and amusingly unreasonable young girl into a mature and respected abbess.

CHAPTER VI

The Autobiographer

belard's *History of My Calamities*, from which we derive most of our information concerning his career up until about 1135, is superficially a letter of consolation addressed to an anonymous friend who has experienced difficulties in the world. This letter appears, however, as the first item in a series of letters, a collection known as *The Letters of Abelard and Heloise*. It should be emphasized that this is not a collection of all the letters Abelard wrote to Heloise, nor of all the letters she addressed to him. We have other letters by Abelard addressed to Heloise and to other persons, and although Heloise as Abbess of the Paraclete must have written many letters, we have only traces of this correspondence, notably a letter written to Peter the Venerable after the death of Abelard. The point is that this is a special collection of letters designed for a specific purpose.

The *History* supposedly inspired the first letter in the collection by Heloise, who begins by referring to it. About half of the entire collection in bulk is taken up by the last two letters. These are letters by Abelard containing a history of the regular life as practiced by women and a special rule for the Paraclete. The manuscript evidence indicates that the *Letters*, including this rule and some traditional material on the life of nuns at the close, was probably a standard volume kept at the Paraclete and at all of the sister houses subsequently established. That is, if one wished to see the Rule of the Paraclete, it was to be found in the volume of *Letters*. In short, the *History*, the letters, the historical information about nuns, and the rule form a single whole. This volume must have been a standard set piece for the nuns of the order to read and study. It should not surprise us, therefore, to find that the whole collection has a thematic as well as a physical unity.

Before we can understand the unity of the whole, however, we must rid our minds of certain prejudices concerning the *History* itself. Modern readers have frequently been puzzled by the question of whether the *History* is actual history or fiction. Contemporary evidence from other sources seems to supply the answer at once. The letters of Fulk of Deuil, Roscelin, Peter the Venerable, the prefatory epistles and other letters addressed by Abelard to Heloise outside the collection, not to mention the surviving records of the Paraclete, all indicate that the outlines of the story Abelard tells us have a basis in fact. Most of the events described in the chapters above probably did occur. There has been an understandable tendency, therefore, to read the *History* as an actual if selective record of things done. But what was the basis for selection? And how does Abelard color the events he describes?

Our difficulty lies essentially in the fact that we have set up two alternatives—history and fiction—as though they were inclusive, with the feeling that the *History* must be one or the other, or a mixture of both. This is a very common error that appears in modern analyses of questions of all kinds, from history to practical engineering. In the present instance, Abelard would have understood neither what we mean by "history" nor what we mean by "fiction." These alternatives are not inclusive but irrelevant. With reference to "history," no one in the Middle Ages had any notion of a detached record of events produced for its own sake. Events in the past belonged to the order of Providence, so that both these events and the persons who participated in them had an exemplary character, immediately relevant to life in the present. To find the "truth" of history was then not simply to discover the facts, but to find the exemplary force of the events adduced, or, in other words, their Providential implications.

With reference to the other alternative, modern fiction is equally remote from the world-view of the twelfth century. In our fiction, we are led through a series of emotional experiences, sometimes delicately structured, to a climactic and emotionally satisfying conclusion, and this is still true when the conclusion provokes only a kind of gaping wonderment about the profound problems of the human condition. Usually, we have watched the developing personality of the protagonist in all of its mysteries and complexities, have been led to experience for ourselves his emotional satisfactions and frustrations, and are much impressed when we feel them to be very like those that we ourselves, along with many of our contemporaries, must inevitably face. Medieval fiction, or "fabulous narrative," as it was often called, was quite different. The characters are usually exemplifications of ideas and are never "personalities," and their actions are for the most part disguised developments of an underlying theme. Medieval readers or listeners—for most fabulous narratives were heard rather than read privately— were much more interested in the significance of actions than they were in the actions themselves, and for them this significance was characteristically conceptual rather than emotional. We are almost never asked to share the experiences of medieval characters vicariously, although we may be asked to observe them in some detail. But even when we are, the emotions represented take a curiously logical or explicitly illogical form in their development. Thus the emotional impact of a medieval work of fiction has little to do with the external trappings of the narrative. It lies instead in the discovery of a valuable attitude or idea beneath what is often an externally confused surface, just as medieval figurative language usually conveys ideas rather than emotions stimulated by its concrete elements. If the protagonist in a narrative is virtuous, we are encouraged to imitate him not in his external behavior but in his virtues. If he is a sinner, we are often led to laugh at him, since sin is unreasonable behavior as seen against the background of a providentially ordered world and is hence ridiculous.

Beginning in the late seventeenth century, as we shall see, there has been a strong tendency to attribute to Abelard's *History* the virtues of both history and fiction. That is, it was felt that all the events in it are literally true and at the same time that they constitute a record of universal human passion. In order to achieve this happy combination, however, it was necessary to rewrite the *History* completely, and a spurious version of it, much more consistent and unified than the orginal as a record of emotions, was popular for over two hundred years. Even after scholars and readers generally began to realize that the spurious version differed widely from the original, much of the attitude toward the spurious version was transferred to the original, in spite of the fact that the original, on the face of it, is hardly devoted to the subject of romantic passion. If we wish to understand the significance of what Abelard wrote, we must abandon our quest for either history or fiction in the modern sense of those words in his book.

But we are still faced with another chimera, "autobiography." Even if we grant that Abelard's *History* is neither history nor fiction, we are likely to say that it is certainly autobiography, and hence an intimate personal record of events reflecting the personality of its author. In fact, the *History* has been hailed recently as a precious example of "psychological realism," a stark revelation of inner psychological life. The fact that Abelard wrote an autobiography at all has been attributed to his castration, which presumably made him introspective. Now all this would undoubtedly have had some substance if Abelard had been a contemporary of Rousseau or Goethe or Kierkegaard. But it has no relevance at all to the twelfth century. In the first place, no one in the twelfth century had a "personality" as a "thing." Each individual had his own peculiar temperament and his moral characteristics, it is true, but these had not then been reduced to a conceptual entity and then objectified. The word *personality* is first used in the eighteenth century to mean the sum of the peculiar characteristics of an individual. In this sense, which is still current, the word is a useful verbal tool. However, the idea soon became objectified, and the verbal tool became a thing, with "depths," "force," and so on. One popular theologian has even found God in the "depths" of the personality. As an objective entity the personality shares the weaknesses of the medieval "universals" when they are considered as realities; it belongs to the realm of poltergeists, leprechauns, and other fantasies of the popular imagination, in spite of the fact that along with many other "things" of the same kind it occupies a prominent place in academic discussions. In his *History* Abelard does exhibit certain traits of temperament and certain moral characteristics. But his concern is not to reveal them for their own sake but to describe a pattern of development based on moral and theological values. Even a cursory examination of the text should be sufficient to show that this is true.

It is quite probable that Abelard did have another "autobiography" in mind when he wrote his own—the *Confessions* of St. Augustine. In discussing the uses of autobiography in the *Convivio*, Dante points out that it is legitimate to write about oneself as St. Augustine did, to provide a useful example. His perception is correct; the *Confessions* is not an autobiography in the modern sense at all, but an exemplary narrative dominated by a theme and containing a great deal of symbolic action. In the course of his book St. Augustine undergoes a conversion from immersion in the world, with its appeals to vanity, sensuality, and avarice, to a firm faith in God. Like Abelard, he was in his youth a teacher of probable argument. He had special difficulties in abandoning his pursuit of women, and once contemplated marriage. His book, moreover, uses an examplary autobiography to introduce a lengthy exposition, and the autobiographical parts of the *Letters* introduce a long expository section also. Abelard rather carefully describes the steps in his own downfall and in his subsequent conversion, and it is almost inconceivable that he did not have the precedent set by St. Augustine in mind.

Our problem becomes much simpler if we visualize Abelard's actual situation at the time he wrote his *History*. He was at St. Gildas, beset by hostile monks, desperately trying to provide the basic documents for his new order at the Paraclete. Since no one else could be relied upon to provide a rule for Heloise and an account of the founders of the order, Abelard would have to furnish these things himself. He needed not only a rule, but an edifying introduction to it that would fortify the nuns in their renunciation of the world and lead them to accept the rigors of the regular life with patience. If he could show how he and Heloise had once been totally immersed in worldly concern but had eventually given up the temptations of the world, as St. Augustine had also done before them, his own early life and that of Heloise would provide salutary examples. Few of the nuns would have lost so much as Abelard and Heloise, and their own difficulties would seem less by comparison. Abelard states very clearly at the beginning of his narrative that it is exemplary in character: "Frequently," he wrote, "human affections are either stimulated or mitigated more efficiently by example than by words." The "affections" in this instance are to be mitigated, since emotional reactions to worldly deprivation or misfortunes constitute what he calls "temptations." As we have seen, the *History* closes with an injunction to accept the trials of the world with patience and to submit to the will of God. Abelard had no wish to arouse sentimental compassion for his difficulties, which, as he clearly states, were an aspect of God's justice and for which he was largely responsible himself.

Specifically, the *History* is presented as a letter of consolation to a friend. Abelard says, addressing this "friend," that "after some verbal consolation delivered to you in person, I have decided to write you a consolatory letter concerning the calamities that I have experienced, so that in comparison with mine, you may recognize your own temptations to be negligible or moderate, and may thus bear them with more tolerance." He is actually, of course, addressing the nuns of the Paraclete, most of whom undoubtedly experienced "temptations" of various kinds when they considered the alternatives they had renounced. The typical themes of consolation popular in the twelfth century were especially suited to Abelard's purpose, since they would apply equally well to someone who had suffered adversity and to someone who had deliberately cut himself off from worldly satisfactions. Specifically, they are the themes developed in *The Consolation of Philosophy* of Boethius, upon which, as we have seen, an excellent commentary had been written by William of Conches at Chartres at the time Abelard was composing his work. The *Consolation* became one of John of Salisbury's favorite books, and was closely associated with Christian humanistic activity throughout the Middle Ages and the Renaissance. In order to understand Abelard's use of this work, however, we should not search the *History* for direct quotations, parallel passages, or imitations of Boethian machinery. We should look instead for basic ideas or doctrines. As Lady Philosophy herself says in the *Consolation,* "I do not need a place in your library with ivory and glass, but rather a place in your mind, in which I have located not books, but that which makes books precious, the lessons of my books." These "lessons" from Boethius were a part of the intellectual fabric of Abelard's time; he had no need to quote Boethius in order to call attention to them.

Nevertheless, there are faint but unmistakable traces of Boethius in the language of the *History.* Thus when he has described his remarkable success as a master at Paris and is about to introduce Heloise, Abelard says that "flattering Fortune found an occasion by means of which I might be more easily cast down from this summit." Again, he complains that he had suffered "adverse Fortune" for a long time when the monks of St. Denis rose against him. The *History* concludes, moreover, with a strong assertion of faith in Providence. This juxtaposition of Fortune, which casts one down from a summit, and Providence, which makes all Fortune good, should alert us to the possibility that the influence of Boethius may be more than superficial. We are likely to pass over such references as mere figures of speech, or so much rhetoric, as indeed they might be if they were used today, but in the twelfth century they implied a whole realm of conventional doctrine. Thus after the first of the references to Fortune above, Abelard hastens to add, "I should say rather that Divine Piety took vengeance on a most proud man by humiliating him." Has he changed his mind? Or is this, too, a reference to Boethian teaching? We shall find that Boethius will help us to understand not only the *History* but the subsequent letters as well.

Boethius, who was born in Rome about 480 A.D., not only translated Aristotle's *Organon,* but wrote treatises on logic, rhetoric, arithmetic, and music, as well as a series of five theological treatises. He enjoyed a distinguished public career until he was unjustly accused of treason by Theodoric and thrown into prison, where, in his last days, he wrote his most famous book, *The Consolation of Philosophy.* This work, the product of extraordinary literary craftsmanship, is in the form of a dialogue between two figures. The speaker at the opening is called "Boethius," and near the beginning of the book he includes an account of his undeserved misfortunes which are similar to the misfortunes suffered by the actual Boethius. But he is soon quite obviously an exemplary character, and his misfortunes typify those that almost anyone deeply involved in the world may suffer in one way or another. When we first meet him he is complaining bitterly about adverse Fortune. A lady with majestic countenance and flashing eyes, who seems at times to be of ordinary stature and at times to reach the heavens, comes before him to comfort him. He explains that he has been unjustly accused, stripped of his possessions and his honors, separated from his family, and thrown into prison. In the remainder of the dialogue, the Lady, whose name is Philosophy (or "the love of wisdom"), proceeds to console him, pointing out to him that he has not lost anything worthwhile, and urging him to adopt an attitude of virtuous patience.

Beautiful ladies called Philosophy do not ordinarily appear before men to instruct them, and the commentators who wrote about the *Consolation* during the Middle Ages like to point out that the dialogue is carried out as if between two parts of the same person. We should be very careful, however, not to think of these "parts" as psychological entities. Lady Philosophy offers that wisdom to which, presumably, we all have access, although it is not something inside us until we learn to love it and hence to reflect it. Boethius represents at the outset an unthinking reaction to that adversity which all of us must suffer in one way or another, and his complaints are typical of those of any man who must face misfortune. In short, he is a man cast down by adversity seeking a wisdom that he can, if he wishes, find within himself.

There is not space here to summarize the *Consolation* in detail. However, the principal teachings of Lady Philosophy may be sketched briefly. In the first place, she emphasizes the fact, or what was thought to be the fact, that the universe is a rationally ordered whole governed reasonably by a wise God who is truly lovable. In this reasonable world nothing happens by chance, which is a mere word without a referent. But all created things are transitory. Men frequently regard tangible things, which are by nature ephemeral, as true goods, placing their hopes in wealth, power, dignities, fame, or physical pleasure. But these are partial goods, which cannot actually satisfy a reasoning creature. Desire for these partial goods is insatiable once it is unleashed, so that the pursuit of these goods is inevitably frustrating when they are seen as ends rather than as means. The transitory nature of these goods makes them deceptive to those who pursue them, rendering such persons powerless because they cannot achieve the good they desire.

Alternations between worldly prosperity and worldly adversity are attributed to Fortune, whose wheel constantly turns, so that those who cling to it are raised to a condition of prosperity only to be cast down again, regardless of their merits. Good Fortune is actually more deceptive than bad Fortune, since it leads to false hopes. Adverse Fortune on the other hand serves as a wholesome warning that false goods are not to be trusted. No one forces a man to seek happiness in goods of Fortune. When he seeks such gifts for themselves, he involves himself in the flux of created things and must inevitably face the consequences of their mutability. He has, so to speak, subjected himself to Fortune by failing to set his heart on God rather than on His creatures. The solution to the problem raised by alternations in Fortune lies within the individual, who will be able to regard "Fortune's buffets and rewards with equal thanks" if he loves God and the virtues bestowed by God rather than creatures.

Viewed in a larger sense, Fortune, like chance, does not exist. The seemingly irrational fluctuation between prosperity and adversity that everyone must suffer is not in itself a Divine plan to bestow rewards and punishments. The vicious often prosper and the virtuous often suffer. Rather the alternation is a part of the

Providential Order structured to offer a kind of continuous dem-onstration of the fact that temporal satisfactions are necessarily deceptive. God, as George Herbert put it, has given us everything but rest:

> For if I should, said He,
> Bestow this jewel also on my creature,
> He would adore my gifts instead of me,
> And rest in nature, not the God of nature;
> So both should losers be.

To Boethius, the failure of temporal satisfactions, which has caused a great deal of bitter literature in modern times, was a certain indication that true peace was to be found in a reasonable order beyond the illusions of Fortune. As Peter of Blois said in the twelfth century, he called a little treatise of his *On the Deceptions of Fortune* "not because Fortune is anything, or its deceptions, but so that in the elevation or humiliation of men, believed by many to be fortuitous or uncertain, readers may be convinced that all proceeds from divine dispensation."

If Fortune is an illusion, and the alternative to a submission to this illusion is a love of virtue and a faith in Providence, it is absolutely essential that men should have freedom to choose be-tween them. For this reason Boethius devoted a great deal of space in his book to the problem. The issue was a moral issue, not a meta-physical issue, and we shall do him a grave disservice if we regard his metaphysical machinery as an end in itself, or try to analyze it in terms of post-Kantian systems. God, he explains, exists in a realm outside space and time. Hence, to Him what we regard as the past, the present, and the future is a continuous present. He can observe our actions in what seems to us to be the future without influencing those actions, just as we can watch a man walking down the street as we sit unobserved in a window without influenc-ing what he does. Thus, reasoning creatures, of which man is one, have the discretion to choose their actions, even though God, from a mundane point of view, does "foresee" them. But when a man ceases to exercise his reason by becoming passionately immersed in the pursuit of some temporal satisfaction, he loses his ability to choose, blinding himself to the possibility of virtuous restraint and making himself a part of the flux of created things. He alone has responsibility for this choice. No one, least of all God, forces him either to grasp Fortune's wheel or to disregard it. In this freedom, as Pico della Mirandola was to point out, lies not only the possibility of moral action, but the true dignity of man. As Milton's Angel puts it,

> God made thee perfect, not immutable;
> And good he made thee, but to persevere
> He left it in thy power, ordained thy will
> By nature free, not overruled by Fate
> Inextricable, or strict necessity.
> Our voluntary service He requires,
> Not our necessitated; such with Him
> Finds no acceptance, nor can find. For how
> Can hearts not free be tried whether they serve
> Willing or no, who will but what they must
> By Destiny, and can no other choose?

It cannot be emphasized too strongly that for most men in the Middle Ages, not to mention their Renaissance and Baroque successors, virtue implied manliness, and virtuous restraint before temptations, either of prosperity or adversity, implied heroism. Boethius used Hercules as an exemplar. At the close of the Middle Ages Petrarch was to use Scipio.

To return to Abelard's *History,* we can see without difficulty that the Boethian consolation offered to those in adversity, which advocates that they remove their affections from "gifts of Fortune," operates equally to encourage the kind of deliberate worldly renunciation undertaken by nuns. Meanwhile, Abelard's career illustrates well the evil consequences of submission to what he calls "flattering Fortune." The fact that he goes on to say that Divine Piety, rather than Fortune, was responsible simply calls attention to the further Boethian doctrine that Fortune is an illusion. And the concluding positive assertion of faith in the Providential Order is exactly that advocated systematically in the *Consolation.* The

process of Abelard's initial submission to Fortune is rather carefully indicated by value judgments inserted in the *History* itself.
In fact, the *History* is a tightly structured literary work that contains, in addition to its general salutary lesson, much specific
material directly relevant to the Paraclete. If we regard it as a
record of conversion in the Augustinian manner reinforced by
Boethian themes, we shall find it much easier to understand than
if we think of it simply as a personal record. Incidentally, it
should be pointed out that many of the ideas in St. Augustine's
Confessions are repeated in somewhat different form in the *Consolation,* for Boethius was a close student of Augustine's works. It
was only natural that Abelard should have had in mind the two
most famous "autobiographies" in the Christian tradition when he
wrote his own, and it is not surprising that his own work should
reflect the thematic structure of his models. As a matter of fact, it
is unlikely that anyone would have understood the *History* at all
if that structure had not been apparent.

Before we look more closely at the *History,* it will help us to
consider one further point concerning medieval literary technique
—its peculiar employment of humor. When the *History* is regarded as a sentimental or psychological document, its humor disappears. But Abelard had a reputation for jocularity, and this
jocularity does not altogether vanish in the *History,* as we have
seen in our discussion of the little sermon attributed to Heloise.
The appreciation of this humor elsewhere, however, requires a certain adjustment in point of view on our part. Today many persons
think of laughter, the fruit of humor, as a product of release from
tension. But this laughter requires a purely emotional kind of
humor, not based on the intellectual perception of the ridiculous,
but based on feelings. Humor of this kind is actually rare in
medieval literature, and its absence has led to the mistaken impression that medieval people had little sense of humor. As one
step backward in the direction of medieval humor, it will help us
to recall the humor of Henry Fielding, the author of *Tom Jones.*
Fielding tells us that comedy arises from the perception of the
ridiculous, and that the true sources of the ridiculous are vanity

and hypocrisy. During the Middle Ages, these sources can be considerably extended to include other vices, such as lust or avarice, which are sources of the ridiculous in the comedies of Ben Jonson. Before the Renaissance the Devil and his cohorts were often comic characters, and the vices are often portrayed with comic overtones in medieval art. When medieval people laughed at vice of any kind, they were only sharing the laughter of God, for, as the second Psalm tells us (Douay Version), when rebellious worldlings seek to break their bonds, "He that dwelleth in Heaven shall laugh at them."

Our natural inclination today is to sentimentalize or "psychologize" vice, so that it is difficult to be ridiculous without being pathetic. All whores, male and female, have acquired hearts of gold, and sentimental humanitarianism, of which there are no traces in medieval Christianity, smothers the laughter of God in the lugubrious pieties of something called "human understanding." But Abelard does not hesitate, in his *History,* to laugh at himself, and we shall understand him better if we learn to laugh with him.

Historically speaking, the change in the character of humor began to take place during the eighteenth century with the disappearance of any widespread faith in the Order of Providence. When this order is recognized, efforts to evade its consequences seem ridiculous, and, if the immediate results are not too serious, they are laughable. Passion, which became the grand subject of the nineteenth century, was either ludicrous or disastrous when Providence was still taken as an assumption. A significant literary and artistic principle follows from this situation: medieval works of art and literature are seldom emotionally serious, but they are almost always intellectually serious and are amusing at the same time when they involve portrayals of departures from reasonable behavior. Without the intellectual seriousness as a background, the ridiculous could not emerge. During the twelfth century a marked stimulus to the use of humor as a means of attacking vice was afforded by the popularity of Ovid, who was regarded as a "mocker of light loves" and hence an exemplar of attacks on any love that deviated from the love of God. The difference between medieval and modern attittudes is easy to see in the change in approach to Ovid's *Art of Love*. For medieval readers it was a funny book, full of witty ironies; for nineteenth-century readers it was a "dirty" book, and, generally speaking, that attitude still prevails.

Turning now to the *History*, we should not hesitate to smile when the very youthful Abelard is said to have abandoned the trophies of war for those of disputation and gone wandering about like a knight-errant seeking triumphs in the schools. The "knight of the schools" is just as ridiculous as Ovid's "knight of love," and the military imagery with which Abelard describes his youthful encounters only makes them laughable. But he does not hesitate to criticize himself directly, in the event that the reader fails to respond to the imagery. Thus on the establishment of his first school at Melun he says, "Disregarding the limited power of my years and presuming greater force of mind than I had, I aspired, a mere boy, to become a master of students. . . ." Then he moved to the "Camp of Corbeil" so that "my insolence might be vented in more frequent attacks in disputation." Actual "insolence" may or may not have been a feature of Abelard's character, but he is careful to emphasize the trait in order to establish himself as a suitable candidate for Fortune's whims.

The device used to record the result of Abelard's contest with William of Champeaux in 1113 is especially noteworthy. Although William became Bishop of Châlons, a distinction that Abelard would have coveted himself, and Abelard simply retreated to Le Pallet, ostensibly to assist in the installation of his mother Lucia in a nunnery, he describes these events as a victory for himself. He says, "But these words of Ajax I may speak more modestly and proclaim more boldly than he did:

> If you ask the Fortune
> Of this strife, I was not conquered by him."

The quotation is from Ovid's *Metamorphoses* (Book XIII, lines 89–90), where it forms a part of the boast of Ajax in his contest with Ulysses for the arms of Achilles. But as all readers of Ovid

I MEDIEVAL KNIGHTS (*c.* 1215). From the Shrine of Charlemagne at Aachen, showing the Emperor lamenting his slain warriors. Abelard envisages himself in his youth as a knight slaying his opponents in the schools with the arms of dialectic.

MARBURG—ART REFERENCE BUREAU

II SUGER'S ABBEY CHURCH OF ST. DENIS. This first appearance of the Gothic Style heralds the great age of the cathedrals just as Abelard's philosophy heralds the age of scholasticism.

MARBURG—ART REFERENCE BUREAU

III ST. MARTIN-DES-CHAMPS, PARIS (c. 1132). A church Abelard probably knew. The style is basically Romanesque, showing the influence of Cluniac architecture.

MARBURG—ART REFERENCE BUREAU

IV FONTEVRAULT, THE KITCHEN (Restored). It was here in a convent established by Robert of Arbrissel that a nun, one Petronilla, ruled over both monks and other nuns.

GIRAUDON—ART REFERENCE BUREAU

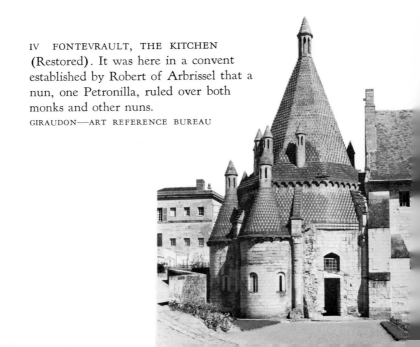

V ROGER DE RABUTIN (Bussy-Rabutin). One of his witty letters to Madame de Sévigné afforded a profound stimulus to the development of the legend of Heloise.

VI POPE'S "ELOISA" (1719). This engraving appeared with the second edition of Pope's poem. The artist made no effort to evoke sentiment, but allowed the figure and the landscape to be governed by a swirling line interrupted by the regular lines of the building, suggesting the contrast between passion and reason in the poem.

VII ROCOCO WIT. Boucher, "Mars and Venus." The lovers are here caught before the act to heighten the humorous effect. The highly improbable setting contributes to the detachment of the painting, which is witty rather than sensual. The story of Mars and Venus is mentioned by Abelard in his *History*.

THE WALLACE COLLECTION. CROWN COPYRIGHT

VIII A VENERIAN LANDSCAPE. Watteau, "Pilgrimage to Cythera" (1717). The scenery near the Paraclete in Pope's poem bears no resemblance to the actual setting of the Paraclete. Eloisa's landscape is blighted by Melancholy, thoughts of death and the futility of passion.

ALINARI—ART REFERENCE BUREAU

IX SENTIMENT AND SENSUALITY. Greuze, "Chapeau Blanc." The sentiment of the picture, its wistfully sweet submissiveness, contrasts with the convincing flesh of exposed breast and shoulder, and the full lower lip. This lady is a stylistic contemporary of Colardeau's Heloise.

MUSEUM OF FINE ARTS, BOSTON

X VIOLENCE IN THE AGE OF SENTIMENT. Moreau le Jeune, "The Castration of Abelard" (1797). The expressions of the figures suggest the emotional impact of violence at a time when sentiment was giving way to sentimentality.

XI   THE TRIUMPH OF INNOCENCE. Grevedon, "Héloïse" (1834). The innocence of Colardeau's Heloise triumphed over her other characteristics in the early nineteenth century to produce this saintly figure.
BIBLIOTHÈQUE NATIONALE, PARIS

XII   THE IRRESISTIBLE LOVER. Grevedon, "Abeilard" (companion piece to his "Héloïse"). The large, mysterious eyes and downy rounded cheeks suggest a romantic passion impatient with the restraint of the cloak and the distraction of the book.
BIBLIOTHÈQUE NATIONALE—ART REFERENCE BUREAU

XIII LENOIR'S MONUMENT (1839). This elaborate structure was erected as a memorial to the undying love of Heloise and Abelard.

XIV PILGRIMS AT THE SHRINE OF HELOISE AND ABELARD. Gigoux (1839). Thousands of lovers and tourists are said to have flocked to the shrine.

XV DEMURE SENTIMEN-
TALITY. Gigoux, "Heloise"
(1839). Here our heroine
is not only innocent but
obviously gifted with very
refined sensibilities. In the
twentieth century these
are lost, replaced by natural human instincts that
enjoy an inherent right to
unfettered expression.

XVI EXPRESSIONISTIC SENSUALITY. From the play, *Abelard and Heloise,* produced during 1970 and 1971, with Diana Rigg and Keith Michell. Helen Waddell's novel, upon which the play is based, emphasizes the transcendent character of sexual passion.
STEVEN KEULL

knew—and, as we have seen, this meant almost anyone in the twelfth century who could read Abelard's Latin—Ajax lost this contest. The arms of Achilles were granted to Ulysses and Ajax killed himself. For Ajax was an early *miles gloriosus*, or "braggart soldier," and in associating himself with him, Abelard simply emerges as a "braggart soldier" of dialectic. This effect, which is humorous, was unquestionably deliberate.

A similar device, somewhat more subtle in character, is used to turn Abelard's condemnation of Anselm of Laon into an indirect reflection on himself. Of Anselm he says, "His tree full of leaves seemed conspicuous to those seeing it from a distance, but to those diligently searching it was found to be unfruitful. Thus when I went to gather fruit from it, I discovered it to be that fig which Our Lord cursed [Matt. 21:19], or that old oak with which Lucan compared Pompey, saying,

> He stood, the shadow of a great name,
> Like an oak towering in a fruitful field."

There are two references here, one to the Gospel of St. Matthew and another to Lucan. In the first place, the "leafy tree" was a fairly common image for a man full of insubstantial words. The troubadour Marcabru, for example, described men who either produce no good works or works that are disappointing as willows and elders. But the Scriptural passage reads: "And seeing a certain tree by the wayside, he came to it and found on it nothing but leaves only, and he said to it: May no fruit grow on thee henceforth forever! And immediately the fig-tree withered away." This passage is discussed in Abelard's sermon *On the Lord's Passion,* included among the sermons prepared for the Paraclete shortly before the *History* was written. There Abelard explains that the fig-tree represents the unrepentant, who are, as it were, sterile, bearing only words. It is pretty obvious that this warning has no relevance to Anselm, but that it does describe the youthful Abelard well, for he had not yet repented his verbose insolence. Those readers familiar with the Scriptural passage and with the conventional interpretation reflected in Abelard's sermon—and again, this means almost all readers of his Latin—would have recognized, no doubt with some amusement, that the bitter condemnation of Anselm actually condemns the youthful Abelard. The quotation from Lucan also applies to Abelard, who, as the Peripatetic of Pallet, was "the shadow of a great name"—Aristotle. But he was an "Aristotle" whose sole interest at the time was in self-aggrandizement. Readers would have been reminded once more of the significance of the quotation when Heloise later, in injured vanity, compared Abelard with Pompey.

Abelard is especially vehement in self-condemnation when he considers the affair with Heloise. He calls attention to the "pecuniary rewards" and "glory" that resulted from his lectures at Paris, calls himself a "fool" puffed up by prosperity, and describes himself after the seduction of Heloise as "laboring completely in pride and lechery." These maladies, he says, were cured by Divine Piety: "It cured first lechery and then pride. It cured lechery by depriving me of the means by which to exercise it, and it cured pride . . . by humiliating me in the burning of that book in which I chiefly gloried." These are remarks made in retrospect. At the time of his castration and later, at Soissons, he was by no means ready to attribute his difficulties to Divine Piety. Rather, he was disturbed by injuries to his vanity, entering the monastery out of "shame," and almost denying Divine Grace altogether after the Council of Soissons.

In fact, Abelard does his best to show himself overcome by the attractions of the world in his youth. He makes of himself a ridiculous vain boaster, an avaricious clerk interested in wealth, fame, and station, and a completely self-absorbed lecher. Conventionally, the three temptations before which Adam fell and over which Christ triumphed in the wilderness were gluttony, or immersion in fleshly satisfaction, vainglory, and avarice, a vice that might include desire for worldly elevation. Abelard shows himself overcome by all three, but it is the first, in the form of lechery, that finally brings him down. In the *Consolation* Boethius points out that concentration on one false worldly good leads first to the neglect of the rest and finally to the loss of the one sought. Lechery deprives Abelard of his fame, his fortune, and his opportunity for ecclesiastical advancement. And it is also lechery that leads to the ultimate destruction of his lecherous inclinations. This lesson could hardly be more emphatically illustrated than it is in the *History*.

At the time the *History* was written, Heloise was a widely respected abbess. If this achievement had been an easy one, reached without struggle, she could hardly serve as an examplar to the nuns of the Paraclete. In order to make her conversion more spectacular, Abelard probably exaggerated her early worldliness, just as he probably exaggerated his own disagreeable character in youth. The literary devices we have just examined emphasize the artificial, or "stylized," character of the *History* and are consistent with its purpose as an exemplary narrative. The plight of the young Heloise is somewhat ameliorated by circumstances; she was not only very young when Abelard met her, but she was almost forced into becoming his mistress. Nevertheless, once this position is established, she is made to demonstrate a rather devastating, if amusing, hypocrisy in her sermon on marriage, and a great deal of vanity in her motivation for taking the veil. Although it is doubtful that the actual Heloise behaved in quite this way, the character Abelard creates is sufficiently submerged in her own self-satisfaction to make her conversion a spectacular example of reform. Her progress from a worldly youth to a wise maturity in actual life was to make an enormous impression on Peter the Venerable of Cluny. It undoubtedly impressed other contemporaries in the same way, and it would undoubtedly impress the nuns of the Paraclete when they read Abelard's somewhat exaggerated account.

But Abelard is careful not to make himself "utterly depraved" in his narrative. He probably regarded the fact that he inspired William of Champeaux to alter his teaching concerning the "universals" as a genuine achievement, felt that his success at Paris was based on real talent, and thought of his book *On the Divine Unity and Trinity* as a valuable contribution to understanding. The nuns had before them in the *History* a picture of a man with an excellent mind, but a man lacking in moral maturity. His most dangerous moral crisis followed the Council of Soissons. As he puts it, "O God, who judges equity, with what gall, with what bitterness of mind did I insanely denounce you, wrathfully accuse you, frequently repeating the demand of St. Anthony, 'Good Jesus, where were you?'" This, as we have seen, is the worst sin of all, the denial of that Paraclete from whom the nuns took their name. From this point forward there is a gradual recovery. The squabble over St. Denis, while in itself trivial, led to the establishment of Abelard's oratory, and from the point of his location there, he was able to insert positive teachings for the nuns in his story.

The first of these doctrinal passages appears in the description of student behavior at the oratory. Abelard probably exaggerated the devotion of the students in his account, not for the purpose of "distorting history," but for the purpose of instructing his nuns. He says of his students that "you would believe that they imitated those ancient philosophers described by St. Jerome in the second book of his treatise *Against Jovinian*." He then proceeds to quote the description at length. It is worth quoting once more to show its applicability to the nuns enduring their self-imposed hardships at the Paraclete and, presumably, devoting themselves to study under the direction of Heloise:

> Through the senses as if through certain windows there is formed an entrance into the soul for vices. The capital and stronghold and fortress of the mind cannot be seized unless the hostile army passes through its gates. If anyone is delighted by the circus, by the contest of athletes, by the gestures of actors, by the beauty of women, by the splendor of gems, or of clothes, or of other similar things, the liberty of the mind is captured through the windows of the eyes, and the prophetic saying is fulfilled: "Death is come up through our windows" [Jer. 9:21]. Thus when battle wedges of the passions enter into the fortress of our minds through these portals, where is the mind's liberty? its fortitude? its thought of God? Especially when the sense of touch pictures for itself past pleasures, and through memory forces the mind in a certain way to suffer them and in a way to experience them, what does the mind not actually perform?
>
> Moved by these reasons many philosophers have relin-

quished the crowds of the cities and the gardens of the suburbs where there are grassy plots, leafy trees, the whisper of birds, the mirrors of pools, the murmur of streams, and many other delights for the eyes and ears, lest through the excess and abundance of opportunities the fortitude of the mind be softened and its shame be ravished. For it is useless to gaze frequently on something by which you may some time be made captive, or to commit yourself to the experience of something you can do without only with difficulty.

The Pythagoreans, declining this kind of resort, used to live in solitary and deserted places. Even Plato himself, although he may have been a wealthy man whose couch Diogenes used to trample down with muddy feet, in order that he might devote himself to philosophy chose for his Academy a villa remote from the city that was not only a wasteland but unhealthy as well, so that the force of libido might be broken through the care and anxiety of diseases, and so that his disciples might find no other pleasures except in those things they learned.

Abelard goes on at once to compare this austere life with the life led by monks, thus reinforcing the relevance of the passage to Heloise and her nuns, to whom the words of St. Jerome probably suggested that if pagan philosophers could so deprive themselves for the sake of study, they should be able to endure similar if less severe deprivations for the sake of devotion.

Almost immediately following this description there appears the long discussion of the name *Paraclete* and its significance. This would have been of special interest to Heloise and her nuns, who used the name for their order, and could find here an authoritative account of it by their founder. The examplary life of the students at the oratory and the implications of the name applied to it would have together afforded them a firm basis for the further development of their own peculiar ideals and aspirations. Meanwhile, with reference to Abelard's own development, the celebration of a life very different from that he had led at Paris before his downfall and the exaltation of God "the Comforter," almost abandoned after the burning of his book, demonstrated a firm basis for his qualification as a spiritual guide. In part the description of the life of the monks at St. Gildas affords a contrast to the life of the students at the Paraclete. The degeneracy and misery of Abelard's Breton charges illustrate very well the consequences to be expected when contemplatives abandon their ideals. Again, the extended discussion of the suitability of eunuchs and holy men as instructors for women reinforces Abelard's own authority as the founder of the Paraclete. And his final acceptance of the Providential Order under very wretched circumstances must have assured the nuns of the genuineness of his conversion and served as an inspiration to their own.

Viewed as a whole, therefore, the content of the *History* is singularly appropriate to the use to which it was put. Abelard undoubtedly wrote it, not to console some anonymous friend, but to supply the beginning of a basic document for his new order. If anything more was needed, in addition to the rule, it was an account of the conversion of Heloise under Abelard's direction. This deficiency is supplied in the subsequent letters, which we shall now consider. Meanwhile, there is no justification whatever for regarding the *History* either as a record of romantic passion or as a revelation of Abelard's "psychological development." These ideas are in fact equally absurd in the light of the text itself, almost as absurd as the notion, sometimes expressed, that the *History* illustrates the principles of "courtly love."

CHAPTER VII

The Correspondent

With a few exceptions the medieval "letter" has no real counterpart among either those stacks of neatly typed messages that emerge from modern office buildings today, nor among the little handwritten personal records, descriptions of local and family affairs, autobiographical detail, and more or less intimate expressions of condolence, affection, or sometimes, wrath, that fill suburban and city corner mailboxes. The exceptions are mostly student letters asking for money, which may have certain modern counterparts, and probably a few love letters, although genuine specimens of these do not survive from the Middle Ages. People did send each other short written messages, often stating very briefly what was needed, but, to be understood fully, these required verbal elaboration on the part of the messenger. The formal letter, or "epistle," was a different thing entirely. Such epistles, assembled in collections, constituted a rather popular form in the eleventh and twelfth centuries, but they were carefully modeled on the epistles of St. Augustine or St. Jerome. They did not, like the letter collections popular in the seventeenth and eighteenth centuries, reveal the details of personal history so as to form a narrative of sorts. Instead, they were in effect treatises. St. Augustine's letters often became authoritative sources for points of doctrine, and the surviving letters of high-ranking ecclesiastics during the twelfth century are frequently expository and obviously instructive. The letters of men like Yvo of Chartres, Bernard of Clairvaux, Peter the Venerable, or Peter of Blois circulated in collections cherished because they contained authoritative statements on a wide variety of topics as well as exemplary treatments of matters of current or recurrent interest. A collection of letters thus often resembled a collection of authoritative essays. The fact that the letters might comment on persons of importance gave them, moreover, an historical interest at a time when "traditions" of all kinds were highly regarded.

The letters of a bishop or abbot were often dictated to a secretary, or outlined to him, so that the secretary might have more to do with the actual wording than the bishop or abbot himself. When such letters were collected, either by the author or by a secretary, they were carefully selected, arranged, and sometimes thoroughly revised. Some letters included might not be actual letters at all, but were instead exercises in exposition on a certain topic or problem, or merely a series of appropriate observations addressed to a person of a certain type. Medieval collections often contain letters addressed to "a certain clerk" or "a certain monk" containing advice suitable for clerks or monks in situations of a kind clerks or monks frequently encountered. The collected letters of a bishop would form an important document for his cathedral library. The letters of St. Bernard were especially useful to members of his own order, although others might find them interesting as well. The letters of Peter of Blois, written in the twelfth century, circulated widely in England in the fourteenth century, not only because of their historical interest, but because they contained salutary essays on a variety of topics. They tell us very little, incidentally, about the intimate personal life of Peter of Blois, although they do reveal a great deal about King Henry II of England.

The Letters of Abelard and Heloise obviously forms a "collection" made for a special purpose. It does not contain a surviving letter written to Heloise advising her on the conduct of Scriptural studies at the Paraclete, or another later letter in which Abelard affirms the orthodoxy of his faith. It begins, as we have just seen, with a "Letter to a Friend" purporting to be a letter of consolation but actually revealing the spiritual conversion of the author. The first of the subsequent letters is joined to it by the device of having Heloise encounter the "Letter to a Friend" by chance and write a reply to it. This is clearly an artificial stratagem designed to give the collection as a whole an external as well as an internal unity. Abelard and Heloise had undoubtedly engaged in frequent correspondence while he was at St. Gildas. The founding of the Paraclete as a nunnery with its problems of organization, both physical and spiritual, must have required a great deal of correspondence, but we have none of it. What we have instead is a collection of "epistles" designed for deposit at the Paraclete for the use of the nuns there. There is no reason whatsoever for thinking that the letters attributed to Heloise in this collection were actually composed as genuine letters by her. It is quite possible, on the other hand, that she may have made useful suggestions to Abelard, both in person and in correspondence, about their content and technique. She would have done this, moreover, with exactly that kind of detachment displayed by Abelard himself when he describes his own youthful waywardness. This does not imply "cynicism" about the "truth" on the part of either of them; on the contrary, they were seeking to get at what they regarded as the truth as best they could. Genuine emotional "sincerity" with reference to literal events had not yet become a literary virtue.

One of the great puzzles of Abelardian criticism has been the chronology of the correspondence, the puzzle having been enhanced by the assumption that the letters attributed to Heloise are genuine letters. Her first letters are still full of amorous passion, but they could not have been written until after she had become a respected abbess, many years after Abelard's castration. This fact has given her a reputation for remarkable "enduring human passion," a rather polite, if somewhat amusing way modern ecclesiastics have of referring to the persistence of lust centered on a single object. The situation also attracted readers from the seventeenth century onward who were interested in "hopeless love." However, we should do well to disregard the chronological problem altogether. Both Abelard and Heloise were interested in the theme developed in the correspondence, not in its value as a record of actual events. If a record of the spiritual conversion of Heloise was to be made available, it was necessary to plunge her once more into the snares of the world and then extract her from this situation under Abelard's guidance. Insofar as the intended audience of nuns was concerned, this worldly involvement would be much more relevant to themselves if it took place not at Argenteuil but at the Paraclete itself, where the conversion of the first abbess under the direction of the founder could become a part of local tradition. The actual chronology is therefore not important, although it seems probable that Abelard had the volume of letters either completed or well on the way to completion before he left St. Gildas. Some of it may have been written later, however, between 1135 and the Council of Sens in 1140, a period during which Abelard seems to have been especially busy as an author. Heloise was not officially installed as Abbess at the Paraclete immediately after she and her nuns went there, but she is considered to be Abbess when the first letter attributed to her was written. It may be that Abelard completed the last two letters in the collection and the *History* first, and then added the intervening correspondence.

When we read the first letters of Heloise we may remember that in actual fact Abelard was a eunuch, an old man by medieval standards, probably not in very good health, and that Heloise had already achieved a reputation for sanctity. But these "facts" had best be forgotten, and we should concentrate instead on the themes adduced. At the opening of her first letter Heloise, or rather the character representing her in the *Letters,* whom we shall call "Heloise" for convenience, states that a copy of the *History* had been brought to her by chance. She summarizes Abelard's difficulties very briefly and asks for a letter so that she may share his joys and woes. This is again a very obvious artificial device, since Abelard undoubtedly visited the Paraclete as often as he could during the course of its establishment and had kept up a correspondence with Heloise while he was preparing the hymns, sequences, sermons, and so on that he wrote for her use. However, she goes on to say that the *History* has caused fresh wounds by reminding her of the past. Again, this is a fairly obvious device for leading Heloise once more into her immersion in worldly concern. Continuing, she says that since the Paraclete is his own foundation, he owes more to his daughters than to the anonymous friend to whom the *History* is addressed. Since the *History* was very clearly prepared for these "daughters" in any event, the "friend" being a device to avoid the embarrassment of saying to the nuns, in effect, "This is the kind of man I, your founder, was," this statement constitutes a further thematic rationalization for linking the *History* with the following letters. Finally, in her preliminary remarks, Heloise argues that since the Fathers consoled holy women, Abelard has ample precedent for consoling his nuns. Here the correspondence picks up a theme already elaborated in the *History,* but used to introduce the further "consolation" to be developed in the letters themselves. In considering this statement, we should remember that "consolation" implied the diversion of the mind away from the "false goods of the world" toward the immutable goods of the realm of the intelligible. Readers who have been disappointed because the subsequent consolation offered by Abelard is not more sentimental have simply misunderstood the nature of twelfth-century consolation in the first place, and the theme and function of the *Letters* in the second.

At this point it may be well to digress once more on the subject of history. If the introduction to the first letter of Heloise is so patently artificial, why did the nuns who read it fail to criticize it on the ground that it could not be "really true"? This is a little like asking why twelfth-century people did not object to the highly stylized sculpture on their churches because it did not look like the productions of Rodin. But the answer to this query has already been discussed. Medieval people were much more interested in significance than in facts. In modern times the artifice of the link between the *History* and the first letter, which is quite admirable in a technical sense, has been overlooked because modern readers, aside from being literal-minded, are so absorbed by a combination of romantic and psychological concerns and by a concentration on "personality development" that they are just as willing as the nuns were to overlook factual improbabilities. This was not true during the seventeenth and eighteenth centuries, when the opening of the first letter was changed in various ways to give it greater surface rationality.

Having established the link between the *History* and her letter and adduced reasons for the further development of the themes of the *History* with reference to herself and her nuns, Heloise proceeds to describe her own predicament specifically by elaborating the ideas of her little sermon on marriage in the *History*. This takes us back thematically to the conclusion of that sermon, and the succeeding letters detail the process by which she recovers from the ludicrous position she adopted there. Historically speaking, it should be emphasized once more that the actual Heloise, as distinct from the character manufactured by Abelard, in all probability never adopted this absurd position. It is true, however, that all healthy nuns, especially those who have been sexually awakened, are subject to regrets about their decision to enter the religious life. Such regrets probably distracted Heloise early in her career. In fact, Abelard says something about them in the instructional poem he wrote for his son Astrolabe shortly before his death. But there is no reason to suppose that Heloise was still much disturbed by the time she became Abbess of the Paraclete, and still less reason to think that she might have rationalized her intransigence either in the manner of her sermon or in the manner developed in the letters attributed to her. The "character" Heloise, like the "character" Abelard, serves as an extreme example, both in degradation and in the final triumph of reasonableness.

To return to the letter, Heloise says that Abelard owes her a special debt because of her love for him; he alone can comfort her, for she always obeyed him, even to the madness of becoming a nun at his request. Her only desire, she says, was to carry out his wishes. We should notice that this argument places the blame squarely on Abelard for the miseries of his former mistress, and that this attitude persists throughout the first letter. The miseries are described at once in one of the most famous passages in the *Letters*: "God knows, I asked for nothing of you except yourself, desiring not that which was yours, but you alone. And although the name of *wife* may seem more holy and more impressive, the name *friend* has always seemed to me to be of more value, or even, if it does not offend you, the word *concubine* or *whore*. For the more I humbled myself on your account, the greater grace you might have in consequence, and thus I should injure your fame less." Abelard had long since given up any interest in the kind of fame to which Heloise here refers, and it is not difficult to see that her concern for that fame constitutes a kind of vanity.

But the most interesting feature of the statement is the fact that it is probably a literary echo and hence a piece of artifice. Where would Abelard (who composed this letter) have heard of a woman who so humbled herself that she wished to become the concubine of her lover in order not to injure him? The answer is to be found in the writings of that favorite poet of the twelfth-century schools, Ovid. One of his most admired works was a series of epistles, mostly attributed to forlorn ladies, the hopelessness of whose predicaments was well known to Ovid's readers. Since the loves were hopeless, the laments of the ladies produce a certain irony. One of them, Dido, whose complete abandonment by Aeneas for very good reasons was well known to all, has this to say to her departed lover:

Of what crime do you accuse me except to have loved?
. . . .
If the name of wife shame you, I shall be called your hostess;
While Dido may be yours, she will bear anything.

Here the word hostess is more or less the equivalent of "concubine," so that Heloise in effect makes of herself another Dido, abandoned by a man whose *pietas* demanded more honorable pursuits. Again, one might ask, what would the nuns have thought if they had recognized Dido lurking behind the posture of Heloise?

The answer is that the indirect allusion to Dido simply serves to emphasize the foolishness of the attitude Heloise attributes to herself, and that it would probably have had the further effect of eliciting a salutary smile.

But there is more, and worse, to come. For Heloise continues, "And you yourself were not altogether forgetful of that grace in the epistle directed to a friend for consolation I mentioned above. There you did not disdain to explain some reasons by means of which I sought to restrain you from our wedding and unfortunate marriage bed, but you omitted some, in accordance with which I preferred love to marriage, liberty to bondage. May God be my witness, if Caesar Augustus presiding over the whole world had held me worthy of the honor of marriage, and had confirmed the whole world to me perpetually, it would have seemed dearer to me and more worthy to be called your prostitute than his Empress." This "world well lost" theme, dear to sentimental critics of Shakespeare's *Antony and Cleopatra,* is ludicrous enough in itself, and was indeed so regarded during the later Middle Ages, but it is especially ludicrous if we remember that Heloise once sought to associate it with the ideals of the philosophical life. In its present context it evinces an enormously vain exaggeration of the solaces Heloise has lost. The exaggeration is obvious and would not have escaped the nuns, some of whom were undoubtedly inclined to exaggerate their own sacrifices. Just exactly what were the great attractions of Abelard that inspired such willingness to sacrifice? Heloise goes on to explain.

She insists first that the proper object of a woman's love should be a man, not wealth, a principle with which most medieval theologians would agree heartily, since they sometimes satirized men and women who married purses instead of human beings. In this way, Heloise continues, the more truly her love was directed toward Abelard, the more free it was from error. This again is a good principle, provided that the object of love was made attractive by virtue. But as Heloise describes Abelard's peculiar attractions, it becomes strikingly apparent that although they did not constitute wealth, they were nevertheless very worldly, appealing to pride and lechery rather than to covetousness. Abelard, she says, was more famous than kings or philosophers. Any kingdom, city, or village would burn to see him. All wives and maidens yearned for him in his absence and burned for him in his presence. Queens envied Heloise her joys with Abelard in bed. Moreover, she says, Abelard could sing songs and thus captivate the heart of any woman. All should pity Heloise for having lost such delights. These arguments reveal exactly the kind of pride and lechery from which Abelard himself suffered at the time of his affair with Heloise, and the intention here was undoubtedly to show how desperately Heloise needed instruction. Her willingness to give up the world of Caesar for the kind of fame Abelard achieved as a "knight of dialectic" and his sexual attractiveness is not romantic but pathetic. Caesar's world might be abandoned for much better reasons.

Finally, Heloise adduces the principle that it is the intention and not the act that makes the crime. Her intentions, she says, were always known to Abelard and were pure. This assertion has sometimes been taken as a reflection of a theory in Abelard's *Ethics* to the effect that since a sin is something done with deliberate consent in contempt of God, a sinful act performed in invincible ignorance is without guilt. Abelard does not deny, however, that such acts are objectively sinful or that they reasonably deserve punishment. The basic principle involved is, in fact, not new. Abelard is simply saying in another way that a mortal sin results from the consent of the reason to an unreasonable action per- formed in knowing disregard of or contempt for God. But Heloise could not really claim invincible ignorance, and she does not do so. She simply says in effect that since she was under the guidance of Abelard, who was irresistible, he was at fault. The accusatory tone continues at the close of the letter, where she points out that everyone thinks that Abelard's love for her was mere concupiscence rather than friendship because when the object of his desire ceased, all else went with it. She entered the religious life, she says, not from devotion to God, but only at his command. She now needs the refreshment of his word so that she can serve God. We

should take this final plea literally. The first letter of Heloise exhibits a self-righteous unwillingness on her part to assume any
responsibility for her condition, and that condition, as she describes
it, or rather as Abelard describes it, is one of extreme spiritual
weakness.

Abelard's reply to this letter, unfortunately for the authors of
the legendary history we shall examine later, betrays no traces of
any romantic passion for Heloise. Indeed, if we have read the
History with any care, we can see that any such passion was not
only physically impossible but also spiritually inappropriate. The
modern reader misses sentiment, even in the absence of passion,
but Abelard lived many years before sentiment became fashionable.
It is also true that a sentimental reply would have been funda-
mentally unkind. In his reply Abelard quite naturally emphasizes
the first duty of the contemplative: prayer. He says first that he
had not written previously (a statement, incidentally, whose
"truth" lies only in the context of the present collection of letters),
because Heloise had demonstrated her prudence by first becoming
prioress at Argenteuil and then abbess at the Paraclete. However,
he now agrees to write to her concerning "those things that pertain
to God," as Heloise had requested. He asks that Divine Mercy
may enable both of them to put Satan beneath their feet and calls
attention to a Psalterium he is sending her, apparently at her request. We should not forget that in the Middle Ages the Psalms
were used regularly as prayers. The book to which he refers was
probably not merely a collection of Psalms, but a series of Psalms
accompanied by "collects," or prayers to be used in conjunction
with them. The letter proceeds with a long discussion of the
efficacy of prayer. With reference to his personal situation, Abelard asks particularly that Heloise pray for him, suggesting certain
prayers for the purpose. Finally, he asks to be buried in the Paraclete, and concludes by requesting prayers when he has gone.

The reply of Heloise exhibits a vigorous unwillingness on her
part to submit to reason. Her first letter had been concerned with
the past, but she now describes present difficulties, which may be
considered typical if somewhat extreme exemplifications of troubles

experienced by many nuns who were uncertain of their calling. First, however, she chides Abelard for placing her name before his in the salutation of his letter. This may seem a trivial point, but Abelard's answer will demonstrate that it contributes to the logical development of the correspondence. She goes on to complain that his letter has brought her only tears and no real solace, since she does not wish either the Paraclete or herself to survive him when he dies. Moreover, she asserts that thoughts of his death hinder the services among the nuns. The function of these objections is to emphasize her continuing temporal concern, a concern that is emphasized even further when she complains that their punishment has been unfair, for God spared them in their fornication but punished them after they were married. Here she falls into the same kind of feeling of injured innocence that Abelard experienced after the Council of Soissons, with a similar suggestion that God was at fault.

But with a certain inconsistency Heloise proceeds to blame herself for what happened, pointing out that women, especially wives, have frequently led men astray, citing the examples of Solomon, David, and Job, and recalling the sufferings they were made to undergo because of women. In view of her guilt, which she now admits freely, she wishes that she could do penance, but her mind distracts her with memories. We should notice that in terms of moral progress, self-blame and a desire for contrition mark a definite step beyond her earlier tendency to blame either Abelard or God for her miseries. However, the distractions she proceeds to describe hardly suggest that she had emphasized friendship rather than concupiscence in her relations with Abelard, or that, as she asserted in her first letter, she had always been concerned to please him rather than herself. The passage is among the most famous in the *Letters*: "Those amorous pleasures that we experienced were so sweet to me that they can neither displease me nor pass entirely from my memory. Wherever I turn, they, together with the desire for them. always come before me. Nor do their illusions spare me even in sleep. Even in the very solemnities of the Mass, when prayer should be more pure, obscene phantasms of these pleasures so enthrall my mind that I devote myself to their vileness rather than to prayer, and when I should lament the things I have done, I sigh rather for the things I have not done. Not only the things we did, but the places and times in which we did them as well, are so firmly implanted in my mind with you that I re-enact every-thing with you; nor do I rest from these things when I am asleep. Sometimes the thoughts of my mind are betrayed by the very motion of my body; nor can I restrain myself from sudden words." The passion here described is clearly physical rather than romantic or sentimental, a fact that should serve to place it in perspective. That is, Heloise is here made to demonstrate how difficult the physical renunciation of nuns can be. Neither she nor Abelard would have had any inclination to gloss over troubles of this kind, or to pretend that they did not exist.

Nevertheless, there is a certain literary artificiality about the amorous dreams of Heloise, for they may very well be a distant echo of the similar visions experienced by Sappho in Ovid's *Heroides*. Abandoned by her lover Phaon, who was never to re-turn, Sappho also thinks of times and places:

You are my concern, Phaon. My dreams bring you back, dreams brighter than the glowing day. There I find you, though you are actually far away. But the joys of sleep are not long enough. Often your arms support my neck, often I seem to hold yours in mine. I fondle you and urge you with soft words, and my lips alert the senses. I seek the kisses your tongue was wont to bestow, apt to receive, apt to give. I blush to tell the rest, yet all is done. It pleases me so that I cannot be without you. But when the sun shows itself I pursue the dreams that have left me so quickly. I flee to the caves and groves (as if caves and groves could help me) that witnessed your delights. . . . There my eyes see caves overhung with rugged cliffs that once for me surpassed Mygdonian marble. I find the grove that often afforded us a couch, shading it beneath its foliage, but I do not find the lord both of the grove and of myself.

Sappho's dreams are more vivid than those Heloise allows us to see and are not characterized as being "vile" or "obscene"; but Abelard had no wish to make his description provocative, and if any of his readers recalled Sappho, they would have remembered also that her dreams were futile and led her only to a leap from a high cliff.

Heloise goes on to allege that Abelard is more fortunate than she is because his injury has cured him of the lust from which she still suffers, and which makes of her a hypocrite, pure in the flesh only. She adds that she always sought more to please him than to please God, repeating the accusation that she entered the cloister only at his command. She deceives others by simulating and needs his help, not his praise, for it is perilous to praise her because of her unworthiness. She wishes, she says, only to avoid danger, not to strive for victory. She is asking, of course, for spiritual help, not help of any other kind. And Abelard proceeds to supply it with a combination of Scriptural authority and logical argument. Passion, in the twelfth century, was thought to be subject to the control of reason, so that no one should be surprised or disappointed to find Abelard using logic rather than sentiment.

His reply is lengthy and systematic, forming the keystone of the correspondence. He begins by dividing Heloise's letter into four points: (1) she complains that he placed her name first in the salutation of his letter; (2) she complains that he increased her misery by alluding to the possibility of his death; (3) she complains against God concerning the manner of their conversion; and (4) she complains that he should not praise her. With reference to the first point, Abelard explains, citing St. Jerome's famous letter to Eustochium as authority, that she became his superior when she took her vows and became a Bride of Christ. The argument is reinforced with an exposition of some verses from the first chapter of the Canticle of Canticles: "I am black but beautiful, O ye daughters of Jerusalem . . . therefore the King hath brought me into his storerooms. Do not consider that I am brown because the sun has altered my color." In the Middle Ages these verses became a standard theme for expounding the ideals of the cloistered life for women, and Abelard uses them to good effect. The outward blackness indicating humility, the renunciation of the world, and penance is contrasted with the whiteness of inward virtue and beauty. All nuns were, in effect, brides of Christ, and as such incurred an obligation to be "fair within" while remaining "black without," or unattractive and unpretentious in the eyes of the world. The doctrine was not, in medieval terms, either trivial or insubstantial. Its efficacy as an encouragement for the regular life where women were concerned is attested by its widespread use.

Turning to the second point, Abelard recalls that Heloise asked to share his adversities. In view of his illness and suffering, he says, she should not wish to prolong his miseries for selfish reasons. If she does so, she can only be an enemy, not a friend. Implicit in this argument is the Ciceronian doctrine that true friendship is based on an admiration for virtue, not on physical presence or physical attributes. Reserving the third point for more extended discussion, Abelard considers next what Heloise had to say about praise. Her objection, she had said, shows humility. But he warns her that this humility may be false, and that her objection may simply express a desire for more praise. His praise, he adds, has not been of a kind that could cause her to become proud. That is, he has praised her for her efforts toward virtue. Again, the argument reinforces the general tenor of the letter, which directs the reader's attention toward inward virtue rather than toward externals.

The third complaint of Heloise, which is the most serious, is answered at some length. Heloise, Abelard says, has presumed to accuse God rather than to praise Him for the manner of their conversion. She must lay aside her bitterness about this if she wishes to please him, as she says she wishes to do. If, as she says, she believes that he is hastening toward God, she should seek in piety to follow him so that they may be together in Heaven. In its own way this plea is a counterpart of the desire expressed by Fortunatus to be led by Radegunde's virtues to Heaven, and an anticipation, in reverse, of the similar desire of Dante to follow his Beatrice there, or that of Petrarch to be led there by his Laura.

Abelard was no Petrarch, and he is here in the awkward position of seeking to make of himself a Beatrice or a Laura. Nevertheless, the concept had a strong appeal to the medieval mind, and, indeed, formed the basis for the moving conclusion of the long letter to Heloise by Peter the Venerable.

As for their personal history, Abelard asserts that God was actually more justly avenged against them in their marriage than in their fornication. He recalls especially his intemperance on a visit to Argenteuil and their shameless behavior in a refectory there dedicated to the Blessed Virgin, which was a token of dire punishment. With reference to their earlier fornications and pollutions, as he calls them, in Fulbert's house before their marriage, he argues, as Roscelin had done in his letter, that his wound was a just punishment for his betrayal of trust. Heloise, he says, feigned herself a nun when they fled to Brittany. Justice, therefore, led her to embrace the religious life she had feigned. Altogether, what happened to them demonstrated grace rather than harshness, for God has now removed them from great dangers. The physical injury done to him has, in effect, healed two souls, so that she should marvel at God's mercy rather than complain. He asks her to remember how they once showed no reverence even for the days of Our Lord's Passion, and how he often made her please him with threats and blows. Altogether, Abelard's picture of himself as a lover is hardly romantic, or even attractive, and would certainly not encourage any further Sapphic dreams. He goes on to say that since he preferred obscene pleasures to God, he was justly deprived of the instruments of lust. But his castration made possible his salvation by setting him free from concupiscence so that he obtained without the blameworthy action of Origen, who castrated himself, what Origen and other holy men earnestly desired. As for Heloise, Abelard points out that it is fortunate that she took her vows before he decided to enter St. Denis. If she had waited until after he became a monk, she might have clung to the world and its pleasures. Now, he assures her, she has "turned the curse of Eve to the blessing of Mary," a phrase that reflects the commonplace idea that if man fell through Eve, his salvation was made possible by another woman, the Blessed Virgin, who was, among other things, the great exemplar of all nuns.

The letter continues with a plea that Heloise may turn her compassion toward Christ, who redeemed her with Himself. "He loved you truly and not I. My love, which involved us both in sins, should be called concupiscence, not love. I fulfilled my miserable pleasures in you, and that was all I loved. You say that I have suffered for you, and perhaps that is true. But rather I suffered through you and that unwillingly, not out of love for you, but by my own compulsion, not for your salvation, but for your grief." In other words, Abelard was motivated by lust and self-gratification, regardless of the consequences for Heloise. His suffering was not something he sought, and was not endured for her sake. Christ, on the other hand, as he goes on to say, suffered willingly for her salvation, so that her devotion and compassion should be directed toward Him. If she can turn her love toward Christ, she can accept her misfortunes and his with patience. The letter closes with a prayer in which Abelard asks for mercy. God joined them together in marriage and then separated them. He asks that both may be joined with Him in Heaven.

In terms of the correspondence Abelard's letter proved efficacious, for in her reply Heloise says nothing further about her personal difficulties, but asks instead for instruction on the origin of nuns, and for a rule that she and her nuns may follow at the Paraclete. She is especially concerned about modifications of the Benedictine Rule to make it more appropriate for women, inquiring about them in some detail. There is no further talk about abandoning the Paraclete, but instead an expressed desire for Abelard, the founder, to establish its rule so that the nuns may not have to accept one from a second master who might be less solicitous for their welfare. Heloise, that is, has now resolutely turned away from worldly joy and worldly sorrow to devote herself wholeheartedly to her profession. When the *Letters* were composed, Abelard undoubtedly hoped that the nuns who read them would experience a similar renewal of determination when they read his letter. The two final letters, which close the correspondence, consist of the treatise on the origin of nuns and the rule for the Paraclete. If we consider Abelard's first two letters, from the initial injunction to prayer, which is the first duty of contemplatives, to the final injunction to love Christ, whose bride any nun is supposed to be, it is not difficult to see them as a series of preliminary instructions for nuns leading up to the practical information in the final letters.

The *Letters* as a whole, then, have a logical and reasonable thematic structure. The "Letter to a Friend" describes the spiritual conversion of Abelard and contains, incidentally, a great deal of information of special interest to the nuns at the Paraclete. The conversion of Heloise is not here detailed, but in the subsequent letters we can mark her progress from a position resembling that attributed to her in her little sermon on marriage to that of a nun deeply interested in the practical details of the contemplative life. When Abelard was at St. Gildas, it was Heloise whose example led him to the conversion expressed at the close. And in the subsequent letters it is the example and teaching of Abelard that leads Heloise to a sincere interest in her profession. What began as a rather unattractive union in lust ended with a mutual concern for the life of the spirit. How much of this is "historically" true we do not know, and we are especially ignorant about Heloise, although it is probable that her actual conversion took place much earlier than the date implied by these letters. The *Letters* display a great deal of artifice, undoubtedly conceived by Abelard himself. But this fact would not have detracted from their usefulness insofar as the nuns of the Paraclete were concerned. Underlying them is one of the great themes of the *Consolation* of Boethius, a theme that every nun could recognize and appreciate: he who loves the world and its attractions for themselves will suffer adversity, but he who sets his heart on the invisible things of God cannot be harmed by Fortune.

CHAPTER VIII

The Philosopher

The years between Abelard's departure from St. Gildas in 1135 or 1136 and the Council of Sens in 1140 are obscure. We do not know how he managed to abandon his abbey, but it is quite likely that both Duke Conan and the ecclesiastical authorities agreed that he could no longer rule his monks effectively. It is probable that he was ill. Nor do we know who succeeded him as Abbot or whether his successor was more efficient than he had been in keeping St. Gildas in order. Perhaps he returned for a time to his brother's house in Nantes, or sought once more the rural peace of Le Pallet. After some rest, he undoubtedly wished to resume his writing, both for Heloise and for the preservation of his own ideas. Abelard had a very active mind in spite of his physical difficulties. He probably needed rest first of all and then money to provide the leisure necessary for study and writing. He now had a repository for his books and a sympathetic audience at the Paraclete. Moreover, his conversion at St. Gildas brought with it a serenity he had never known before. The prospect of high ecclesiastical office no longer intrigued him, and his fame was important only insofar as it would enhance the prestige of his new order.

We know that in 1136 John of Salisbury found Abelard lecturing in Paris, not at the Cathedral, but at Mont Ste. Geneviève. John's attitude is entirely respectful: "When, still but a youth, I journeyed to Gaul for the sake of study, in the year following the death of the illustrious King of the English, Henry, 'the Lion of Justice,' I betook myself to the Peripatetic of Pallet, who was then teaching at Mont Ste. Geneviève. The latter was a famous and learned master, admired by all. At his feet I learned the elementary principles of this art [i.e., dialectic], drinking in, with consuming avidity, every word that fell from his lips. After his departure, which seemed all too soon, I became the disciple of master Alberic, who had a very high reputation as the best of the other dialecticians." In the same year Abelard was attacked about a theological matter by Walter of Mortagne, later Bishop of Laon, who had studied under Alberic, but the attack was a mild one and not unfriendly, unlike a more violent attack made in one of Walter's books some ten years before. We hear no more of violent controversies between Abelard and Alberic of Rheims, who was probably the master to whom John of Salisbury refers. Meanwhile, we do not know where Abelard went in 1137 when he left Paris.

In any event, he soon returned, probably in the following year. He probably visited the Paraclete from time to time, now sufficiently old and worn-looking to be above any kind of suspicion. Teaching may well have provided the income for periods of study and writing, and it certainly stimulated his fame once more. At Paris he lectured on the Scriptures as well as on dialectic, certainly on the Epistle to the Romans, upon which he wrote a commentary, and probably on the Pauline Epistles generally. He also composed his *Hexaemeron* on Genesis for Heloise and her nuns, elaborated his theological treatise, composed an *Ethics* called *Scito te ipsum*, or "Know Thyself," answered some Scriptural questions for Heloise in a work called *Problemata*, and may well have written his *Dialogue*, or argument among a Christian, a pagan, and a Jew concerning the Christian faith. Some authorities place this last work and the *Hexaemeron* later, however, when Abelard was at Cluny. Among these works the *Theology* and the *Ethics* are pioneering enterprises. In a way the former looks forward to the development

of theology as an independent discipline, not merely as an introduction to the study of the Scriptures, and the *Ethics* was an early
attempt to develop a systematic basis for Christian morality, a
subject that later became associated commonly with discussions of
the Sacrament of Penance. The commentary on Romans exhibits
Abelard's fondness for *quaestiones*, which were to become a fairly
common, although by no means universal, feature of exegetical
writings. Abelard's originality in both thought and technique is
impressive. He became a rival of Hugh of St. Victor, although
Hugh was not the kind of man to become involved in bitter personal controversy. Instead, he sought to examine and if possible to
improve Abelard's teachings, with the result that Abelard exerted
a strong indirect influence on later theology through the stimulus
he gave to Hugh and his followers at St. Victor.

In modern times Abelard's most famous work, aside from the
Letters, is his *Sic et non*, or "Yes and No," which is a series of
conflicting Patristic opinions on a variety of topics. Of the ten
manuscripts of this work that survive, none affords a complete
text, although it is likely that Abelard revised it on various occasions. We do not know when it was written, but it may belong,
in its original form, to the period during which Abelard taught at
his oratory before he went to St. Gildas de Ruis. Modern readers
are often astonished that Abelard dared to show that the Fathers
do not always agree, but this attitude disregards the fact that the
recognition of such disagreement had long been commonplace, and
misses the point of the book. The traditional view may be represented in a statement by John the Scot (*c.* 800–870), who said,
"We simply compare the conclusions of the Fathers among ourselves, but it is not our intention to decide which one should be
believed. Each one abounds in lessons, and may those who come
after choose which they will, leaving contentions aside." The new
approach in Abelard's book lay in the fact that, as he indicates in
his Preface, he sought the possibility of reconciling or sifting the
conflicting opinions by taking note of such matters as the varying
meanings of words at different times or in different contexts, the
establishment of reliable texts, and the comparison of texts on a

given subject by a single author in order to establish his mature opinion, or his opinion as it appears in relation to other arguments. All this does sound a little like "philology." In a very limited sense, although the *Sic et non* does little more than state the prob- lem, Abelard here looks forward to the techniques of the later scholastics. His book may thus be thought of as a forward step, but it is not, actually, a very revolutionary work, and it did not cause as much furor among his contemporaries as did some of his opinions, especially with regard to the Trinity, expressed in other works. Even there, his manner of expression was often more provocative than what he actually said.

As a result of his originality, both in thought and expression, he once more began to arouse hostility. In 1138 or 1139 a former Abbot of St. Thierry, William, who had been converted by Bernard of Clairvaux and become a Cistercian, interrupted his work of commenting on the Canticle of Canticles to write a letter condemning Abelard. William was a very learned man, especially in the classics and the writings of the Greek Fathers, with a flair for eloquence that attracted the admiration of many of his con- temporaries. The letter was based on some ideas he had found in Abelard's *Theology* and on others appearing in a book of *Senten- tiae* that he attributed to Abelard but which was not actually his. William's epistle contained a *disputatio* against Abelard and a list of doubtful propositions supposedly derived from his writings. He sent copies to Bernard of Clairvaux and to Geoffrey of Lèves at Chartres. At first this effort produced little reaction, but after William had visited Bernard to make a complaint in person, the latter arranged to meet Abelard to discuss their differences. The sources differ on how many meetings took place and on Abelard's reactions to them. His ultimate reaction, however, was not to submit to Bernard. Bernard was not the man to agree to the dissemination of doctrines he regarded as being perverse, and he had gained by this time enormous power both in the ecclesiastical hierarchy and among the nobility.

Abelard's position was not made any more secure by the fact that he was apparently supported by Arnold of Brescia, an extreme reformer and a militant critic of ecclesiastical abuses. Bernard was able to achieve a strong advantage by linking the names of Arnold and Abelard as being equally scandalous. We do not know what attracted Arnold to Abelard, although it has been suggested that he may have been interested in a view expressed in the *Ethics* to the effect that only those bishops who merit being successors to the Apostles actually have the power of the keys. This view was not accepted by the medieval Church, which maintained that the character of the priest or bishop has no bearing on the efficacy of the sacramental act he performs. A view similar to Abelard's was introduced with great vigor in the fourteenth century by John Wyclif, creating widespread disturbance. There may have been other reasons for the relationship between the two men, although the suggestion that Arnold had once been Abelard's pupil has not been widely accepted. As events were to turn out, Arnold was condemned along with Abelard at the Council of Sens and was finally hanged in Rome in 1155 because of his revolutionary activities.

The tendency of nineteenth-century historians to regard both Arnold and Abelard as rationalistic rebels should be emphatically discouraged. Arnold was a troublemaker and something of a rabble-rouser. Abelard was in part the victim of his own past and in part the victim of his innovations in theological technique. His innovations, which undoubtedly disturbed Bernard deeply, were first the large-scale introduction of "probable argument," or dialectic, into the discussion of fundamental matters of faith and in part his rather free use of pagan philosophical sources. The first of these techniques looks forward to the full development of scholastic theology; the second anticipates in a way the anti-scholastic humanism of the later Middle Ages and the Renaissance as represented by such men as Petrarch, Ficino, and Erasmus. Petrarch would have been repelled by Abelard's use of dialectic, since he thought syllogisms childish, but he would have admired his use of classical sources. Thus Abelard is very difficult to classify in terms of later history.

The events leading up to the Council of Sens in 1140 are obscure. Abelard compiled a version of his *Theology* in which he sought to answer some of the criticisms that had been directed against him. Bernard probably began compiling his *Treatise Concerning the Errors of Peter Abelard*, in which he made use of the list of propositions attacked by William of St. Thierry and added some new material derived from the *Ethics* and the commentary on Romans. He may have also composed some of the letters condemning Abelard he sent to members of the Papal Curia after the council. In preparation for his defense at Sens, where he looked forward to a public confrontation with Bernard, Abelard sent a letter to many of his disciples, urging them to attend. Most of the propositions attributed to Abelard by Bernard were unfair; that is, they do not accurately represent Abelard's teaching. Bernard has been severely criticized on this account, but it is probably true that the list of condemned views was largely the fruit of hasty "secretarial assistance," so to speak, and not the result of deliberate study on Bernard's part. He suffered here from a perennial weakness of the administrator. A few of the accusations were just, however.

We do not know exactly what happened at the council. A facetious account of the proceedings by one of Abelard's followers, Berengar of Poitiers, survives, but it is largely jocular, and even Berengar had to admit that some of Abelard's views were unsound. Evidently Abelard found himself faced by administrative strategies similar to those he had encountered at Soissons. But he was no longer the brash person he had been then, and he probably recognized the fact that the kind of patience advocated by Geoffrey of Lèves twenty years before was his best course. He refused to speak for himself, apparently, and decided to present his case to the Papal Curia. It has been suggested that weakness due to physical illness may have been a factor in this decision. He had not been well since his last months at St. Gildas, and he was certainly ill shortly after the council. It is also likely that after his conversion at St. Gildas he was able to regard personal attacks with a certain detachment. Bernard, however, hastened to anticipate Abelard's appeal, sending his case against him to the Pope and writing a series of strongly worded letters to members of the Curia. The result was to be an official condemnation of Abelard's teachings. However, a number of respected and moderate ecclesiastics thought that the council had been unfair, and there is some validity in the view expressed by modern students of St. Bernard, that the condemnation of Abelard was one of Bernard's less admirable achievements.

Abelard returned to Paris, where he gave up his lodgings to Arnold of Brescia before setting out on his long journey to Rome. At some time during the controversy he wrote a formal *Confession of Faith* for Heloise and, perhaps later, an *Apology* that was answered almost immediately by Thomas of Morigny. We can imagine him finally setting out once more, perhaps accompanied by a clerk and one or two servants, leaving the black mud of Paris for the last time, tired, ill, and dejected, but perhaps smiling a little as he rode up the hill past the Palais de Hautefeuille, heading southward on the road he and Heloise had taken many years before, when she was a mere girl, pregnant and apprehensive in her prophetic nun's costume. Now, however, he would turn eastward away from Le Pallet and the lands of Duke Conan, who had a few more years to rule, toward Burgundy, Lombardy, and Rome. He would sometimes accompany other travelers on the road, merchants with their packhorses, noblemen with their retinues, and ecclesiastics bent on the complex affairs of church and monastery. Abelard, with his varied background and experience, would know how to converse with all of them, and it is likely that many were glad to see the famous master of the schools whose teachings had so shaken the ecclesiastical hierarchy and stimulated the wrath of Bernard of Clairvaux. It is probable that he passed through Nogent and visited Heloise along the way, taking solace once more in her gentleness and steadiness and leaving with her copies of his books. Eventually the road passed near Cluny, the monastery of the famous Abbot Peter, which contained in its library over five hundred volumes, including a large number of manuscripts of the Latin classics. Abbot Peter had just finished revising a treatise against the teachings of some heretics in Provence. He had also attacked the teachings of the Jews, and was soon to depart for Spain to study the Koran so that he could write against the Moslems. This kind of enterprise deeply interested Abelard, who had vigorously defended dialectic as a means of attacking heresy. The abbot was a learned man, a firm and devoted student of St. Augustine, and Abelard probably felt that he and Peter had many interests in common. He was, in any event, very weak, hardly able to continue further, and Peter gave him a warm welcome.

At Cluny Peter and the Abbot of Cîteaux urged Abelard to make peace with Bernard, first removing anything from his writings that might seem contrary to the faith. It is a tribute to Peter's warmth and generosity of spirit that he apparently succeeded in this endeavor, for Abelard is said to have journeyed to Cîteaux, settled his differences with Bernard, and returned to Cluny, where Abbot Peter permitted him to remain, obtaining Papal permission to harbor him. But Abelard's health declined still further. We do not know what was troubling him, although one modern physician has diagnosed his malady as Hodgkins' disease. Diagnosis on the basis of the little evidence we have is difficult, however, and it may be futile to speculate on the exact nature of the malady. The strains of life at St. Gildas had probably taken their toll, and it is likely that when he returned to Paris to immerse himself in teaching, study, and writing, he neglected his health. Finally Peter sent Abelard to St. Marcellus, near Chalon-sur-Saône, where the climate was milder than it was at Cluny, and there, probably on April 21, 1142, the wanderings of the Peripatetic of Pallet came to an end.

In the following year, or perhaps the next, when Abbot Peter returned from Spain, he wrote a long letter to Heloise describing Abelard's last years. The subject is introduced with fine tact, for before saying anything about Abelard, Peter first recalls his admiration for Heloise. When he was a young man, he says, her fame as a student reached him. Then she excelled all women in literary studies and was superior to most men. Later she abandoned these studies for better ones, using her secular learning as so much "gold from Egypt" to erect the tabernacle of the Lord in her heart.

Now, he says, as a true philosopher should, she has trampled on the ancient serpent that tempts women so that it can harm her no more. There follows a long discussion showing that it is appropriate for a woman to rule over women, not, of course, to contradict what Abelard had said about this matter, but to prepare her for life at the Paraclete without Abelard's guidance. Turning to Abelard, Peter describes his activity at Cluny, where he spent his time abstemiously in study, prayer, and devotion. Although Peter does not mention the subject of Abelard's study, it seems likely that he turned once more to the subject that had attracted him in his youth, dialectic, and perfected the final version of his substantial treatise on the subject. This treatise survives in only one imperfect copy from the library at St. Victor, and it seems unlikely that it had much influence on logical studies in the thirteenth century. But in turning to his first love once more, Abelard did demonstrate a curious and rather admirable consistency. Above all, Peter stresses Abelard's humility, truly remarkable, he thought, in a man so learned and famous. The conclusion to the letter picks up a theme from the *Letters*: "Therefore, venerable and most dear sister in the Lord, him to whom you clung after the termination of a fleshly union in a stronger and therefore much better union of divine charity, with whom and under whom you served the Lord, him I say He cherishes in His bosom in your place, as another you, and He keeps him there to restore to you through His grace at the Advent of the Lord, the voice of the Archangel, and the Trump of God descending from Heaven."

Later Peter had Abelard's remains transferred to the Paraclete, where they were interred in a place of honor. And later still Heloise wrote to Peter requesting assistance for her son Astrolabe, now in his twenties and seeking a benefice, and an "open" absolution for Abelard to replace the "closed" or folded and sealed absolution he had sent before, so that she could exhibit it, seal intact, on the tomb. We do not know what happened to Astrolabe, but Abbot Peter sent Heloise her absolution so that all could see that, in spite of Sens and Soissons, the founder of the Paraclete had died in harmony with his Church. Heloise lived until 1164, and under her direction her convent continued to grow and prosper.

When we look back over the career of Abelard, it becomes obvious that whatever cautions we must use in interpreting the *Letters*, including the initial *History of My Calamities*, his affair with Heloise, which was in itself trivial, was partly responsible in the long run for his lasting fame as a philosopher. An elaborate commentary on Ezechiel would have been a poor substitute for the works Abelard composed both directly for Heloise and those more technical studies he produced after he left St. Gildas. He was a great teacher, a very learned man, and a profound scholar, but with a touch of brashness that was probably at once responsible for his personal difficulties and for the originality of his writings. His books were often regarded with suspicion after the condemnation that followed Sens, but they nevertheless exerted a powerful stimulus to the development of theology. The brilliance of Abelard's mind is undeniable, and his originality, often courageous, was impressive, even though he lacked the reliability and caution that enabled some of his contemporaries to obtain much more enduring reputations as theologians.

As a man Abelard is something of a puzzle. The artificial structure of the *Letters* places a veil over the intimate details of his life, even in those passages that seem to be most revealing. But this elusiveness also characterizes his contemporaries. The stylized human figures that adorn late Romanesque churches in statuary, and the flat, geometrically controlled human beings that brighten the illuminated manuscripts of the period do not afford us much insight into what we are inclined to think of as "humanity." But when we look for it there, or in Abelard, we may be searching for something that was never there in the first place. Our "humanity" was not theirs, and it is quite likely that the conventions by means of which we describe ours will some day make us puzzling to our descendants. Concerning Heloise we know very little indeed. But we do have a legend, and this legend tells us a great deal about ourselves if not about Heloise.

PART II

The Legend of Heloise

CHAPTER IX

The Comedy of Love

*I*n modern times Abelard's reputation has little to do either with his philosophical and theological writings or with his success in establishing an order for nuns. Fame, whose fickleness is proverbial, has made him instead the lover of Heloise. The brief account of Heloise in the *History*, combined with the first two letters attributed to her, has grown into a legend remarkable for its enormous popularity, especially during the nineteenth century, and for its curious origin. Meanwhile, the history of the legend affords a kind of paradigm for the stylistic changes that have taken place in Western culture since the seventeenth century. Heloise has changed with changes in style and attitude, and her transformations afford an instructive, if not always encouraging, picture of cultural developments in modern times.

But during the later Middle Ages the story of the lovers passed almost unnoticed. The *Letters of Abelard and Heloise* were probably studied at the Paraclete, and at the sister houses of the order, and for the nuns they did not constitute a love story but a book of elementary instruction. In the thirteenth century that indefatigable translator Jean de Meun, who also made French versions of *The Consolation of Philosophy* of Boethius, St. Ailred of Rievaulx's treatise *On Spiritual Friendship*, and the work of Vegetius on things military, made a lively translation of all but the last letter of the correspondence. But this survives in only a single manuscript, and it is not likely that it enjoyed a very wide audience. Jean de Meun was, however, in addition to being a translator, the author of one of the most famous and influential poems of the late Middle Ages, or at least the bulk of it, *The Romance of the Rose*. The poem had been begun by William of Lorris, about whom we know almost nothing. Jean's continuation is an enormous poem, encyclopedic in scope, constituting a satire on false love of all varieties. Manuscripts of it, many richly illustrated, circulated widely among the nobility of late medieval Europe, and it was the first vernacular book to be "chained" as a standard work of reference in the Sorbonne Library.

Superficially the poem concerns the quest of a "foolish lover" for his "rose," a thinly disguised euphemism for the center of sexual satisfaction in the female of the species. In this quest he is assisted by the God of Love, Venus, and a host of attendant figures, the most efficient of whom is probably a representation of hypocrisy named False-Seeming. Among the Lover's chief advisers, however, is one "Friend," a worldly-wise man who strongly advocates the use of flattery and various other ruses, and who severely condemns resort to marriage. If one marries with the kind of single-minded devotion to self-satisfaction the Lover has, he is likely to be jealous, and it is reasonable that Friend should introduce, in the course of his long lecture, a subsidiary character called "The Jealous Husband." This gentleman also speaks at length in an effort to discourage marriage. The sophistry, cynicism, and just plain foolishness of Friend are often amusing, and the Jealous Husband was already a stock comic figure in the medieval literary tradition, often the butt of ridicule. Since jealous husbands usually regard their wives as property or goods, and are interested in them merely as sources of self-satisfaction, they form a subtype of, or even at times a figure for, another stock comic character, "The Avaricious Man." Jean de Meun had evidently been much amused both by the little sermon of Heloise on marriage, and by the elaboration of the views stated there in her first letter to Abelard. It formed a convenient example for the Jealous Husband to use in his speech, and with that speech Heloise for the first time really enters the Western literary tradition.

To sense the flavor of the Jealous Husband's speech on the disadvantages of marriage, we might consider some of the context. One of the more famous "satires on women," which is actually a satire on men who submit to women because of the pleasant amenities they provide, was the "Epistle of Valerius to Rufinus," included in the twelfth-century *Courtier's Trifles* of Walter Map. The book itself did not circulate widely, but the "Epistle" enjoyed great popularity in the later Middle Ages. The Jealous Husband does not hesitate to cite it: "Valerius, who sorrowed because his companion Rufinus wanted to marry, made a stern speech to him: 'My friend,' he said, 'may omnipotent God keep you from being put in the snare of an all-powerful woman who smashes all things through cunning.'" The patent difficulty here is that there are two Omnipotents, God and the woman; that is, the Jealous Husband is an impotent husband. He can't keep his wife in hand, so that in his view all women are cunning devils. Of course, he wants only one thing from his wife, as we shall see, and is disappointed because she is not simply a convenient whore. He goes on to cite Juvenal: "Juvenal himself writes to Postumus on his marriage: 'Do you want to take a wife, Postumus? Can't you find ropes, cords, or halters for sale? Can't you jump out of one of the high windows that we can see? Or can't you let yourself fall from the bridge? What Fury leads you to this torment and pain?'" The Fury, obviously, is libido, but the Jealous Husband is not about to subdue that one in himself. After citing the example of King Phoroneus "who gave the Greek people their laws," and who lamented ever taking a wife, our Jealous Husband turns to Heloise in her unconverted state, making her a kind of ideal.

Here, at last, was a woman who wished only to be a convenient concubine, demanding nothing whatsoever in return for her services. What more could a man ask?

Pierre Abelard, in turn, admits that Sister Heloise, abbess of the Paraclete and his former sweetheart, did not want to agree for anything that he take her as a wife. Instead, the young lady of good understanding, well educated, loving and well loved in return, brought up arguments to convince him not to marry; and she proved to him with texts and reasons that the conditions of marriage are very hard, no matter how wise the wife may be. For she had seen, studied, and known the books, and she knew the feminine ways, for she had them all in herself. She asked him to love her but not to claim any right of her except those of grace and freedom, without lordship or mastery, so that he might study, entirely his own man, quite free, without tying himself down, and that she might also devote herself to study, for she was not empty of knowledge. She told him also that in any case their joys were more pleasing and their comfort grew greater when they saw each other more rarely.

But, as he has written for us, he loved her so much that he afterward married her in spite of her admonition, and unhappiness resulted. After she had taken the habit of a nun at Argenteuil—by agreement of both of them together, as it seems to me—Pierre's testicles were removed, in his bed in Paris, at night; on this account he endured great suffering and torment. After this misfortune he was a monk at St. Denis in France, then abbot of another abbey; then, it says in his *Life*, he founded a widely known abbey that he named the Abbey of the Paraclete, where Heloise, who was a professed nun before, was abbess. She herself, without shame, in a letter to her lover, whom she loved so much that she called him father and lord, tells a wondrous thing that many consider demented. It is written in the letters, if you search the chapters well, that she sent him by express, even after she was abbess: "If the emperor of Rome, to whom all men should be subject, deigned to wish to take me as his wife and make me mistress of the world, I still would rather," she said, "and I call God to witness, be called your whore than be crowned empress." But by my soul I do not believe that any such woman ever existed afterward; and I think that her learning put her in such a position that she knew better how to overcome and subdue her nature, with its feminine ways. If Pierre had believed her, he would never have married her.

What a woman! What wisdom! She knew all about feminine wiles not only because she had feminine inclinations in herself, but also because she had read the books, and she had subdued her nature to such an extent that she offered to be a free and exclusive whore! But such women are, alas, rare, and the Jealous Husband's wife falls far short of the wisdom of Heloise:

Marriage is an evil bond, so help me Saint Julian, who harbors wandering pilgrims, and St. Leonard, who unshackles prisoners who are truly repentant, when he sees them lamenting. It would have been better for me to go hang, that day I had to take a wife, when I became acquainted with so quaint a woman. With such a coquette I am dead. For Saint Mary's son, what is that quaintness worth to me, that costly, expensive dress that makes you turn your nose up, that is so long and trails behind you, that irks and vexes me so much, that makes you act so overbearing that I become mad with rage? What profit does it give me? No matter how much it profits others, it does me only harm; for when I want to divert myself with you, I find it so encumbering, so annoying and troublesome that I can come to no real result. You make me so many turns and parries with your arms, legs, and hips, and you go twisting so much that I cannot hold you properly. I don't see how all this comes about, but I see very well that my love-making and my comforts are not pleasing to you. Even at night, when I lie down, before I receive you in my bed, as any worthy man does his wife. . . .

If marriage is essentially unsatisfactory and wenches of such wisdom as the unconverted Heloise are not readily available, the amorous male interested only in free sport has no permanent refuge, nothing to which he can cling with confidence. This logical inference, of course, escaped Friend, the Jealous Husband, and the Lover, who was eventually to become impoverished in his pursuit, but Jean's audience would not have sat in open-mouthed wonderment and remained unaware of it.

Thus Heloise became famous in literary history, not for her devotion as an abbess, but for her supposed views on marriage. Among the admirers of *The Romance of the Rose* was Geoffrey

Chaucer of London, a poet who translated at least some of it into English. He also translated *The Consolation of Philosophy* of Boethius, presumably using the French version by Jean de Meun to assist him. Chaucer's poetry is full of echoes of Jean's poem, as well as of the *Consolation*, and among the echoes of the *Romance* there appears a reference to Heloise. It occurs in the Prologue to the tale of the Wife of Bath, in which that good cousin of the unconverted Samaritan woman, whose portrait is in part based on a character best called "the Old Whore" in *The Romance of the Rose*, delivers a sermon on the woes of marriage. The allusion occurs in a description of a book read to her for her correction by her wise but ultimately weak fifth husband. Her first three hus- bands were old, weak, wealthy, and soon worn out. These, in her view, were "good" husbands. The last two were more difficult, especially the fifth, who was a clerk. This fifth husband, one Jankyn, had a book full of traditional wisdom, including the letter of Valerius to Rufinus, St. Jerome's treatise *Against Jovinian*, the Proverbs of Solomon, and Ovid's *Art of Love*. All these either condemn or make fun of men who submit to women because of desire, deprecating the efforts of women to turn men into un- reasoning creatures of the kind Abelard was when he became besotted with Heloise. Here is the Wife's description of the book, roughly translated from Chaucer's Middle English:

> He called it Valerius and Theofraste,
> At which book he always laughed full fast.
> Also there was once a clerk in Rome,
> A Cardinal who was called St. Jerome
> Who made a book against Jovinian,
> In which book also was Tertullian,
> Crisippus, Trotula, and Heloise
> Who was abbess not far from Paris;
> And also the Proverbs of Solomon,
> Ovid's *Art* and books many a one—
> And all were bound in one volume.

The "Heloise" here is probably the Heloise of Jean de Meun, whose wisdom contrasted amusingly with that of the Wife, a woman not about to "subdue her nature with its feminine ways."

There are a few other brief references to Heloise during the Middle Ages. Petrarch owned a copy of Abelard's *History* in which he made some annotations. The reformer Jean de Gerson once wrote contemptuously of Abelard and his "Heloydes," evidently recognizing the similarity between the *Letters* and the *Heroides* of Ovid, a poet whose work he detested. In the Renaissance Villon refers in passing to "wise Heloise." But as the Renaissance flowered, Heloise and her Abelard were largely forgotten. The Latin text of the *Letters* appeared in 1616, but only the learned read them, and the learned were for the most part silent, at least about Abelard. As the seventeenth century wore on, a sharp break developed between literature written for the aristocratic classes and books produced for those below them in rank. This break had already appeared earlier, but now it became decisive. But it is a simplification to speak of popular readers as members of the "middle class," since the commonplace division of society into "upper, middle, and lower" classes makes little sense even in Victorian times, and much less earlier. There was a difference in literary audiences, and this difference was marked by differences in style, since the nobility tended to preserve the traditions of the past, while those in the lower orders of society showed a marked tendency toward greater emotionalism. Sentimental literature appealed first to the lower social ranks, and a taste for it gradually spread upward. In the modern world, in fact, it is fair to say that cultural tastes rise from the bottom upward, where they become more refined through the employment of sophisticated techniques, although it is an unwarranted bit of romanticism to speak of the lower orders as "folk," and to assume that their cultural reactions are more "natural" than those of their more fortunate contemporaries.

The legend of Heloise, as distinct from the medieval joke about Heloise, first appears in a lower stratum of literary culture in the form of a romance by one Alluis called *Les amours d'Abailard et d'Heloise,* published in 1675. In concentrating on the "loves" of his characters Alluis anticipates the future, but his book is full of historical absurdities and is by no means a classic of French letters. For example, he makes Alberic of Rheims a rival to Abelard for the hand of Heloise, preferred, in fact, by Fulbert to the Breton philosopher. To make the story more palatable our author reduces Abelard's age at the time of his first meeting with Heloise to "twenty-seven or twenty-eight," and assures his readers that he had "the air and manner" of a "man of quality." The lovers engage in very gallant conversations, presumably like those of seventeenth-century persons of rank. If the reputation of the lovers had depended upon Alluis, it might soon have vanished, but a far different author was soon to turn his attention to Abelard and Heloise with results that were, to say the least, astonishing.

That author was Roger de Rabutin, Count of Bussy, usually called for brevity Bussy-Rabutin. Since the count was chiefly responsible, although inadvertently so, for the subsequent development of the legend, he deserves more than passing attention. He was born on April 13, 1618, the grandson of Ste. Chantal. After studying at the Collège de Clermont, young Roger took up a military career at sixteen, in which he soon achieved notable success. Like most healthy young aristocrats of his age, he had an amiable weakness for women. It is said, for example, that he once abandoned his garrison to pursue a conveniently complaisant young lady to Paris, and, because his troops misbehaved in his absence, was forced to cool his ardor for five weeks in the Bastille. He at first sought to marry his cousin, Mlle. Chantal, the future Madame de Sévigné, who was to become the author of one of the most famous collections of letters ever written. When she refused him, he married another cousin, Gabrielle de Toulongeon. Later, when Madame de Sévigné's husband became hopelessly involved with Ninon de Lanclos, Bussy approached her once more, this time gallantly offering to become her lover. The offer, however, was refused, for Madame de Sévigné was neither very lustful nor much inclined to indiscretions.

Gabrielle died in 1646. After an unsuccessful if spectacular attempt to carry off and marry a rich widow, Madame de Mira-mion, Bussy married Louise de Rouville. He was alienated for a time from his cousin Madame de Sévigné because she refused to lend him money in a time of great need, and he was forced to borrow from his mistress, Madame de Montglas, a lady he described as being very accomplished and as having "small eyes, black and shining, a nose slightly retroussé, teeth pretty and clean, features fine and delicate, and an agreeably-turned countenance." No real scandal besmirched Bussy's name until 1659, when he and some friends indulged in a drunken party during Holy Week. It was rumored that the party involved monstrous irreligious practices, including some very shocking rituals and songs; but these rumors are now considered to have been groundless, even though they did persist for many years as a legend. The age was given to witchcraft and black magic, but in this instance Bussy and his friends were probably innocent.

The count was famous for his merry stories, some of which were sufficiently indiscreet to alienate a few of his associates. But his tales concerning the ladies at the royal court were highly relished, and he was persuaded by Madame de Montglas to write some of them down. The result was the *Histoire amoureuse des Gaules,* which enjoyed a lively private circulation and later a certain literary distinction. The names of the characters in these tales were carefully concealed, and the stories themselves are witty and good-natured rather than malicious, even though the treatment of the persons involved, including their physical descriptions, is often frank. Among the readers, however, was a certain Mlle. de la Baume, who surreptitiously copied the manuscript after promising solemnly not to do so. Bussy reproached her unmercifully, and shortly thereafter departed on a military campaign.

On his return to Paris the count found himself famous, for the *Histoire* had amused Louis XIV and his courtiers. He was invited to recite his *Maxims of Love* before the court. Their lively wit made a profound impression, and Bussy was named to the Academy. But Mlle. de la Baume, smarting still because of Bussy's treatment of her, took her revenge by supplying a key to the *Histoire,* revealing the names of the various ladies, and publishing it at Liège in 1665. At this the court was scandalized. Private jocularity privately circulated was one thing, but printed exposure to the general public was quite another, and poor Bussy, who was held responsible, was thrown into the Bastille. To make matters worse, various scandalous pamphlets, the first of which involved the King himself, were published as continuations of the *Histoire* under Bussy's name. The King held Bussy responsible and exiled him from the court on September 6, 1666. Bussy spent twenty-seven years secluded on his estates, his military career ruined, and his social activities severely restricted. Madame de Sévigné and other friends kept him informed by letter of events in Paris. One result of his exile was thus a series of letters, including some to and from Madame de Sévigné, and one, more or less incidentally, that gave an enormous stimulus to the legend of Heloise.

It was the age of Corneille, much admired by Madame de Sévigné, of Racine, whom she thought to be insane, of Molière, of the Countess de la Fayette and her *Princesse de Clèves,* a work that did not appear entirely convincing to Bussy, of La Roche-foucauld, La Fontaine, and Boileau. Bussy admired Poussin, a copy of one of whose paintings adorned a chapel on his estates. The detachment, wit, and elegance that characterizes some of the best literature and art of the age are not lacking in the letters of Bussy. He sent his cousin entertaining translations of Ovid, Martial, and Petronius, as well as diverting narratives of his own composition. As his *Maxims* indicate, he was especially fond of amorous prob-lems. One of these was hopeless love, which he treated in the following manner:

> When you find a lover
> Who says that under your sway
> His heart incessantly sighs
> Without any hope of solace,
> Under a modest appearance
> He actually seeks to surprise you.
> For, as for loving without hope,
> Nobody has ever done it.

Like other writers of the period, Bussy is here seeking to represent a "just idea" of a situation, not his own private idea, nor a commonplace idea, but an original idea, the justice of which, in spite of a certain element of surprise, will appeal spontaneously to others. It is noteworthy that for him "hopeless love" is basically a comic notion. When he sent his letter concerning Abelard and Heloise to Madame de Sévigné on April 12, 1687, the day before his sixty-ninth birthday, he undoubtedly felt that he had constructed a new representation of the idea of hopeless love and wished to put it to the test.

"It is not, my dear Cousin," he began, "that you have not heard of Abelard and Heloise, but I do not think that you have yet seen a translation of their letters. As for me, I do not know of one. I amuse myself by translating some of them that have been giving me much pleasure. I have never seen a more beautiful Latin, above all that of the nun, nor more love and spirit than she exhibits in it. If you do not find this to be so, my dear Cousin, it will be my fault. I pray that our friend Corbinelli read it to you and to the fair Countess [i.e., her daughter] together, and I shall adjust the esteem I have for my amusement according to the sentiments that you three have together." These remarks are followed by a very brief historical introduction. Heloise was, of course, a "girl of quality" and "no one was more amiable than she in body and spirit"; and Abelard was "the most polished and able man of his age." The main events of the *History* are indicated, and an effort is made to account for the correspondence. Abelard, the count says, was accustomed to write to a friend who lived near the Paraclete. A letter addressed to him fell into the hands of Heloise, who, prompted by "the curiosity natural to her sex," opened it and read it. Our translator thus seeks to rationalize the connection between Abelard's *History* and the first letter of Heloise, a rationalization, incidentally, of which those who wish to take the letters as literal historical documents are desperately in need.

The first letter in the count's version follows very generally the opening letter attributed to Heloise in the original. However, the language and emotions are toned down and elaborated in a manner suited to a young woman "of quality." The idea of "civility" which would eventually produce the concept of "civilization," now considerably altered in the modern world, was well developed by Bussy's time. Civility breeds tears, or at least the inclination to tears at appropriate times, so that Heloise writes: "The account you give of all [your sufferings] to your friend is so lively and is written so naturally that I was almost suffocated with sorrow as I read it, and I should have had the pleasure of returning your letter obliterated by my tears if someone had not come to take it from me a little too soon." It is not difficult to see the count smiling a little at this creation of his; but his heroine is a faithful mistress, eager for the welfare of her lover, and shows a strong inclination to vindicate him: "I am determined to publish our disgraces in all tongues to shame the unjust world that has not known you. I shall spare no one, since no one has spared you, and you will win so much pity that no one will speak of my dear Abelard without a tear in his eye." She wrote better than she knew, for the tears, both literary and actual, were to flow more and more copiously with the passage of time.

Like her twelfth-century predecessor, our new Heloise asks for letters. The Latin version contains a quotation from Seneca to the effect that if images of absent friends are pleasant, letters from them are more pleasant. Bussy took a hint from this quotation and made Heloise write: "In waiting for you to give me the same pleasure, I frequently enjoy looking at your portrait. I neglected it when I saw you; your absence makes it dearer. But if the painting gives such pleasure, what joy would your letters not inspire—those that speak, that ignite, and nourish the fire of our passions! Such an innocent pleasure is not forbidden us; let us not lose through our own negligence the only consolation left to us. . . . It is to comfort persons shut up as I am that letters were invented. I shall always carry yours with me. I shall kiss them ceaselessly; but I do not wish that they cost you any pain. Write to me without thought, with negligence, so that your heart may speak to me and not your mind I do not know how I shall live longer unless you tell me that you love me. . . ." Neither the historical Abelard nor any of his contemporaries would have had the faintest inkling of how to go about writing negligently from

the heart, a fact that had a great deal to do with the neglect of
the Latin letters during the eighteenth and early nineteenth centuries. A letter written in this way would have looked as strange
in the twelfth century as a sermon by Tristram Shandy, and it is
not at all certain that Bussy himself did not regard this request of
his heroine with a certain amusement.

His Heloise softens the determination of her original to humble
herself before Abelard. "How often have I protested to you that
it would be sweeter to live with Abelard as his mistress than to be
Empress with Augustus; and that I should find more sweetness in
obeying you than in seeing subject to my laws the master of the
world? True tenderness separates from the lover all that which is
not himself; it seeks neither rank nor fortune. And I am persuaded
that if there is to be any felicity to be hoped for here below, it is
to be achieved only in the union of true hearts that sympathy has
joined together and that merit and reciprocal love render happy."
Our gentler Heloise omits all reference to whores; a "mistress"
was, in the late seventeenth century, not necessarily a woman of
easy virtue who felt ashamed of her status. On the other hand,
mistresses did not ordinarily disregard rank and fortune, so that
the statement of Heloise has a comic air. Bussy shows no inclination to let his heroine reflect much of the frank concupiscence of
the source. His Heloise does speak of Abelard's verse, calling it the
most gallant in the world and citing "cette jolie Rose," by which
she means, of all things, *The Romance of the Rose,* as an example.
If she is gentle, she is not lacking in spirit, for she envisages herself in Abelard's chamber at the time of his wounding, where, she
says, she would have defended him with her life. When she became a nun, she says, she had a letter of Abelard's saying that he
would always be with her. Thus when she made her profession, she
made his too. Nevertheless, she should think of God. But her letter
closes with a lively representation of her desperate need to be assured of Abelard's love, and an affirmation that it would be
blasphemy on her part not to love him.

This gallant if somewhat injudicious epistle certainly deserved
a warm reply. Unfortunately, Abelard's original reply is hardly

a billet-doux, as we have seen. His reticence in this respect has brought many condemnations upon his head from admirers of Heloise, but we should remember that he was never confronted with the idea that human felicity consists exclusively in the "union of true hearts." Bussy lacked Abelard's reticence, and he did not hesitate to concoct a completely original response, beginning as follows: "If I had thought that a letter not addressed to you would fall into your hands, I should have been careful to include nothing in it that could bring back the memory of our past pleasures. I spoke in confidence to my friend of my misfortunes to make his own less painful by comparison. If I have caused evil for you in seeking to do good for him, I beg your pardon. It is enough that I have made you suffer, even though I have done so unwittingly; I suffer for having done so. For do not be deceived, Heloise, I adore you with more ardor than I have ever felt before. I must open my heart to you. I have hidden my passion from the world since my retreat through vanity, and from you through tenderness. I wished to heal you through my affected indifference, and to spare you the cruel evils of a love without hope." This is in part a rationalization to explain why Abelard had not written before. But the count is very assiduously constructing an entirely new Abelard. He may be in some ways the result of an effort to avoid what seemed to be inconsistencies in the original, but he is much more than that. The philosophical integrity of the original is abandoned altogether so that Abelard may become an exemplar of a truly hopeless passion, not for the sake of sentiment, but for the sake of amusement. Bussy's Abelard, in fact, places himself exactly in the dilemma we usually associate with Heloise: "I have myself, not being able to hope any longer to live with you, sought to efface you from my heart. I have searched in Philosophy and Religion for arms to combat passion which our misfortunes have done nothing but ignite further. I have done more: I am obliged by vows to forget you, and I have forgotten nothing but the vows. The solitude where I sought to find a sanctuary from you, abandoned by all the rest of the world, allows you alone to fill my mind. I am convinced that it is useless to strive to love you no more. . . .

I have nothing to hope for from love, and I cannot devote myself to virtue. . . ." There is much more in the same vein.

It is clear that whatever else he may have been doing, the count was not seeking to evoke any tears from Madame de Sévigné and her companions. His Abelard is essentially a comic character produced in the spirit of Molière to show the amusing but fascinating irrationality of hopeless love. Abelard considers the question of why he pressed Heloise to take vows before he did. His answer again constitutes a rationalization of the original, and, at the same time, reflects a further inspiration by the comic muse: "When your uncle had made me an example to rash lovers, my feebleness made me jealous. I thought that if you found in me nothing but desires, you might look elsewhere for a more substantial love. Love believes that which it fears." He asks that Heloise write no further, saying that this will be his last letter, and asking, like Abelard himself, that he may be buried at the Paraclete. The brief reply of Heloise, which concludes this correspondence, represents again a toning down of the original as well as a considerable abbreviation of it. Heloise protests, "You speak of your death to advance mine, for you know well that it would be less sweet to survive you than to die in your arms." The voluptuous dreams of the original almost completely disappear. Heloise alternates between realization of "the emptiness of the world and its false pleasures" and love, concluding, "Love, I abandon myself to you. But alas! What shall become of those vows that I have made to exist only for God? Supreme Divinity, illuminate my spirit less, or give greater strength to my heart. Farewell."

Madame de Sévigné replied to the count's letter, saying in effect that in the opinion of Corbinelli, her tutor, Bussy's French exhibited certain delicacies and turns not to be found in the original, which is, we may observe, putting the matter very politely. Nevertheless, she and her daughter, she says, decided not to study the original, since nothing could be better than Bussy's composition. The count's jocular little device had thus achieved its primary purpose—to amuse his cousin. But it achieved something else as well. For if the comedy could be removed from those letters of his

and the sentiment could be enhanced, the result might be the basis
for a new series of love-letters looking much more like the intimate
narratives appearing in popular letter collections of the day. Meanwhile, if we except the wit of Alexander Pope and certain slap-
stick productions that appeared many years later, it is fair to say
that the comic muse abandoned Heloise and Abelard altogether
after the concoction of Bussy-Rabutin. The humor of Abelard's
picture of Heloise in her unconverted state became lost in philology
and sentiment, and the jocularity of Jean de Meun was forgotten.
When Jean was remembered once more in modern times, his jokes
were promptly smothered in academic chatter about "courtly love,"
so that he himself, rather than simply his Jealous Husband, was
transformed into a serious admirer of "wise Heloise." By providing
a love-letter by Abelard, Bussy provided the framework for a
legend of a new kind. In the light of what was to happen later,
through no fault of his, he emerges as a man of rather heroic
proportions. He had a cultivated taste for civilized comedy.

CHAPTER X

Baroque Passion

To the aristocratic mind of the late Baroque era, passion was either comic or disastrous. If Molière could show the comedy of passion, Racine, with unflinching vigor, could demonstrate its dangers. Readers of the *Princesse de Clèves*—sometimes rather inappropriately called a "psychological" novel, although its preoccupation is moral—are made aware in very vivid terms of just how destructive passion can be. But such readers are also aware that the heroine of this novel views her own passion with enormous objectivity, is fully conscious of its dangers, and resolutely refuses in the end to submit to it. And nowhere in the narrative is the passion clouded by much sentiment. The age of sentiment did not begin until about the middle of the eighteenth century, when "benevolence" began to take the place of traditional ideas of charity among large segments of the population. Meanwhile, however, a tendency toward a more sentimental attitude had been steadily growing among the more popular ranks of the Baroque audience. Bussy's little collection of Abelardian letters was rather quickly revised and expanded to meet the demands of this wider and steadily more influential reading public.

One Nicolas Rémond des Cours published an elaboration of the count's letters at La Haye in 1693 under the title *Histoire d'Eloise et d'Abelard.* But others were at work, too. If the attractive devices of Bussy were to be fully enjoyed, they needed extension to make them resemble, at least superficially, the whole original correspondence, except for the last two letters, which were not subject to much stylistic revision and could in any event be neglected. Two new letters were concocted to close the correspondence, and an entirely new *History of My Calamities* was composed in which the love element was developed and carried to the conclusion of the narrative. The new *History* was called a *Lettre à Philinthe*, in which the name of Abelard's "friend" is supplied for the first time. Thus in 1695 one F. N. Du Bois was able to publish at La Haye his enormously successful *Histoire des amours et infortunes d'Abélard et d'Heloise* containing (1) a long "historical" introduction drawing on Alluis and allegedly on the authority of Peter Bayle; (2) the *Lettre à Philinthe*; (3) a somewhat long-winded elaboration of Bussy's letters; and (4) two new letters to complete the collection. This highly fanciful production was translated into English by John Hughes and published in 1713. It was to become the chief source of information about Abelard and Heloise for ordinary English readers for over two hundred years, being published for the last time in the Temple Classics in 1922. The astonishing success of this book amply illustrates the fact that each age customarily disregards the messages signalled to it from the past either by revising them completely to make them "relevant" or by leaving them alone superficially but interpreting them in subtle ways so that they seem to say something palatable. The latter alternative was not to be available on a large scale, however, until after the development of sophisticated techniques of literary criticism in the nineteenth century. In defense of Bussy-Rabutin, who actually made the collection possible by writing a love letter for Abelard, it may be said that he was patently and unashamedly indulging in a joke. No such excuses can be made for Du Bois and his translator.

The English translator Hughes was clearly interested in the letters as valid representations of human passion, of sentiments once actually experienced by distinguished persons, for their authenticity made them true guides to "human nature." He says in his Preface, "It is very surprising that *The Letters of Abelard and Heloise* have not appeared sooner in English, since it is generally allowed by all who have seen them in other languages, that they are written with the greatest passion of any of this kind that are extant." In this respect, he says, they are far superior to the *Letters from a Nun to a Cavalier*, first published in 1669, which relate the passionate history of the nun Marianna Alcoferado, and which made an enormous impression on readers of the late seventeenth century. "Whatever those were," Hughes says, "these are known to be genuine pieces occasioned by an amour that had very extraordinary consequences and that made great noise at the time when it happened, being between the most distinguished persons of that age." Needless to say, the persons were not quite so distinguished as Hughes indicates, and the resemblance between his "genuine pieces" and the original was superficial. Nevertheless, he sought eagerly to convince his readers of their authenticity, insisting on their eternal validity as records of human experience: "These letters, being truly written by the persons themselves . . . are everywhere full of sentiments of the heart (which are not to be imitated in a feigned story), and touches of Nature, much more moving than any which could flow from the pen of a writer of novels, or enter into the imagination of any who had not felt the like emotions and distresses." Thus he could find in the letters "surprising mixtures of devotions and tenderness, of penitence and remaining frailty, and a lively picture of human nature in its contrarieties of passion and reason, its infirmities, and its sufferings." These are moving words, auspicious neither for the comic muse nor for any real understanding of Abelard and Heloise.

The historical introduction Hughes translated from Du Bois affords very telling examples of the excesses of the historical imagination. Some kind of imaginative reconstruction is always necessary in historical writings, and it is very difficult indeed, even today, to avoid shaping such reconstructions in accordance with current tastes and prejudices. "Abelard," we are told, "besides his uncommon merit as a scholar had all the accomplishments of a gentleman." There is a certain amount of truth here, but a "gentle-man" of the twelfth century was hardly the same thing as a "gentleman" of the seventeenth century. Hughes continues by describing the best qualities of the aristocracy as they were thought of among those inferior to them socially at the time: "He had a greatness of soul which nothing could shock; his passions were delicate, his judgment solid, and taste exquisite." The vainglory, avarice, and sheer lechery that Abelard attributed to himself are here overlooked; in fact they are directly contradicted: "He was of graceful person, and carried himself with the air of a man of quality. His conversation was sweet, complaisant, easy, and gentle-manlike. It seemed that Nature had designed him for more elevated employment than that of teaching the sciences." Anselm of Laon would have been interested to hear that Abelard was "sweet, com-plaisant, and easy." The remark about teachers of the sciences undoubtedly appealed to most of Hughes' audience, for Thwack-ums and Squares of one kind or another had probably rendered an indelible impression on society before Fielding immortalized them in *Tom Jones*. The account continues, even more wide of the mark concerning Abelard: "He looked upon riches and grandeur with contempt and had no higher ambition than to make his name famous among learned men, and to be reputed the greatest doctor of his age."

Our history hastens to add, however, that in spite of Abelard's taste, grace, and so on, he had "human frailty"—an increasingly attractive weakness from Hughes' day to this—"and all his philosophy could not guard him from the attacks of love. For some time he defended himself from this passion pretty well, when the temptation was but slight; but upon a more intimate familiarity with such agreeable objects, he found his reason fail him. . . ." The calculating manner in which the original Abelard selected the original Heloise is here overlooked completely. This "agreeable object" puzzled the seventeenth century a little, for no one knew what to make of her ancestry, a matter of some importance at the time. For, as Hughes translates, "It was well known in those times, as well as since, that the niece of an ecclesiastic is sometimes more nearly related to him." However, Heloise easily made up for doubts concerning her origin: "Whatever she was for birth, she was a very engaging woman; and if she was not a perfect beauty, she appeared as such at least in Abelard's eyes." Our historians readily supply details, for each age has been quick to adorn Heloise with those attributes best suited to its own standards of beauty: "Her person was well proportioned, her features regular, her eyes sparkling, her lips vermilion and well-formed, her complexion animated, her air fine, and her aspect sweet and agreeable. She had a surprising quickness of wit, an incredible memory, and a considerable share of learning, joined with humility; and all these accomplishments were attended with something so graceful and moving that it was impossible for those who kept her company not to be in love with her." This description, which is almost enough to make a man wish he had lived in the late seventeenth century, betrays no traces of the obvious vanity of the youthful Heloise as Abelard portrays her.

In spite of the attractions of Heloise, however, they were insufficient to insure that she was the single object of Abelard's affection. Many ladies, we are told, pitied Abelard at the time of his castration, and there were some who had special reasons for feeling deprived: "And it is probable that among the great number of ladies who pitied Abelard, there were some with whom he had been very intimate; for his philosophy did not make him scrupulous enough to esteem every small infidelity a crime, when it did not lessen his constant love of Heloise." Persons of quality, everyone knew, were not prudes. Abelard himself says nothing about ladies among the mourners who came to visit him, but it probably seemed incredible to seventeenth-century writers that they should not have been there.

Our history dwells at length on the question of why Heloise did not wish to marry Abelard. There are no hints of the humor of her sermon on marriage and no reflections at all of the jocularity of Jean de Meun. Instead, we are told finally exactly what we might have anticipated: "And excess of passion, never heard of before, made her choose to be Abelard's mistress rather than his wife." This view, allied with ideas concerning human frailty, has prevailed ever since, although it has sometimes been fortified by ideas of rebelliousness against convention, natural paganism, or unsullied human instinct. The "gentlemanly" qualities of Abelard as contrasted with the "passion" of Heloise eventually brought Abelard into disfavor among promulgators of the legend. But the attitude toward passion in Hughes is not yet romantic; it is accompanied by attractive sentiment, but it has not yet acquired the complete innocence and blamelessness it was to acquire later. Meanwhile, the historical introduction provided for the letters is sufficiently colored by the tastes of its own time to make the characters seem "universal" to the contemporary reader.

The "Epistle to Philintus," which replaces the original *History,* contains a brief "factual" account of Abelard's early career, omitting many details and glossing over entirely the amusing parallel between Abelard's disputations and the activities of an armed knight. Although the general technique is one of condensation, a few new details are added. For example, the entry of Abelard's parents into a life of religion is described as follows: "About this time my father Berengar, who at the age of sixty had lived very agreeably, retired from the world and shut himself up in a cloister, where he offered up to Heaven the languid remains of a life he could no longer make use of. My mother, who was yet young, took the same resolution. She turned a Religious, but did not entirely abandon the satisfactions of life. Her friends were continually at the gate; and the monastery, when one has an inclination to make it so, is exceedingly charming and pleasant." It is one of the ironies of this new version of the *Letters* that although the original was obviously designed for the instruction of nuns, this one consistently assumes either a cynical or, at times, an openly antagonistic attitude toward the religious life.

The encounter with Anselm of Laon is passed over lightly, Abelard achieves fame quickly and without any reference to the content of his teaching, and we are soon introduced to the central subject: love. "And now, my friend, I am going to expose to you all my weaknesses. All men, I believe, are under a necessity of paying tribute, at some time or other, to Love, and it is vain to strive to avoid it." As the result of the action of this foe, we are told, Abelard became "a singular example of the vengeance of Heaven." The implication is clear, however, that this vengeance was unjust: "I will tell you, my friend, the particulars of my story, and leave you to judge whether I deserved so severe a correction." This attitude resembles the original not at all, where Abelard points out that Divine Piety devised a remedy for his maladies. The exemplary pattern and the doctrinal implications of the original are, in fact, abandoned completely. This does not mean that no one in the late seventeenth and early eighteenth centuries would have understood them. Madame de Sévigné, as readers of her letters are aware, was much interested in reassurances concerning the Providential Order, and there were many persons in the upper circles of society to whom Boethius was not unknown. But if Du Bois and Hughes had tried to imitate the intellectual content of the original, as well as its "story," they would automatically have restricted their audience. They also lacked the classical background necessary to understand Abelard's allusions. For example, the quotation from Lucan's Cornelia spoken by Heloise is retained, but we are told that Cornelia spoke these words "after the death of Pompey the Great," when, as a matter of fact, she was addressing him. Again, the quotation from Ovid's Ajax is used, but without any evidence of an awareness of its significance.

The concentration of this new *History* on the love story led to embellishments, some of which are today rather entertaining, although they were at the time serious representations of "human nature." We are told of the manner in which Abelard gained access to Fulbert's house, although all mention of the "rod" is omitted. Instead we have the following charming picture of Abelard's first approach to his beloved:

As I was with her one day alone, "Charming Heloise," said I, blushing, "if you know yourself, you will not be surprised what passion you have inspired me with. Uncommon as it is, I can express it but with the common terms—I love you, adorable Heloise! Till now I thought philosophy made us masters of all our passions, and that it was a refuge from the storms in which weak mortals are tossed and shipwrecked. But you have destroyed my security and broken this philo-sophic courage. I have despised riches; honor and its pageant-ries could never raise a weak thought in me. Beauty alone has fired my soul. Happy, if she who raised this passion kindly receives the declaration, but if it is an offense—"

"No," replied Heloise, "she must be very ignorant of your merit who can be offended at your passion. But, for my own repose, I wish either that you had not made this declaration, or that I were at liberty not to suspect your sincerity."

"Ah, divine Heloise," said I, flinging myself at her feet, "I swear by yourself—"

I was going to convince her of the truth of my passion, but heard a noise, and it was Fulbert. There was no avoiding it, but I must do a violence to my desire, and change the dis-course to some other subject.

This sort of thing produced a "happy understanding" and an enjoyment of "the sweets of love" while Fulbert slept. Our new Abelard "quitted Aristotle and his dry maxims to practice the precepts of the more ingenious Ovid," but was, like Mars, dis-covered and in consequence forced to leave Fulbert's house. The stratagems Abelard used to gain access to his mistress are com-pletely original in this new version, involving, first of all, an effort to bribe a servant girl, who, however, presents unacceptable coun-terproposals.

It being impossible that I could live without seeing Heloise, I endeavored to engage her servant, whose name was Agaton, in my interest. She was brown, well-shaped, a person superior to the ordinary rank, her features regular and her eyes sparkling, fit to raise love in any man whose heart was not prepossessed by another passion. I met her alone, and en-treated her to have pity on a distressed lover. She answered she would undertake anything to serve me, but there was a reward. At these words I opened my purse and showed the shining metal, which lays asleep guards, forces a way through rocks, and softens the heart of the most obdurate fair.

"You are mistaken," said she, smiling and shaking her head. "You do not know me. Could gold tempt me, a rich abbot takes his nightly station, and sings under my window. He offers to send me to his abbey, which, he says, is situate in the most pleasant country in the world. A courtier offers me a considerable sum of money, and assures me I need have no apprehensions, for if our amours have consequences he will marry me to his gentleman and give me a handsome employment. To say nothing of a young officer who patrols about here every night and makes his attacks after all imaginable forms. It must be Love only which could oblige him to follow me, for I have not like your great ladies any rings or jewels to tempt him. Yet, during all his siege of love, his feather and his embroidered coat have not made any breach in my heart. I shall not quickly be brought to capitulate, I am too faithful to my first conqueror—"

And then she looked at me. I answered, I did not understand her discourse. She replied, "For a man of sense and gallantry you have a very slow apprehension. I am in love with you, Abelard. I know you adore Heloise. I do not blame you. I desire only to enjoy the second place in your affections. I have a tender heart as well as my mistress; you may without difficulty make returns to my passion. Do not perplex yourself with unfashionable scruples; a prudent man ought to love several at the same time. If one should fail, he is not then left unprovided."

Unfortunately, Abelard paid no attention to these seductive arguments, but left Agaton abruptly. She went immediately to Fulbert to tell of his attempt and also began to act the part of a watchman in her nocturnal vigils. As our gallant Abelard puts it, "Let no lover hereafter follow my example. A woman rejected is an outrageous creature." However, he soon bribed Heloise's singing-master, of all people, to carry a message for him to his beloved, and by scaling a wall with a rope ladder managed to meet her at the "end of the garden." There his happiness was short, however, for she informed him of her pregnancy, the news of which, he says, plunged him "into a thousand distractions." Thus he was forced to carry Heloise off to Brittany.

The delightful little sermon on the subject of marriage is con-densed and rationalized by the omission of any remarks about continence: "She urged all that was possible to divert me from marriage: that it was a bond always fatal to a philosopher, that the cries of children and the cares of a family were utterly in-consistent with the tranquility and application which the study of philosophy required. She quoted to me all that was written on the subject by Theophrastus, Cicero, and above all, she insisted on the unfortunate Socrates, who quitted life with joy, because by that means he left Xantippe." Socrates is here somewhat more unfortunate than usual, and the audience being addressed would not have had the faintest notion of what Theophrastus or Cicero said about marriage. Heloise goes on to offer to be Abelard's mistress, using the argument that "pleasures tasted sparingly, and with difficulty, have always a higher relish, while every thing, by being easy and common, grows flat and insipid." Some of the burden is taken from Heloise as a scorner of marriage by a new character, Abelard's sister Lucilla, who argues that the beauty of Heloise will soon fade, that Abelard will have to use discretion in speech before her if she is his wife, and that Heloise, as a wife, will "be a woman" and hence probably unfaithful. These argu-ments, of course, are of no avail.

The lovers come to Paris, marry, and then, without the provoca-tion of the sequestration of his niece in Argenteuil, Fulbert takes his vengeance. The operation leaves Abelard still suffering from desire: "The desire was left with me, but not the possibility of satisfying the passion." This arrangement, in contrast to the original, where Abelard never evinces any further sexual appetites, was necessary to account for the love expressed by the new Abelard in his letters; that is, historically speaking, the preservation of Abelard's lust was due to the fertile wit of Bussy-Rabutin. This survival also provided once more a motive for Abelard's placing Heloise in a nunnery, also derived from Bussy but expressed with-out that author's comic smile: "Jealousy took possession of my mind; at the very expense of her happiness, I decreed to disappoint all rivals. Before I put myself in a cloister, I obliged her to take the habit and retire into the nunnery at Argenteuil."

The burning of Abelard's treatise is turned into a vague burning of his "books" that were "condemned by a council." Nothing is said of the quarrel over St. Dionysius, but Abelard is simply forced to "retire near Nogent." Suger's action concerning Argenteuil is omitted, and there is no long discussion of the name "Paraclete." Abelard says, "The rage of my enemies now awakened again and forced me to quit this retreat. This I did with much difficulty. But first the Bishop of Troyes gave me leave to establish there a nunnery, which I did, and committed the care of it to my dear Heloise." To make the first letter of Heloise follow this one more reasonably, Abelard adds, "When I had settled her down—can you believe it, Philintus?—I left her without taking any leave." Abelard's alleged casualness concerning Heloise when he visited her at the Paraclete is still used today as an hypothesis to explain her complaint concerning his neglect of her in her first letter.

After a brief description of St. Gildas, the letter draws to a close, but the seventeenth century was not content without some picturesque detail: "The doors and walls are without any ornament except the heads of boars and hinds' feet, which are nailed up against them, and the heads of frightful animals. The cells are hung with skins of deer." Nothing is said, of course, about the appropriateness of male spiritual instructors for women. The conclusion is again moving, but this time it is sentimental rather than philosophical. The lessons of St. Augustine's *Confessions* and the *Consolation* of Boethius were too severe for the relatively untrained audience Du Bois and Hughes were addressing. Moreover, it was necessary, because of Bussy-Rabutin's picture of an ever-loving Abelard, to keep the love theme intact. Here it is in all its hopeless glory:

Ah, Philintus! does not the love of Heloise still burn in my heart? I have not yet triumphed over that unhappy passion. In the midst of my retirement I sigh, I weep, I pine. I speak the dear name of Heloise, and pleased to hear the sound, I complain of the severity of Heaven. But, oh! let us not deceive ourselves; I have not made a right use of grace. I am thoroughly wretched. I have not yet torn from my heart the deep roots which vice has planted in it. For if my conversion was sincere, how could I take a pleasure to relate past follies? Could I not more easily comfort myself in my afflictions? Could I not turn to my advantage those words of God Him-self: "If they have persecuted me, they will also persecute you; if the world hate you, ye know that it hated me also." Come, Philintus, let us make a strong effort, turn our mis-fortunes to our advantage, make them meritorious, or at least wipe out our offenses; let us receive without murmuring what comes from the hand of God, and let us not oppose our will to His. Adieu. I give you good advice, which could I myself follow, I should be happy.

The first letters that follow are elaborations of the letters of Bussy, deprived of their comedy and rendered with more words and greater feeling. The two concluding letters, the first of which is attributed to Heloise, may be briefly summarized. Heloise begins by pointing out that Abelard has not answered her last letter, but her own correspondence is renewed only with a denial that it can continue: "It is happiness to me that you show so much insensi-tivity to the fatal passion which has engaged me to you. At last, Abelard, you have lost Heloise forever." She explains that she now loves God: "Some few days after you sent me your last letter I fell dangerously ill; the physicians gave me over, and I expected certain death. Then it was that my passion, which always before seemed innocent, appeared criminal to me." Since the time she entered the cloister she has spent her days in grief and sighing, looking upon her refuge as a "prison." But now, she assures him, she has gained a "complete victory." Referring to complaints about ir-regularities in her convent, she assures Abelard that they are to be expected: "Do fathers consult the inclinations of their children when they settle them? Are not interest and policy their only rules?" This is a direct attack on the religious life that would have astonished Abelard and shocked the Abbess of the Paraclete. Our new Heloise, however, says that she has found no irregularities. Turning to the subject of his miseries, she offers herself as an ex-ample: "Let me see no more in your letters, dear Abelard, such murmurs against Fortune; you are not the only one she has persecuted, and you ought to forget her outrages. What a shame is it for a philosopher not to be comforted for an accident which might happen to any man! Govern yourself by my example. I was born with violent passions; I daily strive with the most tender emotions, and glory in triumphing and subjecting them to reason."

Her good example soon fades, however, when she begins to think of what it would mean to see Abelard no more, and she con-fesses that she still dreams of him at night: "I will own to you what makes the greatest pleasure I have in my retirement. After having passed the day in thinking of you, full of the dear idea, I give myself up at night to sleep. Then it is that Heloise, who dares not without trembling think of you by day, resigns herself entirely to the pleasure of hearing you and speaking to you. I see you, Abelard, and glut my eyes with the sight. Sometimes you entertain me with the story of your secret troubles and grievances and create in me a sensible sorrow; sometimes forgetting the perpetual obstacles to our desires, you press me to make you happy, and I easily yield to your transports. Sleep gives you what your enemies' rage deprived you of; and our souls, animated by the same passion, are sensible of the same pleasure. But oh! you delightful illusions, soft errors, how soon you vanish away! At my awaking I open my eyes and see no Abelard; I stretch out my arms to take hold of him, but he is not there; I call him, he hears me not." We are back with Sappho again, or at least with a distant echo of her dreams. Abelard, she says, does not suffer in this way. If he could come to the nunnery, then all her desires would be innocent. A young nun, she says, recently escaped the convent and ran away with an Englishman. If Abelard could be there, such things would not happen. At the close of her letter, Heloise, in spite of her illness and the fears it brought, and in spite of her triumphs over Fortune, still wavers: "I am sensible of the motions both of grace and passion, and by turns yield to each."

Abelard's reply to this wavering epistle exhibits an emotional religiosity that would have appalled his twelfth-century prede-cessor and probably amused Bussy. "Write no more to me,

Heloise," he begins, "write no more to me; it is time to end a commerce which makes our mortifications of no advantage to us." He wishes he could be at the Paraclete to instruct her and her nuns, but "your heart," he writes, "still burns with that fatal fire which you cannot extinguish, and mine is full of uneasiness." He sighs and weeps over her letters, but to no avail. "Endeavor," he urges, "with all your strength to become a perfect Christian." Her true husband is Christ, who should not be renounced, for if Heloise despises His grace, "He will say to you, 'Go, proud creature, dwell in everlasting flames. I separated you from the world to purify you in solitude, and you did not second my design; I endeavored to save you, and you took pains to destroy yourself; go, wretch, and take the portion of the reprobates.'" If she can forget him, Abelard assures her, "every virtue will become easy," and she will hear her Savior say, "'Come, partake of my glory, and enjoy the eternal reward I have appointed for the virtues you have practiced.'" We may observe certain Pelagian inclinations in our late Baroque Abelard, but these are helpful to heighten the emotional effect. In any event, he bids Heloise farewell for the last time, concluding by urging further tears: "May you shed as many tears for your salvation as you have done during the course of our misfortunes!" Thus has passion brought our lovers to an unhappy conclusion, and on this very moist note our new version of *The Letters of Abelard and Heloise* subsides in what might be called "sensible feeling."

Although the comedy of love was to sparkle once more, somewhat sporadically, in Alexander Pope's *Eloisa*, the new version of the *Letters* produced by Du Bois in France and Hughes in England effectively erected a barrier between most readers and the comic aspects of Abelard's love affair. The barrier still stands. More important, perhaps, is the fact that Du Bois and Hughes inverted the meaning of the *Letters*. Their collection could hardly be followed by a history of the cloistered life for women and a rule for the Paraclete. The "Letter to Philintus," with its unsuccessful conversion, would not serve very well as a spiritual history of the founder of a religious order. The new letters offer an emotional experience instead of a spiritual experience. The progress of the affections was much more convincing to the popular audience being addressed than any reasonable or logical argument could possibly be, even though it might be based on some of the most revered principles of Christian philosophy. It is still much more convincing to audiences today. In fact, there is a sense in which this curious fabrication, in part a corruption of the comic spirit of Bussy-Rabutin, heralds the dawn of the modern world.

CHAPTER XI

Rococo Wit

Art historians call the style manifested in the arts during the early eighteenth century, especially among the aristocracy, "Rococo." They often regard it with small enthusiasm, emphasizing its sensuality, its triviality, and its lack of anything resembling "redeeming social value." Of course, social value depends to some extent on which segments of society one wishes to redeem, but, leaving such questions aside, it is probably true that Rococo art was the last manifestation of major European cultural traditions that had extended from antiquity through the Middle Ages, the Renaissance, and the Baroque Era. And it is also true that art historians have sometimes neglected its wit. There is an element of humorous detachment even in the paintings of Boucher, and, indeed, it is sometimes possible to detect an actual joke lurking in the implications of his tableaux. Wit and sensuality do not mix well, for as Mr. Shandy points out in *Tristram Shandy*, there is nothing so serious as lust. It follows that Rococo art is often not sensual at all, even when the nude ladies that disport in its representations seem almost unbelievably inviting, if somewhat disconcerting in their perfection of form and surface. Surface perfection, in fact, sets them off in another world, as it were, and the scenes in which we find them are often very obviously not locations in the ordinary world we know. Gravity sometimes forgets its laws, odd statues appear in wild groves, and nature generally arranges herself in interesting but factually dubious decorative landscapes. Sensuality goes much better with sentiment, and with believable backgrounds, than with wit, and sentiment duly replaced wit as the eighteenth century wore on.

The *Eloisa to Abelard* of Alexander Pope is an excellent example of a Rococo poem, perhaps a little dampened by its English ambience. It is based on the *Letters* as they appear in Hughes, but Pope's transformation of Hughes is one of the more fascinating events in the history of the legend, matched only, perhaps, by the transformation of Pope's own poem into a masterpiece of sentiment by his French translator, Colardeau. Pope was a Roman Catholic, somewhat alienated for this reason from the English society of his time. He was also largely self-educated, assisted by Jesuit tutors, and the training he received was highly traditional. His classical readings included many works that Abelard must have studied at Angers or elsewhere, and his theological and philosophical background also included works that Abelard had read and enjoyed. He lacked, moreover, Hughes' obvious contempt for the cloistered life. Altogether, Pope was in a position to restore just a touch of the spirit of Abelard's original letters, in spite of the fact that he never read them.

There is one sense in which Pope's poem was made possible by Ovid, understood in the old way as a witty and detached observer of amorous affairs. Cultivated men of the late seventeenth and early eighteenth centuries relished his verse, not yet transformed by the nineteenth century into "dirty poetry." One of the most successful poetic anthologies of the period was a volume of English translations of Ovid's *Epistles* or *Heroides*, first published in 1680 and reaching a seventh edition in 1705. It contained a preface by the poet John Dryden, who translated three of the epistles. When the eighth edition was being prepared, a new translation of the first epistle, "Sapho to Phaon" (now usually numbered XV, with the spelling *Sappho*, which will be adopted hereafter), was requested, since the old translation by Sir Cass Scrope was incomplete and frequently merely a paraphrase of the Latin text. Pope, who had already made a preliminary translation of this epistle, offered to supply it. His translation appeared in the edition of 1712.

When the *Letters* of Hughes, who was an acquaintance of Pope's, appeared in 1713, Pope undoubtedly noticed the resemblance between the dreams of Heloise and those of Sappho, as well as the general resemblance between the forlorn Heloise and the forlorn ladies of Ovid's epistles. One of them, Helen, even alternates between the demands of ancient piety and the seductive allurements offered by Paris, to which we know she succumbed with very disastrous consequences. What could be more natural than a lament of Heloise, or Eloisa, in Ovidian form? He could imitate what appeared to be a record of nature in Hughes and a classical poet at the same time, thus, as he might have said, dressing nature to advantage.

Perhaps it will help us to remember that according to legend Sappho, whose tastes had previously been "Lesbian," fell desperately in love with a youth named Phaon. Phaon left her, however, and she fell into despair, eventually leaping from a high cliff into the sea. In her descent she hoped to be rescued by Eros, who would take her safely to Apollo. The legend, probably stimulated by Ovid's epistle, became a favorite one among late antique Pythagoreans, who found in it a philosophical message. The leap is depicted, for example, in the apse of a late Pythagorean basilica, discovered in modern times under a railway track in Rome when the gravel in the roadbed began to disappear mysteriously into the earth. It may be that Ovid's poem actually conveyed certain Pythagorean attitudes, in accordance with which Sappho was saved, since there is some evidence to indicate that he may have been involved with the sect, but these attitudes would have been lost to early Christian readers, who were probably skeptical about Sappho's hopes for assistance from the fragile wings of Cupid.

In Pope's translation of the epistle, we find Sappho writing to the departed Phaon, lamenting that she has abandoned her songs for "elegies of woe." She burns with love so that music pleases her no more. Moreover, "soft scenes of solitude" no longer please her, since

Love enters there, and I'm my own disease.

This line, which is not in the original, where Sappho enumerates some of her "guilty loves" with girls, suggests an idea elaborated later in the poem and developed even further in *Eloisa*. Wild scenery that is delightful in the presence of the beloved because of the privacy it affords becomes sad and forbidding when the lover is absent. We are inclined to regard this as a simple psychological effect, or even as a matter of existential "reality." But for Ovid and for Pope, the scenery remains the same, and both its transient attractiveness under the stimulus of satisfied passion and its sorrowful aspect in frustration afford amusingly ironic comments on the irrationality of passion itself. Hence the statement, "I am my own disease." There is nothing intrinsically emotional about the scenery. All this was to change in the course of the eighteenth century, when it became possible to attribute a melancholy character to scenery alone, as Gray does, for example, in his celebrated "Elegy in a Country Churchyard." And in the next century the isolated figure set in a vast landscape or seascape became a standard bit of iconography for conveying the essential melancholy loneliness of the human condition, a loneliness that was deliberately cultivated.

Sappho mentions briefly in Pope's translation her former "guilty love" for "Lesbian dames," now transferred to Phaon, whose beauty is extolled extravagantly. He is a "brighter Phoebus," for example. Meanwhile, she calls attention to her own fame and poetic power. She is brown and short, but exceedingly famous because of her skill at song. Even so, Phaon stopped her songs with kisses, and she learned to please in everything, as she reminds him in vivid terms:

> In all I pleased, but most in what was best;
> And the last joy was dearer than the rest.
> Then with each word, each glance, each motion fired,
> You still enjoyed and yet you still desired,
> Till all dissolving in a trance we lay,
> And in tumultuous raptures died away.

These lines, although they do follow the original Latin, afford, in this form, a good example of Rococo "sensuality." We can imagine how they must have shocked nineteenth-century readers who had been taught that respectable women do not enjoy sexual pleasure. Neither Ovid nor Pope, however, had heard of this doctrine, and no one in the audience of either would have missed the point that the pleasures so fetchingly described here had led Sappho into an extremely desperate position.

Sappho goes on to discuss that desperation. Phaon is now deceiving Sicilian maids, just as he had deceived her, but she has other woes as well. She lost her parents early, her brother was disgraced because of his love for a prostitute, and she has an infant daughter to care for. She no longer dresses in purple robes, adorns herself with jewels, or cares for her hair; she thinks only of love. She implores Phaon to return, castigates him for leaving her without saying farewell, and describes her rage in detail, not to mention the scorn of her brother and her furious despair. Phaon is her "daily longing" and her "dream by night." Since these dreams play a large part in the legend of Heloise, it may be helpful to describe them once more in the language of Pope's translation:

> O Night more pleasing than the brightest day,
> When fancy gives what absence takes away,
> And dressed in all its visionary charms,
> Restores my fair deserted to my arms!
> Then round your neck in wanton wreathes I twine,
> Then you, methinks, as fondly circle mine.
> A thousand tender words I hear and speak,
> A thousand tender kisses give and take.
> Then fiercer joys—I blush to mention these,
> Yet while I blush, confess how much they please!
> But when with day the sweet delusions fly,
> And all things wake to life and joy, but I,
> As if once more forsaken, I complain,
> And close my eyes, to dream of you again.
> Then frantic rise, and like some fury rove
> Through lonely plains, and through the silent grove,
> As if the silent grove, and lonely plains
> That knew my pleasures, could relieve my pains.
> I view the grotto, once the scene of love,
> The rocks around, the hanging roofs above,

That charmed me more, with native moss o'ergrown,
Than Phrygian marble or the Parian stone.
I find the shades that veiled our joys before,
But, Phaon gone, those shades delight no more.
Here the pressed herbs with bending tops betray
Where oft entwined in amorous folds we lay;
I kiss the earth which once was pressed by you,
And all with tears the withering herbs bedew.
For thee the fading trees appear to mourn,
And birds defer their songs till thy return.
Night shades the groves, and all in silence lie,
All, but the mournful Philomel and I.
With mournful Philomel I join my strain,
Of Tereus she, of Phaon I complain.

In the original it is not the nightingale that sings, but her sister
Procne, the swallow; the change was made desirable by the fact
that Pope makes night fall upon the scene to deepen its gloom,
and, further, it associates Sappho with the ravished Philomel. It
was on the basis of suggestions here that he was to elaborate the
remarkable scenery in *Eloisa*.

One more scene remains, a spring

> whose silver waters show
> Clear as glass, the shining sands below.

It is inhabited by a Naiad, or "watery virgin," who gives poor
Sappho some advice. This figure is transformed in *Eloisa* into the
ghost of a nun, who was to become the source of some consoling
sentimental doctrine in Colardeau. In Ovid, however, her advice
is stern. She urges Sappho to go to a famous promontory some
two thousand feet above the sea. There she should cast herself
down as other forlorn lovers have done before her, without dread-
ing the "deeps below." Sappho promises to follow this advice and
to consecrate her lyre to Apollo with the hope that Love, or Cupid,
will waft her over the waves to a place where she will forget her
love. After some final castigation of Phaon, who had doomed poor
Sappho to the "rocks and sea," and a farewell to "Lesbian dames,"
the epistle concludes:

> To raging seas unpitied I'll remove,
> And either cease to live or cease to love!

Whatever the Pythagoreans may have thought, readers of the early eighteenth century would have concluded at once that Sappho ceased to do both. This, indeed, is the verdict reached by Addison in a jocular account of this and other lovers' leaps published in *The Spectator* (1711, no. 233).

Pope not only knew Ovid very well; he was also a careful student of *The Consolation of Philosophy* of Boethius, which is, as we have seen, one of the most successful defenses of Providential justice ever written. Some time before 1710 he translated part of the ninth meter of the third book, beginning and ending as follows:

> O thou, whose all-creating hands sustain
> The radiant heavens, the earth, and ambient main!
> Eternal Reason! whose presiding soul
> Informs great Nature and directs the whole!
>
> . . . .
>
> In thee the righteous find
> Calm rest, and soft serenity of mind;
> Thee they regard alone; to Thee they tend,
> At once our great Original and our End,
> At once our Means, our End, our Way,
> Our utmost Bound, and our eternal Stay!

The poet was so convinced of the reasonable order of creation that he was later able to write, in the *Essay on Man*, a work that shows strong Boethian influence

> All Nature is but art, unknown to thee;
> All chance, direction, which thou canst not see;
> All discord, harmony not understood;
> All partial evil, universal good;
> And spite of pride, in erring reason's spite,
> One truth is clear: "Whatever is, is right."

He concluded also that "virtue only is our bliss below," a view that supplies the ironic smile necessary to a witty view of passionate love. The tortured emotion of Pope's Eloisa is thus some-

[187]

thing we should expect to find regarded with a due detachment and a touch of humor. At the same time, there lurks in the background of Pope's heroine a possibility for devotion much more genuine than anything suggested in the feigned letters of Hughes.

Eloisa to Abelard, which first appeared in the *Works* published in 1717, must rank, along with *The Rape of the Lock*, as a master-piece of English Rococo verse. The scenery, which is at least in part an elaboration of Ovid, sets the figure of Eloisa against a deliberately artificial background somewhat like the landscapes in Watteau's paintings. It is not made up of familiar scenes exag-gerated for the sake of mood, of overpowering landscapes in the style of the Romantics, nor of impressions that reflect the emotions of the observer as distinct from those of Eloisa. The reader is not invited to enter the scene at all. Abstractions find a natural place in it, and there is a sense in which Eloisa herself is an abstraction —a representation of the "idea" of a woman torn between pas-sionate memories of love and equally passionate but futile and unreasoned impulses toward devotion. If we try to consider her as a "personality," or a "psychological reality," we inject a discordant note into the scenery and destroy the fabric of the poem. The process would be a little like inserting a figure by Degas into a painting by Boucher.

The first part of the poem is based largely on the elaboration of Bussy's first letter of Heloise in the version found in Hughes. The setting is "melancholy," but not in the Romantic sense of the word. The melancholy is that of thoughtfulness and contemplation celebrated by Milton in *Il Penseroso*, a mood appropriate to the cloistered life:

> In these deep solitudes and awful cells,
> Where heavenly-pensive, contemplation dwells,
> And ever-musing melancholy reigns,
> What means this tumult in a vestal's veins?
> Why rove my thoughts beyond this last retreat?
> Why feels my heart its long-forgotten heat?
> Yet, yet I love! From Abelard it came,
> And Eloisa yet must kiss the name.

"Ever-musing" melancholy is indeed destroyed immediately, giving way to sorrow as Eloisa wishes to blot out Abelard's name with her tears. Tears are even more copious in Pope than they are in Hughes, but if the reader objects to them on the ground that they do not move his own tears, he should consider the possibility that Pope had no intention of moving them at all. They are a part of the representation, not part of a narrative in which the reader is asked to participate vicariously.

Pope soon returns to the setting, where the Ovidian coloring is now unmistakable, for "grots and caverns" mingle, rather oddly, with the shrines:

> Relentless walls! whose darksome round contains
> Relentless sighs, and voluntary pains.
> Ye rugged rocks! which holy knees have worn,
> Ye grots and caverns shagg'd with horrid thorn!
> Shrines! where their vigils pale-eyed virgins keep,
> And pitying saints, whose statues learn to weep!
> Though cold like you, unmoved, and silent grown,
> I have not yet forgot myself to stone.
> All is not Heaven's while Abelard has part;
> Still rebel nature holds out half my heart.

As Eloisa thinks of Abelard, the landscape grows both more Venerian, or "Sapphic," and more sorrowful at the same time. Pope and his readers were aware that walls are not necessarily "relentless" and that statues do not weep. That is, the scenery creates an irony of its own. The line "I have not forgot myself to stone" may strike a chord of sentimental sympathy today, but it is an echo of Milton, whose "Melancholy," the daughter of Saturn and Vesta in *Il Penseroso*, is urged to undergo just such a transformation:

> Come, pensive Nun, devout and pure,
> Sober, steadfast, and demure,
> All in a robe of darkest grain,
> Flowing with majestic train,
> And sable cape of *Cipres* lawn,

> Over the decent shoulders drawn.
> Come, but keep thy wonted state,
> With even step and musing gait,
> And looks commercing with the skies,
> Thy rapt soul sitting in thine eyes:
> There held in holy passion still
> Forget thyself to marble, till
> With a sad leaden downward cast,
> Thou fix them on the earth as fast.

Eloisa has grown "cold," but not in the raptures of contemplation appropriate to her calling. Her "rebel nature," to which we shall return in a moment, has chilled her with the loss of other delights recalled by Abelard's letter.

We see Eloisa weeping over her letters and asking for more. Her "faded eyes" can only "read and weep," so that, like Bussy's heroine, she needs further letters that will "pour out all the heart." She turns to the subject of her innocence, but her protestation also involves an accusation with amusing overtones:

> Thou knowest how guiltless first I met thy flame,
> When Love approached me under Friendship's name.

In Chaucer's *Troilus* Pandarus is at some pains to win Criseyde's "friendship" for Troilus as an initial step toward seduction, although Criseyde is fully aware of what this "friendship" implies. He is successful. Later on, Diomede employs the same ruse with equal success. The implication that Abelard employed this tactic is thus humorous, since it strongly suggests a complete lack of scruple on his part. There is a further touch of humor in Eloisa's response as she describes it. Abelard seemed to her at first to be "of Angelic kind," she says, and "truths divine came mended" from his tongue, as though he were some supernatural messenger divinely sent. Any precept would move coming from "such lips" which "too soon" taught her that "it was no sin to love." Thus she no longer desired an angel when she loved a man. The implication of hypocrisy in this picture of Abelard's conduct is unmistakable. But Eloisa succumbs to it completely so that the joys of Heaven seem "dim and remote." Just exactly what would result

if Abelard should "pour out all the heart" in further letters is
dubious. Would there be heartfelt "truths divine" or heartfelt
expressions of hopeless and futile passion?

Like her predecessors, Pope's Eloisa scorns marriage:

> How oft, when pressed to marriage, have I said,
> Curse on all laws but those which love has made!
> Love, free as air, at sight of human ties,
> Spreads his light wings, and in a moment flies.

The last two lines here echo a passage in Chaucer's "Franklin's
Tale," whose obtuse Epicurean speaker argues that the "mastery"
of the husband in marriage, which is a sacramental reflection of
the relationship between Christ and the Church, is incompatible
with activities of the God of Love:

> Love will not be constrained by mastery.
> When mastery comes, the God of Love, anon,
> Beats his light wings, and farewell, he is gone!
> Love is a thing as any spirit free;
> Women, by nature, desire their liberty.

It is true that marriage is a sacrament whose function is to control
concupiscence, which is the kind of love inspired by Cupid. But
to argue that marriage is an evil because it does this is to make the
joys of Heaven "dim and remote" indeed. Eloisa's easy submission
to obvious hypocrisy and her clear alliance with those ladies who
follow Eve in their desire for "liberty" were not presented by
Pope to win any sentimental sympathy for her; on the contrary,
Pope's treatment of his protagonist is not only objective but, to
use a term current in his day, "witty."

Eloisa states further, as her predecessors had done before her,
that in her attachment to Abelard she was not seeking wealth,
fame, or honor, but love alone. Pope makes her add, however, that
any other course would have incurred the wrath of Cupid:

> The jealous god, when we profane his fires,
> Those restless passions in revenge inspires,
> And bids them make mistaken mortals groan,
> Who seek in love for ought but love alone.

[191]

It is obvious that Eloisa is now suffering, like Sappho and the other ladies of the *Heroides*, exactly for the reason that she concentrated on love. Blind and winged Cupid had, in the early eighteenth century, no reputation for dependability. Rather was he known for inconstancy and levity, so that the above lines are even at first glance ironic. The irony is intensified, however, if we remember that Boethius insisted that concentration on one "false good," like pleasure, leads first to the loss of all the rest and finally to the one singled out. In his *Epistle to a Lady* published in 1735 Pope made the following observation:

> In men, we various ruling passions find,
> In women, two almost divide the kind;
> Those, only fixed, they first or last obey,
> The love of pleasure, and the love of sway.

Eloisa's concentration on the delights of Cupid and her disdain of marriage make her a good illustration of both of these characteristic feminine weaknesses.

Following Bussy's modification of the original, in the version of Hughes, Eloisa affirms that she would rather be mistress of the man she loves than Caesar's empress, and she envisions a state of bliss in which lovers are concerned with nothing but their mutual satisfactions:

> Oh happy state! when souls each other draw,
> When love is liberty, and nature, law:
> All then is full, possessing and possessed,
> No craving void left aching in the breast.
> Even thought meets thought ere from the lips it part,
> And each warm wish springs mutual from the heart.
> This sure is bliss, if bliss on earth there be,
> And once the lot of Abelard and me.

These lines have a peculiar appeal to the modern mind that they lacked altogether in Pope's time. We have experienced Words-worth's Lucy, or at least her analogues, to whom "nature was both law and impulse," and have come to think that anything "natural" is commendable. But "nature" in this passage is a fallen

nature that must be controlled by reason. The situation described
is inherently ephemeral, a mere dream that cannot be maintained
in the exigencies of living. It may have been "once" the lot of
Pope's Eloisa; it was "once" the lot of Ovid's Sappho. To expect
to maintain it is sheer foolishness, especially if one agreed with
Pope's assertion that "virtue is our only bliss below."

In describing the manner in which Eloisa took the veil, Pope
regains something of the impression of vain defiance that Abelard
conveys in his *History*:

> As with cold lips I kissed the sacred veil,
> The shrines all trembled, and the lamps grew pale:
> Heaven scarce believed the conquest it surveyed,
> And saints with wonder heard the vows I made.

Her eyes, Eloisa says, were not fixed on the Cross, but on Abelard.
The memory of her passion renews it, and leads to one of the
most striking passages in the poem. The love of Eloisa is very
obviously a kind of idolatrous physical passion altogether free of
sentiment:

> Come with thy looks, thy words, relieve my woe;
> Those still at least are left thee to bestow.
> Still on that breast enamored let me lie,
> Still drink delicious poison from thy eye,
> Pant on thy lip, and to thy heart be pressed.
> Give all thou canst—and let me dream the rest.

A clearer invitation to self-frustration would be difficult to imagine.
As we learn later, Eloisa does indeed "dream the rest," like
Sappho before her, but to no very good effect. The lines emphasize
the inevitable frustration of those who pursue "the jealous god"
in search of pleasure to the exclusion of everything else.

But Eloisa shifts at once to a plea for guidance of another kind:

> Ah no! instruct me other joys to prize,
> With other beauties charm my partial eyes,
> Full in my view set the bright abode,
> And make my soul quit Abelard for God.

Her desperate swirl from a desire for physical satisfaction to a desire for grace, which is repeated in various ways in the remainder of the poem, is sometimes thought of as an alternation of "opposites." But this is a modern simplification that would turn Pope into a Manichaean. For him an acceptance of misfortune combined with a desire for grace was reasonable. Lapses from reason did not constitute an "opposite," but a deprivation of a good. To put this in another way, Eloisa's basic desire is intense. It shifts by shifting its end, not its nature, and the shifts so made are not lateral oscillations between opposites but spirals downward on the chain of being followed by upward swirls when reason begins to recover control. Since Eloisa is an "Ovidian" lady in this poem, we may expect her to descend finally and hopelessly to the depths. The recovery we have just witnessed will not last.

Up to this point we have been largely concerned with memories, with the past. From this point forward Eloisa concentrates on the present and on a still more gloomy future. She now pleads for Abelard to return to the Paraclete, first on the ground that his "flock" deserves his care. The nunnery was, after all, his own foundation:

> You raised these hallowed walls; the desert smiled,
> And Paradise was opened in the wild.

Cloisters, which were built around central gardens, were conventionally called "Paradises," or walled gardens, with the implication that one might there return to Paradise in contemplation. But Eloisa has no inclination to make this Paradise in the wilderness a Paradise for herself; like Sappho's grove, it has become a gloomy place without its lord:

> In these lone walls (their day's eternal bound)
> These moss-grown domes with spiry turrets crowned,
> Where awful arches make a noon-day night,
> And the dim windows shed a solemn light,
> Thy eyes diffused a reconciling ray,
> And dreams of glory brightened all the day.
> But now no face divine contentment wears,
> 'Tis all blank sadness or continual tears.

By implication, the nuns all share this gloomy view of the situation. But Eloisa admits her stratagem at once. She has no real
interest in the nuns; she simply wants Abelard to return, although
she is not quite sure just what aspect of her lover she needs most:

> See how the force of others' prayers I try,
> Oh pious fraud of amorous charity!
> But why should I on others' prayers depend?
> Come thou, my father, brother, husband, friend!

The idea of scenery transformed by passion in Ovid's "Sappho
to Phaon" evidently appealed strongly to Pope's imagination, for
he allows Eloisa to elaborate it in one of the finest descriptive
passages in the literature of the time. In Rococo painting there
were certain iconographic conventions associated with the "Venerian" landscape: streams and lakes indicated the watery instability
of the goddess, grottos and caves or dark groves suggested places
of privacy for her pursuits, grassy lawns invited amorous repose,
and flowers marked the bright but fragile beauties of her gifts.
Eloisa conjures up a remarkable landscape of this kind, blighted
by the goddess of meditation, Melancholy, before whose thoughtfulness the illusions of eternal delight darken into a kind of nightmare:

> The darksome pines that o'er yond rocks reclined
> Wave high, and murmur to the hollow wind,
> The wandering streams that shine between the hills,
> The grots that echo to the tinkling rills,
> The dying gales that pant upon the trees,
> The lakes that quiver in the curling breeze—
> No more these scenes my meditation aid,
> Or lull to rest the visionary maid.
> But o'er the twilight groves and dusky caves,
> Black Melancholy sits, and round her throws
> A death-like silence, and a dread repose.
> Her gloomy presence saddens every scene,
> Shades every flower, and darkens every green,
> Deepens the murmur of the falling floods,
> And breathes a browner horror on the woods.

These lines offer a picture in little of Eloisa's love. At first meditation was aided by the pleasant scene, but when passion clouded
meditation, the Venerian qualities returned to the landscape, and
meditation became a blight on the dreams it inspired. Death casts
a shadow over Arcadia that cannot be rationalized away. When
the nymphs and satyrs begin to play in the grove, the tomb that
stands there becomes more ominous.

The thought that she must remain in this melancholy scene,
made gloomy by the futility of her desires, leads to further thoughts
of death. Her cold dust may mix with Abelard's without sin, but
also without any joyful satisfaction. She seeks to pray, but cannot
do so, for she cannot be truly penitent:

> I ought to grieve, but cannot what I ought.
> I mourn the lover, not lament the fault.
> I view my crime, but kindle at the view,
> Repent old pleasures, and solicit new.
> Now turned to heaven, I weep my past offense,
> Now think of thee, and curse my innocence.

It is important to notice here that "innocence" represents an in-
ability to perform the amorous acts about which she dreams, and
that its essential meaning is the old one: freedom from sin. As we
shall see, "innocence" underwent a drastic transformation in the
later history of the legend, when love like that of Eloisa, enhanced
by sentiment, became a virtue made innocent by its sincerity. Here
she wishes to be penitent, but cannot separate contrition from the
sorrow and confusion of her frustration.

She again asks Abelard to come to her, this time to help her to
forget him, a patently futile enterprise under the circumstances:

> Oh come! Oh teach me nature to subdue,
> Renounce my love, my life, my self—and you.
> Fill my fond heart with God alone, for he
> Alone can rival, can succeed to thee.

The unblushing idolatry here displayed would have been far more
impressive to Pope's audience than it is to us. Meanwhile, there
is no possibility at all that the hypocritical Abelard described for

us in the poem would have had any success in turning the passion of Heloise toward God. Here again "nature" is fallen nature, prone to sensuality and uncontrolled passion. As a representation of such nature, or of its "idea," Eloisa has almost no characteristics to set her off as a distinct individual. But nature, like innocence, was a concept that was soon to be transformed. For the attitude that man is naturally good, corrupted by external pressures from outmoded custom or social injustice, swept across later eighteenth-century Europe, stimulated by the most advanced thinkers, and changed the character of Heloise, among other things, completely.

Meanwhile, Pope retained a respect for the aims of the cloistered life. Eloisa contrasts her state with that of the "blameless vestal" whose "spotless mind" enables her to enjoy religious contemplation. The "spotless mind" implies innocence, for to be innocent according to the Scriptures as Pope knew them was to be "without spot," or without the stain of sin, like the maiden in the Middle English poem *Pearl*. To Eloisa all joys are passionate, with the result that her vestal is a little reminiscent of Bernini's *St. Theresa*. But the ecstatic experience suggested in the closing lines was not an uncommon feature in the literature of devotion itself:

> How happy is the blameless vestal's lot!
> The world forgetting, by the world forgot!
> Eternal sunshine of the spotless mind!
> Each prayer accepted, and each wish resigned,
> Labor and rest, that equal periods keep,
> Obedient slumbers that can wake and weep,
> Desires composed, affections ever even,
> Tears that delight, and sighs that waft to Heaven,
> Grace shines around her with serenest beams,
> And whispering Angels prompt her golden dreams.
> For her the unfading rose of Eden blooms,
> And wings of Seraphs shed divine perfumes.
> For her the Spouse prepares the bridal ring,
> For her white virgins Hymenaeals sing;
> To sounds of heavenly harps she dies away,
> And melts in visions of eternal day.

[197]

The dreams of Eloisa as she goes on to describe them are very different indeed, inspired by Demons rather than by Angels, and closing in a nightmare that leads to an awakening to self-inflicted grief little better than the nightmare itself. In this passage the influence of Sappho's dream is vividly apparent, and memories of it would have strongly suggested to the reader an unhappy fate soon to come:

> Far other dreams my erring soul employ,
> Far other raptures, of unholy joy.
> When at the close of each sad, sorrowing day,
> Fancy restores what vengeance snatched away,
> Then conscience sleeps, and leaving nature free,
> All my loose soul unbounded springs to thee.
> O curst, dear horrors of all-conscious night!
> How glowing guilt exalts the keen delight!
> Provoking Daemons all restraint remove,
> And stir within me every source of love.
> I hear thee, view thee, gaze o'er all thy charms,
> And round thy phantom glue my clasping arms.
> I wake—no more I hear, no more I view,
> The phantom flies me, as unkind as you.
> I call aloud; it hears not what I say.
> I stretch my empty arms; it glides away.
> To dream once more I close my willing eyes—
> Ye soft illusions, dear deceits, arise!
> Alas no more!—methinks we wandering go
> Through dreary wastes, and weep each other's woe,
> Where round some mouldering tower pale ivy creeps,
> And low-brow'd rocks hang nodding o'er the deeps.
> Sudden you mount! you beckon from the skies;
> Clouds interpose, waves roar, and winds arise.
> I shriek, start up, the same sad prospect find,
> And wake to all the griefs I left behind.

The dreary wastes, mouldering tower, and nodding rocks are not Romantic, but are the visionary equivalent of the wasteland of passion. Abelard's ascension beyond the turbulence of the scene below, as if through the clouds of a ceiling in a Rococo church, does not enable Eloisa to follow him, or even to wish to do so. Abelard as Pope describes him was hardly capable of much inspiration in this direction.

Eloisa contrasts the "long, dead calm" of Abelard's life with her own torment. Her flames are hopeless, her joys "cut from the root" by Abelard's castration. Nevertheless, the "dear ideas" of their joys rise not only "in the grove" but before the altar:

> Thy image steals between my God and me.

In a confused vortex of hopeless passion she urges her lover to snatch her away from her incipient penitence, a gesture that, in view of his condition, would have been singularly empty:

> While prostrate here in humble grief I lie,
> Kind, virtuous drops just gathering in my eye,
> While praying, trembling, in the dust I roll,
> And dawning grace is opening on my soul,
> Come, if thou darest, all charming as thou art!
> Oppose thyself to Heaven, dispute my heart.
> Come, with one glance of those deluding eyes,
> Blot out each bright idea of the skies.
> Take back that grace, those sorrows, and those tears,
> Take back my fruitless penitence and prayers,
> Snatch me, just mounting, from the blest abode,
> Assist the Fiends that tear me from my God!

But she retracts this plea at once, with a desperate demand that Abelard fly from her "far as Pole from Pole" so that she may find "grace serene" and "oblivion of low-thoughted care." Both appeals are passionate; neither is founded on reason. Hence both are futile.

The voice of one dead, an echo of the Naiad who advises Sappho to throw herself down from "high Leucadia," seems to call Eloisa to an "eternal sleep," where love and superstitious fear are both forgotten and God is the judge who is merciful:

> See in her cell sad Eloisa spread,
> Propped on some tomb, a neighbor of the dead!
> In each low wind methinks a spirit calls,
> And more than echoes talk along the walls.

Here, as I watched the dying lamps around,
From yonder shrine I heard a hollow sound.
Come, sister, come! it said, or seemed to say,
Thy place is here; sad sister, come away!
Once like thyself I trembled, wept, and prayed,
Love's victim then, though now a sainted maid:
But all is calm in this eternal sleep;
Here grief forgets to groan, and love to weep;
Even superstition loses every fear:
For God, not man, absolves our frailties here.

Like Sappho, Eloisa is tempted by a vision of oblivion, the only solution to her dilemma that offers any hope at all.

But as she thinks of herself about to die, Abelard is far from forgotten. He appears first as a lover and then as a teacher, but as an object of passion in either guise:

I come, I come! prepare your roseate bowers,
Celestial palms, and ever-blooming flowers.
Thither, where sinners may have rest, I go,
Where flames refined in breasts Seraphic glow.
Thou, Abelard! the last sad office pay,
And smooth my passage to the realm of day.
See my lips tremble, and my eye-balls roll,
Suck my last breath, and catch my flying soul!
Ah no—in sacred vestments may'st thou stand,
The hallowed taper trembling in thy hand.
Present the Cross before my lifted eye;
Teach me at once, and learn of me to die.
Ah then, thy once loved Eloisa see!
It will be then no crime to gaze on me.
See from my cheek the transient roses fly!
See the last sparkle languish in my eye!
Till every motion, pulse, and breath be o'er,
And even my Abelard be loved no more.
O death all-eloquent! you only prove
What dust we dote on, when 'tis man we love.

Thus even at the end, at least as she envisages it, Eloisa cannot see Abelard clearly either as a guide or as a lover. The hypocrisy

evident in his transformation from an angel furbishing divine truth
to a lover providing physical joys has produced a confusion that
she is powerless to conquer. At least the lesson of death is now
unmistakable. When man is the object of passion, the charms that
inspire it must be replaced by something that has no charms at all.
But this fact does not lead Eloisa to meditate on its implications.
Hers is a vision of passion; her motions toward devotion are just
as passionate and unreasoning as are her motions toward love. She
shows no inclination at all to reflect the "Eternal Reason" that
guides "great Nature." Perhaps it would be well to emphasize
once more that she is not a person, but the representation of an
idea.

Thus when she thinks of Abelard's death, she can conceive of it
only as an erotic experience:

> In trance ecstatic may thy pangs be drowned,
> Bright clouds descend, and Angels watch thee round,
> From opening skies may streaming glories shine,
> And Saints embrace thee with a love like mine.

Needless to say, this is a perverse wish, for saints would hardly
be capable of the kind of love that Eloisa represents.

At the close, Eloisa imagines herself and Abelard united at last
in the grave, where lovers may come to say,

> Oh may we never love as these have loved!

And even the devoted, as they glance at the monument, may shed
"one human tear" and be forgiven. Perhaps, she thinks, some poet
will sing their loves:

> And sure if fate some future Bard shall join
> In sad similitude of griefs to mine,
> Condemned whole years in absence to deplore,
> And image charms he must behold no more—
> Such if there be, who loves so long, so well,
> Let him our sad, our tender story tell.
> The well-sung woes will sooth my pensive ghost;
> He best can paint 'em, who shall feel 'em most.

Thus the fairest literary reflection of the legend of Heloise closes with a flash of wit in the last line. The idea is Eloisa's, not Pope's, and we deceive ourselves if we think of it merely as an echo of a critical principle to be found in Aristotle or Quintilian without inquiring into its relevance in this poem specifically. Eloisa had not read the critics. Perhaps we should consider a subsidiary question first. Are we to sympathize with Eloisa? The answer, actually, is neither "yes" nor "no"; for we have asked the wrong question. Should we sympathize with Venus in a Rococo painting? Venus, however beautiful she may be, is not a woman but the representation of an idea. The idea, however, represents in turn something that most of us experience: the pleasure of sexual love. In the same way, Eloisa represents the idea of uncontrolled and hopeless passion, as well as the painful frustration that accompanies it. Eloisa does not say that her woes can be best represented or "painted" by those who sympathize with her, but by those who can "feel" them, or, in other words by those who have suffered, for a long time, from the kind of frustration she represents.

In a Providential world, as in the world of Ovid's *Heroides,* frustrated passion uncontrolled by reason is more than a little ridiculous, and Pope was the "bard" to whom his Eloisa clearly refers. In the last line of his poem, therefore, Eloisa is asking us, quite inadvertently, to smile a little at Alexander Pope. If Eloisa was unaware of this implication, Pope was certainly not; we may assume that he led the chorus of smiles. The matter, however, does not rest there, for most of Pope's readers were probably familiar with rationalizations made by themselves of a kind not unlike those represented in the initial hypocrisy of Abelard, not to mention the fact that they could also recognize in themselves, at least occasionally, ensuing woes and frustrations resembling those represented in Eloisa. The smile thus extended to engulf any reader who had wit enough to understand it. As Mr. Addison had written in *The Spectator* (1711, no. 227) in a preface to his later account of lovers' leaps, "Ridicule, perhaps, is a better expedient against love than sober advice." We should not doubt that Pope had learned this lesson well from Ovid.

By giving us a picture of the painful consequences of sensuality, Pope restored, at least by implication, the central issue of the original *Letters*, which involved basically the struggle of reason to control passion. As a letter to "Mr. Spectator" in 1712 (no. 408), often attributed to Pope puts it, "The strength of the passions will never be accepted as an excuse for complying with them; they were designed for subjection, and if a man suffers them to get the upper hand, he then betrays the liberty of his own soul." Eloisa clearly represents this betrayal. Since Pope did not know the original *Letters*, however, he could not have realized that reason was there made triumphant in the end, first in Abelard and then in Heloise under Abelard's guidance. Thus Pope's Abelard is not a very admirable character. His seduction of Eloisa is cynical and hypocritical, and he shows no inclination to bring his former wife to her senses. In fact, if Pope had allowed him to do so, he would have destroyed the meaning of his poem.

The general pattern established by Pope, which involved a more or less unattractive Abelard and an unrepentant Heloise, furnished the outline for the later legend, at least until this century, when, through the magic of expressionism, both lovers were made attrac-tive once more. But the intellectual content that Pope attached to his pattern disappeared completely. The publication in 1718 of a new edition of the Latin letters, actually a reprint of the edition of 1616 disguised slightly with a false claim to reliance on a newly discovered manuscript, had no effect on the legend. Pope's poem, however, achieved considerable popularity, and in later years it was customarily reprinted in editions of Hughes, which continued to be numerous well into the nineteenth century. It has been said, for example, that there were at least seventeen editions between 1800 and 1824. The passion of Hughes and the wit of Pope came down to us, so to speak, hand in hand. But with the rise of senti-ment and revolutionary ardor in Europe, wit was soon forgotten or misunderstood to make way for more serious and "sincere" forms of emotionalism. Both the false aristocratic airs of the lovers in Hughes and the genuine aristocratic wit of Pope disappeared in a burst of sentiment that turned Heloise into an innocent victim of convention and Pope's poem into a harbinger of Romanticism.

CHAPTER XII

The Saint of Love

The mid-eighteenth century marked the really decisive turning-point in the fortunes of Heloise, and this turning-point is merely one further, although very minor, indicator of a profound change that took place in European culture generally. In an economic sense, the change is obvious. The "old regime" of economic and social organization based ultimately on the structure of the patriarchal family was gradually but decisively giving way to a new industrial society. Europe began to experience a sustained economic growth, and, concomitant with it, a growth in population sufficiently marked to be characterized by modern economic historians as a "demographic" or "vital" revolution. The potentiality of the new economy for improving the standard of living, which rose fairly steadily between the 1730s and the 1760s, produced a new "rationalism," a firm belief that if reason and ingenuity could produce technological advances, they could also produce social and cultural advances on a large scale. But industry produced a new class, a rootless proletariat cut off from the cultural traditions of the past, which it could not understand, and desperately seeking to establish cultural values of its own. The new industrial employers were not much better off in this respect themselves. A side effect of the new industry, especially during the early nineteenth century, was the growth of mass poverty in the cities. All this afforded a profound stimulus to a new emotionalism in human relationships and, at the same time, a new rationalism in political theory. The old hierarchies, it was felt, should be attacked directly and rational means discovered for reorganizing society. The theoreticians of the French Revolution are in a sense the ancestors of the rationalism of the Great Exhibitions of the nineteenth and twentieth centuries. Reason promised the liberation of mankind, available in the near future, as soon, that is, as social and political ideas caught up with technology. The attitude is still current.

Oddly, but quite logically, the new rationalism was accompanied by an increasing emphasis on sentiment and emotion. The sentiment of the late eighteenth century developed into the passion of Romanticism, a passion now regarded as a good in itself and the wellspring of art. Romanticism led to intense sentimentality on the one hand, and to the merciless and disillusioned exposés of realism on the other. Both merged in the more recent extravagances of expressionism. The inner hierarchy in which wisdom, or knowledge of things human and divine, dominated the passions disappeared concomitantly with the old social hierarchies. One consequence of these developments was the loss of any real faith in, or even understanding of, the Providential Order. In comparing Dr. Johnson's *Rasselas* with Voltaire's *Candide,* Boswell observed in 1759 that "Voltaire . . . meant only by a wanton profaneness to obtain a sportive victory over religion, and to discredit the belief in a superintending Providence; Johnson meant, by showing the unsatisfactory nature of things temporal, to direct the hopes of man to things eternal." *Rasselas* is thus a work of consolation in the older manner, but the voice of Voltaire was more powerful, and men increasingly sought solace in the rational manipulation of "things temporal." But if the Providential Order began to disappear, men also turned to each other for satisfaction. A concern for temporal life as the highest good produced the beginnings of sentimental humanitarianism, the great religion of the nineteenth and twentieth centuries. With the loss of small, familial groups as working units and the growth of "masses" for the first time, men, as individuals, grew increasingly lonely and uncertain of their rôles, so that loneliness became one of the grand themes of modern art and letters. Religious experience, increasingly emotional even in Christianity itself, tended more and more to become "meaningful contact" with other human beings, the word for which most commonly was *love*. When in the nineteenth century Matthew Arnold found faith receding and the world in chaos, he could only picture his spokesman turning to his beloved to say, "Let us be true to one another."

The beginnings of this cultural change are evident in one of the most popular poems written in France during the latter half of the eighteenth century. It was an adaptation of Pope's *Eloisa*, first published in 1758. The author was a relatively obscure poet, no longer much read, one Colardeau. But his poem made a profound impression on his contemporaries, won him an election to the French Academy, and radically transformed the character of Heloise. It opens with a reference to "innocence," which here begins to take on a new meaning, for we are convinced in the end that Heloise was innocent too, despite her differences from her less passionate sisters. We see her contemplating Abelard's *History*:

> In these places inhabited by simple innocence,
> Where there reigns, with peace, an eternal silence,
> Where hearts, enslaved by severe laws,
> Are virtuous by duty as well as by choice,
> What frightful tempest, fatal to my rest,
> Arises in the senses of a feeble vestal?

The "enslavement" of hearts by severe laws is an obvious and overt protest against the restrictions of the contemplative life, a protest made doubly incisive because "hearts" rather than persons are enslaved. Heloise now expresses her passion in broken exclamations, straight from her own still unfettered heart. We can almost hear her voice in breathless decrescendo:

> O Love, cruel love, are you reborn in my heart?
> Alas! I was deceiving myself. I love. I burn still.
> O dear fatal name . . . Abelard . . . I adore you.

[207]

The spirit of Ovid, who regarded passionate love with amused detachment, has here given way to a much more serious-minded attitude that makes love a basic human freedom. Pope's "relentless walls," made oppressive by Eloisa's unreasoning passion, here become oppressive in fact, a scene of human destruction, which is "unreasoning" in an entirely new way:

> Emprisonments, where virtue, a voluntary victim,
> Sighs, and repents though free of crime,
> Where man, the imprudent destroyer of his being,
> Casts nothing toward Heaven but cries of pain;
> Inanimate marbles, and you cold relics,
> That we adorn with flowers, honored by our hymns—
> When I adore Abelard, when he is my spouse,
> Why am I not insensible and cold like you?

This is, to say the least, a curious attitude to adopt in telling a tale originally designed to encourage the renunciation undertaken by nuns. Unlike Pope's statues, Colardeau's "marbles" refuse to weep, thus eliminating the Ovidian irony from the passage. This scene is "actually" cold and forbidding. We can imagine Heloise, who has here become a person rather than a representation of anything, withering like the flowers on the cold stone as she imprudently destroys herself.

Pope's Eloisa thinks of her lover's conversion in four regretful lines:

> Now warm in love, now withering in thy bloom,
> Lost in the convent's solitary gloom!
> There stern religion quenched th'unwilling flame,
> There died the best of passions, Love and Fame.

Pope's attitude toward fame was probably not very different from that of the converted Abelard; at least he knew, having composed a poem based on Chaucer's *House of Fame,* that fame could be closely allied with Fortune and was often the object of vanity. But Colardeau took fame very seriously. He elaborates Pope's lines at some length to the further detriment of religion, conjuring up first a picture of Abelard like some oddly admirable Mars prostrated before Venus, his fame indicated by a myrtle crown:

THE SAINT OF LOVE

Now I seem to see you crowned with myrtle,
Happy and satisfied, prostrate at my feet;
Now you are in desert places, grim and solitary,
Your forehead covered with ashes, your body in a hair shirt,
Withered in your flower, pale and disfigured,
In the shadow of the altars, ignored in the cloister.
It is there that religion, jealous of their happiness,
The ties that bound them having been severed,
Wishes Abelard and his faithful spouse
To live indifferent, each forgetful of the other.
There, detesting and bewailing their victory,
They trample underfoot both love and fame!

If love and fame are accepted as true values, as they are here, we can see that the plight of the lovers begins to take on aspects of that most revered of modern art forms: tragedy.

It is not surprising that Heloise's complaint about marriage, originally little more than a joke, becomes in Colardeau's version of the story a revolutionary outcry against social and political bondage. The enemy is no longer passion, which is now natural and just, but the new tyrant Convention, and the victim is human sentiment, stronger and more genuine than anything artificially and externally applied:

You know this: When your spirit chained to mine
Pressed me to bind the hymenaeal knots,
I said to you, "Dear lover, alas! What do you demand?
Love is not a crime; it is a virtue.
Why then enslave it in tyrannic laws?
Why make it captive in bonds of politics?
Love is no slave, and pure sentiment
In human hearts is born free and independent.

The French author had not read Chaucer, and could not have recognized the irony of "Love is a thing as any spirit free," nor that of the echo of this idea in Pope. His readers probably responded with warm enthusiasm to this defense of the freedom of human love, which is the essence of the fundamental freedom of the human heart, an ideal which few people today would dare to question publicly.

The rather startling passage in which Pope's Eloisa asks Abe-lard to come to her and "do all he can" allowing her to "dream the rest" becomes much more convincing in the French version, which brings the action into sharper focus so that we can almost see it as Heloise "pants" before our very eyes:

Let me recline on your amorous breast,
Swoon on your mouth and breathe our fires.
What moments! Abelard! Do you feel them? What joy!
O sweet voluptuousness . . . pleasures . . . where I drown myself!
Fold me in your arms! Press me to your heart!
We deceive ourselves together, but what sweet error!
I no longer remember your fatal destiny.
Cover me with kisses . . . I shall dream the rest.

This passage is much more "sensual" than the original largely be-cause it is reinforced by a sense of sentimental rightness. There is evident in it an essential element present to a greater or lesser extent in "progressive" political, social, moral, and psychological theories from Colardeau's day to this: the human right to self-gratification. It may appear in fairly sophisticated forms, with a certain intellectual appeal, or it may be expressed crudely in rather childish demands for self-indulgence. But it had a great deal to do with the popularity of the legend of Heloise as Colardeau's version of it became more widely known.

Colardeau's lack of sympathy for the religious life, and for traditional Christian ideals generally, appears very clearly in his treatment of Pope's "blameless vestal," who is transformed from a single figure into the listless sisters of Heloise as a group:

Dear sisters, innocent companions of my chains,
Beneath these holy portals, mourning doves,
You, who know only those feeble virtues
Granted by religion . . . which I have no more,
You, who in the languors of a monastic spirit
Are ignorant of the tyrannic sway of love,
You, after all, having only God for a lover,
Love by custom and not through sentiment—
How your hearts are happy because they are insensible!

Such nuns hardly enjoy "the eternal sunshine of a spotless mind," find rapture in "sounds of heavenly harps," or "melt in visions of eternal day." They lack any feeling at all. In general, the absence of any sense of positive religious value in traditional terms gives Colardeau's work a shape very unlike that of his original. Pope's Eloisa reminds us of the twisting curves of a statue by Egid Quirin Asam, fixed in the frozen swirls of her dilemma. Colardeau's heroine, with her seductive combination of sensuality and sentiment, resembles more a portrait by Greuze, if we may compare, for the purpose of calling attention to stylistic similarity, the work of a minor poet with that of a great painter. The French lady is much more "human" than her model.

Since his Heloise is oriented, so to speak, in only one direction, Colardeau was faced with the problem of how to bring his poem to a conclusion. The final vision of Pope's Eloisa, in which she imagines herself attended by an ambiguous Abelard in her dying moments, now kissing her and now holding up the Cross, with its dismal lesson—"What dust we dote on when 'tis man we love"— would hardly suit either his new heroine or his new audience. He solved the difficulty by elaborating the voice from the tomb and making it carry conviction. This new and unwitting descendant of Ovid's Naiad urges Heloise to abandon her "credulous piety" and the fears it brings. Pope's fearful "superstition" becomes ordinary Christian belief, and the spirit that "seemed" to say something in Pope here becomes authoritative:

One night . . . I was sleeping beside a tomb.
The funerary torch, obscure and black flambeau,
Put forth at times a dying and somber flame.
Struggling, it fluttered out and vanished in the dark.
Long-drawn cries from a grave brought the voice I heard.
"Cease, dear sister, cease!" it said to me,
"My ashes await yours, my grave calls to you.
Here is the abode of that repose which escapes you:
I have lived, like you, a victim of love;
I have burned, like you, with a hopeless fire.
It is in the depths of an eternal silence

[211]

That I have found the end of my fearful torments.
Here one knows no more the sighs of lovers;
Here ends love, its sighs, its complaints,
And credulous piety here loses its fears.
Die, but without fearing death or the future.
That God shown us armed for our punishment,
Far from lighting vengeful fires for us here,
Deadens our sorrow and pardons our weakness."

The Good Lord Himself has here grown a little sentimental; He
had to do so by popular demand, so that the world's Heloises could
pursue their dreams of bliss and their tender sentiments in freedom
and innocence. What had been sheer lust in the original letters and
in Pope is here transformed by sentiment into an expression of
human freedom. As sentiment grew into sentimentality toward
the close of the next century, lust was almost extinguished in its
sweetness, to the great profit of Freud, who was to shock the world
by pointing out that it was still there. Nevertheless, the appeal of
Colardeau's heroine is unmistakable. Her sweet sensuality, which
did not disappear altogether as an ideal until recently, has a
nostalgic attractiveness.

Colardeau's poem ends on a tragic note as Heloise welcomes in
imagination a last visit from an unambiguous Abelard and death
in his arms:

O, my God, if this is true, if such is your bounty,
Hasten the instant of my tranquility.
O Luminous Grace! O Profound Wisdom!
Virtue, Daughter of Heaven! Holy forgetfulness of the world!
You, who promise me eternal pleasures,
Lift Heloise in the midst of the immortals!
I die . . . Abelard, come close my eyelids;
I shall lose my love as I lose my life.
In these last moments, come at least to gather
Both my last kiss and my last sigh.
And you, when death has withered your charms,
Those seducing charms, the source of my tears,
When the death of your days has extinguished this torch,
When one shall unite us at last in the night of the grave,

May the hand of Love there write our story.
And may the traveller, weeping in our memory,
Say, "They loved too well; they were unfortunate.
Let us lament o'er their tomb and love not as they did."

The ingredients of modern tragedy are before us: an essentially innocent protagonist like ourselves has been crushed by an inscrutable world whose injustices are reinforced by convention. This tragic pattern was made possible by the disappearance of the Providential Order. Shakespeare's tragic protagonists, whatever the critics may say about them, are never innocent. Through some weakness they subject themselves to Fortune and suffer the Providential consequences. But the scholars of the eighteenth and nineteenth centuries, not to mention our own, busied themselves to obscure this old pattern in the plays. A great deal of our earlier literature, in fact, has undergone transformations exactly analogous with the transformations of Heloise. The Abbess of the Paraclete had one more step to take. She became a saint, not a saint of the Church, but a saint of the new religion of love.

Colardeau revised his version of Pope's *Eloisa* in 1772, and in 1776 he was named to the French Academy. His death, four days before his formal reception, served to enhance the popularity of his poem, which came to be included prominently in anthologies of materials concerning the lovers—other imitations of Pope, of which there were several, "answers" attributed to Abelard, the letters of Bussy, "historical" accounts of the lovers, and so on. Just as Pope's poem continued to be published in editions of Hughes, Colardeau's became a center of attraction in French volumes devoted to the lovers. The diffident if not antagonistic attitude toward organized religion in Hughes and Colardeau suited both the revolutionary tastes of the times and the growing interest in sentimental humanitarianism. As the reputation of Heloise grew, that of Abelard declined. Diderot's reaction to Abelard had been, "How that man was loved!" Rousseau's Saint-Preux writes to Julie that Heloise "had a heart for love," but that Abelard was "a wretch worthy of his fate." In more scholarly circles, however, Abelard gained a reputation as a revolutionary in philosophy, just as Heloise was a revolutionary in love, and we are still urged at times to look on both the philosopher with his rationalism and the abbess with her sentiment as heralds of our own age. Sentimentality and material-istic rationalism are "opposites" only as the two ends of a see-saw are "opposites." Both ends belong to something that rests on a single fulcrum.

The Romantics did not produce any famous literary tributes to Heloise. Pope's *Eloisa* could easily be read "Romantically," even without Colardeau's textual alterations, by those so inclined, and Pope was a formidable rival. Colardeau's poem could much more easily be carried a step beyond its language by the Romantic imagination, which in any event tended to make a cult of love. Most Romantics, moreover, were preoccupied with their own passions. What they failed to do in verse they more than com-pensated for in direct action, for the grave of Heloise became a pilgrimage shrine to which worshippers came from all parts of Europe. The story of how this came about can be related very briefly.

The church containing the remains of Abelard and Heloise was destroyed by the English in 1357, and when it was rebuilt in the next century, the bones of the founder and the first abbess were placed on either side of the choir. In 1621 the remains were re-moved once more to a crypt beneath the chapel behind the choir. There they rested until 1780, when the twelfth-century theologian and his abbess had become famous throughout the world. The bones were taken up once more and placed beneath an altar in the nun's chapel above which stood a statue of the Trinity, once thought to date from the time of Abelard himself. The black marble tomb bore an inscription especially provided by the Aca-démie des Inscriptions. A "Vie d'Abeilard et d'Héloise," published in 1780, informs us that "almost all foreigners who come to France, above all the English, consider it a duty to visit the Paraclete, where they contemplate with a tearful eye the sorrowful tomb of these fatal victims of love and vengeance." In deference to this custom, the entire convent was decorated with pictures of the lovers. Although the revolutionaries of 1792 made Heloise their own, as well they might, the Paraclete was sold in the general dissolution, and the bones of the lovers were carried with great ceremony to the Church of St. Laurent at Nogent, along with the statue of the Trinity. The latter was soon destroyed as a monument to superstition by the vandals of Reason, who somehow failed to ransack the tomb as well.

A young artist, Alexandre Lenoir, succeeded in establishing a "Museum of French Monuments" in Paris during the last years of the century. It contained a series of rooms devoted to sculpture collected from the religious houses of the country and an adjoining garden to serve as a graveyard containing the tombs of famous persons. After some negotiations, Lenoir obtained permission to transfer the bones of the lovers from Nogent to his garden in Paris. They were found in a lead case with a dividing partition down the middle. During some months after he obtained these remains, Lenoir left them unburied, taking the opportunity to distribute "relics," not of religion but of love, to various friends, some of whom had "sanctuaries" made to contain them. Meanwhile, it is said that Lenoir was careful to preserve a collection of small bones for himself. Bonaparte is said to have strewn some flowers over the bones of Heloise. In 1802 the remains, now in two containers, were placed in a sarcophagus in the garden, decorated with two sculptured figures, male and female, and surrounded by a little chapel, supposedly made up of materials from St. Denis and the Paraclete. The stone plinth bore the names of the lovers repeated with the Greek words for "forever united" inscribed between them.

For a few years Lenoir had the satisfaction of welcoming large numbers of pilgrims to his garden, but in 1817 his museum had to be abandoned, and the Peripatetic of Pallet, still ironically peripatetic, took, with his Heloise, his last journey till now. A hearse carried the remains to the Church of St.-Germain-des-Prés, where High Mass was celebrated over them, after which they were moved in solemn procession to the cemetery now called Père-Lachaise. The little chapel was rebuilt at the new site, and again pilgrims, now fired with the passions of the Romantic era, flocked to weep before the shrine. They became so numerous and so avid in their devotion that it was necessary to erect a small iron fence to protect the monument from the zeal of those who wished to take away mementos. The grave remained a popular place of worship and quiet lamentation for well over fifty years.

A prominent French historian described Heloise as "the Saint of Love," but the attitude of many of the pilgrims to the grave of the lovers is probably best expressed by Lamartine, who wrote an essay on the pair. He found Abelard lacking in courage, an idea not actually inconsistent with the Abelard of the *History of My Calamities,* who certainly had his amorous victim at a disadvantage. He also called Heloise, rather perceptively, "the Sappho of the twelfth century," although the Sappho in the mind of Lamartine was probably quite different from the Sappho of Ovid, Abelard, or Pope. At the grave of the lovers he discovered "a posthumous union of two hearts who transferred the conjugal tenderness of the senses to the soul, who spiritualized the most burning of sensual passions, and who made a holocaust, a martyrdom, and almost a saintliness of love." The idea that physical passion in its extremely intense forms becomes "spiritual" became a favorite notion of the nineteenth century. It still survives today in some classroom discussions of Shakespeare's *Romeo and Juliet.* With the disappearance of the Providential Order, sex acquired a mystique of its own; but the spiritual claims of sexual passion, like those of surrealistic and expressionistic art, do not herald the downfall of religion. They are symptoms of a new religion that is a natural outgrowth of materialistic rationalism. Actually, as compared with more recent proponents of this theme, Lamartine was rather restrained.

The grave at Père-Lachaise was still a popular shrine when Samuel Clemens recorded his experiences there in *Innocents Abroad* (1869). His attitude was skeptical and not much influenced by the more refined attitudes of his European contemporaries. The grave of Abelard and Heloise, he wrote, "has been more revered, more widely known, more written and sung about and wept over, for seven hundred years, than any other in Christendom, save only that of the Savior." Not being a lover himself, Clemens did not take the mourners there very seriously: "Go when you will, you find somebody snuffling over that tomb. Go when you will, you find it furnished with those bouquets and immortelles. Go when you will, you find a gravel-train from Marseilles arriving to supply the memento-cabbaging vandals whose affections have miscarried."

In order to better inform his readers, our author tells them the story of the love affair. The objections of Heloise to marriage are regarded with a sternly practical eye: "She refused the marriage at first; she said Fulbert would betray the secret to save her, and, besides, she did not wish to drag down a lover who was so gifted, so honored by the world, and who had such a splendid career before him. It was a noble, self-sacrificing love, and characteristic of the pure-minded Heloise, but it was not good sense." Clemens was fully aware that it was the attempt to conceal the marriage after it had taken place that precipitated the vengeance of Fulbert, here called, incidentally, George W. Fulbert. He regarded the castration as just, offering to shed some tears over the last resting-place of the perpetrators, if it could be found.

To the American humorist from Missouri the *Letters of Abelard and Heloise* simply illustrated the continuing villainy of Abelard. He tells us that Heloise entered a convent where she remained for twelve years. There "she happened one day to see a letter" written by Abelard: "She cried over it, and wrote him. He answered, addressing her as his 'sister in Christ.' They continued to correspond, she in the unweighed language of unwavering affection, he in the chilly phraseology of the polished rhetorician. She poured out her heart in passionate, disjointed sentences; he replied with finished essays divided deliberately into heads and subheads, premises and argument. She showered upon him the tenderest epithets that love could devise, he addressed her from the North Pole of his frozen heart as the 'Spouse of Christ!' The abandoned villain!" The cultural gap between nineteenth-century America and twelfth-century France could not be better displayed than it is here. Clemens naturally thought of Heloise in terms of the wholesome young American girls he had known, full of genuine sentiment and warm, practical affection. Abelard must have seemed to him a fair representation of the snobbish, hypocritical preacher, scheming, cold of heart, and full of pseudo-learning and false piety.

Surprisingly, Clemens includes an account of the contest with Bernard of Clairvaux: "Urged by kings and princes to meet the subtle St. Bernard in debate and crush him, he stood up in the presence of a royal and illustrious assemblage, and when his antagonist had finished he looked about him, and stammered a commencement; but his courage failed him, the cunning of his tongue was gone; with his speech unspoken, he trembled and sat down, a disgraced and vanquished champion." As a result of his defeat, "He died a nobody." Concluding his history, Clemens castigates the "nauseous sentimentality that would enshrine for our loving worship a dastardly seducer like Pierre Abelard," although he does not begrudge the tears shed for "the misused, faithful girl." For the practical American mentality of the time Heloise was not a "saint of love," as she was to many Europeans, but she was an excellent example of the innocent girl led astray. Her erotic inclinations are simply disregarded, perhaps beyond the real comprehension of the American mind of the eighteen-sixties, which cherished affectionate, practical, and cheerfully hard-working females who could manage large households efficiently and raise wholesome and enterprising children. The extent to which American women once succeeded in this rôle is astonishing, and the ideal persists today, although now that the economic and social justifications for it are disappearing, women are beginning to rebel against it.

The romantic Abelard did not die, however, in spite of the strictures raised against him; and the mystique of sex was reinforced in the earlier twentieth century by a widespread substitution of "aesthetic" for moral and other traditional values, and by a new and burgeoning cult of the "natural" and the "primitive." These tendencies became closely associated with social and political ideals emphasizing a "freedom" of the individual that implied his right to "fulfillment" or the enjoyment of his own peculiar personal satisfactions. The integrity and fundamental innocence of the "personality" served as basic assumptions in a society whose members found themselves increasingly suspicious of conventional forms of community activity and hence increasingly isolated. All of these trends are easily discernible in the various forms of expressionism that characterize the modern arts, in spite of the remarkable diversity of surface techniques that mark transient "styles." In an atmosphere of this kind Abelard's weaknesses in the traditional legend again lent themselves to sympathetic treatment, and the character of Heloise changed to meet the demands of the new ideals.

The beginnings of the new Abelard and Heloise are evident in George Moore's novel *Heloise and Abelard* (1921), a book that takes obvious liberties with the original story but that nevertheless implies an interpretation of the chief characters. Moore's Heloise is a free and innocent "pagan" spirit, nurtured on the classics, which are here regarded rather myopically as expressions of unspoiled and free humanity. She is, above all, an advocate of "reason." But "reason" here has nothing to do either with Abelard's logic or with that reason familiar to authors from Antiquity through the Rococo era whose function was to control the passions and hence prevent foolishness. Instead it seeks to justify the passions as a natural prerogative of humanity in its quest for beauty. Moore's Abelard, whose lectures at Paris attract the youthful Heloise because of their liberal attitudes, was a professional troubadour in his youth. His early associates among the poets, who are innocent and devoted pursuers of beauty and human liberty themselves, assist the lovers in their trials. The novel is full of sentimental touches, including nostalgic descriptions of nature, which affords a sympathetic background to the "natural" inclinations of the lovers. "Medieval" atmosphere is provided by "courts of love," imaginary adornments of medieval life fashionable among academic historians at the time the novel was written. Moore was quite obviously, however, writing a novel and not history. His troubadours do not much resemble troubadours as we know them in actual fact, and he once shows Abelard guised as a friar at a time when the fraternal orders had not yet been established.

Nevertheless, his contribution to the legend was genuine, since it did present a pair of lovers consistent with the sentimental aestheticism of his time.

A far more influential novel, *Peter Abelard* by Helen Waddell appeared in 1933. Moore's themes are here presented with greater conviction and effectiveness, not to mention some modifications in the direction of frankness, by an author who enjoyed a reputation as a medievalist and whose work could demand a high degree of credibility. The story opens after Abelard's return to Paris from Laon and concludes at the time of the establishment of his oratory near Nogent. The technique involves the development of a series of highly colorful and impressionistically conceived episodes, each with moments of poignant emotional intensity achieved by the suggestive manipulation of dialogue and atmospheric detail. This detail includes snatches of medieval song, a subject with which the author was thoroughly familiar, apt quotations from medieval texts, reminiscent flashes of pagan legend, and vivid descriptions of places and people. Alberic of Rheims, for example, appears as a thoroughly contemptible little man with appropriate physical characteristics.

Helen Waddell was capable of lending descriptions of nature and ordinary events the kind of intense emotional overtones familiar among the more successful works of the imagist poets, who were very popular in the early thirties. The concrete detail serves to enhance the reader's feeling for the characters. For example, we once observe Heloise, who has returned for a day at Argenteuil to meditate concerning Abelard's demand that she submit to him that evening, listening attentively, and with joy, to the sound of drops splashing in the deep waters of a well as a full bucket is drawn to the surface. She nostalgically recalls her delight in the same sound during her childhood at the nunnery. Again, in the closing episode of the book, we see Abelard comforting in his arms a dying rabbit whose screams he had heard when it was caught in a trap. Both the rescue of the rabbit, which nestles its head against Abelard's arm as it dies, and the subsequent meditations to the effect that pain among creatures is God's Cross, contribute to the reader's sympathy for the character. The appeal in both of these instances is that of sentimental humanitarianism, an ideal that pervades the book and underlies its emotional impact, but that is, at the same time, completely foreign to the twelfth century. The novel is thus actually no better as a guide to an understanding of the original characters than is the romance of Alluis, in spite of its attractive use of historical detail.

The more specific attitudes of Helen Waddell's characters are even more remote from the medieval world-view, and it is clear that her Heloise is a linear descendant of Colardeau's heroine, much more thoroughly sentimental, but at the same time liberated by Freudian teachings. Abelard's first real encounter with sexual intercourse occurs as he watches his servant Guibert copulating with a whore one night in the street below his window. Although he is repulsed by Guibert's lechery, it seems to him as he watches that the amorous couple momentarily enjoy "eternity," while he is left involved in "time." This impression is soon confirmed by a worldly-wise old Epicurean canon, Gilles de Vannes, who becomes the spiritual mentor of the lovers in the story. His wisdom transcends that of the saints and the schoolmen, since it is based on a profound human understanding. Even a whore can give a man "eternity," he assures Abelard, since her ability to bestow grace is not dependent on her merit. Later on, he explains to Heloise that the root of love is lust. But, he assures her, a rose is no less beautiful because of its root, and it flowers best when it is manured. In the same way, lust produces beautiful but transient flowers of love. When Heloise inquires concerning happiness, Gilles assures her that true happiness lies not in contentment but in ecstasy, and that marriage is a futile device to capture something that is by nature evanescent. Our lovers thus come to represent "free" human beings, who can find for a time "a heaven of body and spirit" in each other's arms, undeterred by what Abelard once calls "the insufferable patronage of the saints." Couched as it is in the delicately sensitive and gracefully wrought atmosphere of the novel, this doctrine had an enormous sentimental appeal. The book served several generations of students as a pleasant substitute for history, and it has even appeared in "scholarly" bibliographies of Abelard. As a matter of fact, it represents attitudes characteristic of the academic mentality in the years since its publication. Under the circumstances no one should find it strange that young people scorn what they regard as the hypocrisy of society, seeking "ecstasy" in various forms and cul-tivating what seems to them to be "natural" behavior. This is exactly the sort of thing they have been taught to do.

Scholarly works do not, strictly speaking, fall within the scope of this chapter, since they do not, or should not, form a part of the legend of Heloise. However, one such work, *Heloise et Abélard* by the distinguished medievalist Etienne Gilson (1938), has pro-moted the credibility of the general tenor of the legend in modern times because of its conclusions. Except when he is engaged in strictly philological analysis, Gilson's writing has some of the suggestive qualities of Helen Waddell's prose, so that it is not al-ways easy to summarize his arguments. The book opens, however, with a systematic attack on the conclusions of two other scholars, B. Schmeidler and Charlotte Charrier, who had maintained that the letters of Heloise as they appear in *The Letters of Abelard and Heloise* were all written by Abelard. Their conclusion was based on the apparent inconsistency between the opening of the first letter of Heloise and Abelard's statements about his visits to the Paraclete in the *History,* and on the further point that all the letters exhibit the same peculiarities of style. The details of Gilson's attack need not concern us, since the authenticity of the corre-spondence may be questioned on other grounds entirely. But Gilson did succeed in convincing many scholars that the letters are gen-uine so that they may be taken as sincere expressions of personal feeling. This attitude serves as an effective bar to the discernment of the thematic unity of the collection as a whole.

If the letters are regarded in this way, moreover, Heloise be-comes something of a mystery in her twelfth-century setting. Gilson finds a parallel between the "total" love of Heloise and the teach-ings of Cicero in his treatise *On Friendship.* But in view of the fact that Cicero insists that virtue is the only true basis for friendship and displays a strong distaste for Epicurean motivations of any kind, this parallel is hardly convincing. The love of Heloise is also, Gilson assures us, "pure," since her intention was good. In this connection he seeks to discover a reflection of a doctrine to the effect that sin is a matter of intent in Abelard's *Ethics,* a point we have discussed earlier in connection with the letters themselves. Finally, Gilson, who disregarded the thematic development of Heloise's attitude in her letters, casts doubt upon the genuineness of her conversion. Her phrase in her last letter, *"Domino specia-liter, sua singulariter,"* indicating that she belongs to God "especially," or in accordance with her profession as a nun, but to Abelard "individually," as she is a woman who was once his wife, leads Gilson to suspect that Heloise may be a nun only because of her love for Abelard. In other words, she was convinced by Abelard's wishes, but not by the doctrine in his letters. Actually, the phrase implies nothing more than is implied by Abelard's prayer at the conclusion of the preceding letter, asking that he and Heloise, who were once united sacramentally in the flesh, may be reunited in Heaven. This idea is repeated by Peter the Venerable, who was far from questioning the genuineness of Heloise's conversion. In other words, Gilson has left us with a correspondence that can be regarded as a "psychological" document, looking forward to the Renaissance with its emphasis on the individual, and an Heloise whom we are at liberty to make free and innocent, still a saint of love. There is a mystery here, but it is "history." Stylistically speaking, Gilson and Helen Waddell belong to the same milieu. The trappings of "scientific philology" offer no defense against the subtle powers of a prevailing style. On the contrary, they often serve merely to lend current stylistic attitudes greater superficial rationality and cogency.

Each age has made the lovers over in its own image, using Heloise especially as a vehicle for its ideals. Abelard may have abused Heloise in her youth, but she has been abused much more outrageously by history. Ironically, moreover, the worst abuses she has suffered have been thrust upon her since the rise of modern scientific history and popular education. Her career over the centuries may well lead us to wonder whether other historical and literary characters have not suffered the same fate, so that a great deal of humanistic education actually consists of little more than a projection of our own attitudes on the past, superstitiously fortified with pedantry. Perhaps it is actually fortunate, in a sense, that earlier literature and history are falling into neglect in academic curricula, to make way for more "relevant" subjects.

In these brief chapters we have touched only the high points of the legend. Since the days of Pope it has produced minor works of all kinds, serious, humorous, and scurrilous; but to examine all of them would require a substantial volume. The legend has been largely self-perpetuating, with only occasional and indecisive ref-erence to the original documents. Abelard's highest praise of Heloise has been forgotten: "God allowed such grace to fall over that sister of mine, who was over the other nuns, that bishops loved her like a daughter, abbots like a sister, and laymen like a mother; and all were astonished equally by her religion, prudence, and the incomparable gentleness of her patience." This assessment is sub-stantiated in the long letter written to Heloise by Peter the Venerable. The qualities of a good abbess, which are, in many ways, simply the qualities of a good woman, were much more enthusiastically admired in the twelfth century, when many people were genuinely concerned about the welfare of their souls, than they are today. We must admit that Abelard worked very hard to encourage them. On the other hand, if Heloise had not submitted to his amorous advances in the first place, she would very probably have become just another matron, somewhat more learned than her gossips, among the wives whose husbands met regularly to dis-cuss matters of commercial interest at the Palais de Hautefeuille, soon forgotten and lost to both history and legend.

As for Abelard, since he does all he can to show himself a rebellious worldling in his youth, we do not know much about the actual circumstances under which he seduced Heloise. He was unquestionably a somewhat headstrong and energetic man, who might well have become a worthy knight if his interests had led him toward Nantes rather than toward the schools of the east.

As matters stand, he neither deserves his reputation as a lover nor the calumny directed against him by Samuel Clemens. Meanwhile, the literary skill and intellectual discipline of the *Letters* have been completely overlooked. Abelard was not a great Latin stylist, but he had a flair for disciplined organization, humor, and that thoughtful indirection which is one of the most attractive features of the literary productions of his time. The play of the intellect, whether serious or humorous, never falters in his pages. Perhaps now the extravagances of sentiment, sentimentality, and romantic passion may begin to subside somewhat, and we can begin to appreciate Abelard and his Heloise for what they were in terms that they, and their contemporaries, could understand.

Bibliographical Note

The standard modern edition of Abelard's works is still that by Victor Cousin (1834, 1849, 1859). There are more recent editions of some individual works, among which the edition of the *Dialectic* by L. M. De Rijk (1956) is outstanding. The *Letters of Abelard and Heloise,* except for the final Rule for the Paraclete, have been edited with an introduction by J. T. Muckle in the journal *Mediaeval Studies* (1950, 1953, 1955), and the Rule, edited by T. P. McLaughlin, appeared in the same journal in 1956. A still more recent edition of Abelard's *History* has been prepared by J. Monfrin (second edition, 1962). The standard English translation of the letters is that by C. K. Scott Moncrieff (1926), although a more recent and scholarly translation of the *History,* or first letter, by J. T. Muckle (1954) is now available, and a new transla-tion of the entire collection has been announced.

Scholars have been troubled by the question of the authenticity of the *Letters* since the mid-nineteenth century. A careful and well-documented attack on the view that they are "real letters" appeared in Charlotte Charrier, *Héloïse dans l'histoire et dans la légende* (1933), a book that also presents a great deal of docu-mentary material concerning the Paraclete and a rapid but thor-ough survey of the legend of Heloise. The authenticity of the

[227]

correspondence was defended by Enid McLeod in her *Héloïse* (1938), and in a brilliant study by E. Gilson, *Héloïse et Abélard* (1938), available in an excellent English translation by L. K. Shook (1951).

We very much need a new account of Abelard's life and works. The standard book, J. G. Sikes, *Peter Abailard* (1932) has been outdated in various ways by more recent studies. Those interested in philosophy will find the sections on Abelard in Paul Vignaux, *Philosophy in the Middle Ages* (English translation, 1959), and David Knowles, *The Evolution of Medieval Thought* (1963), stimulating and suggestive. A much more advanced and technical discussion of the subject is provided in Jean Jolivet, *Arts du langage et théologie chez Abélard* (1969). The highly technical study by D. E. Luscombe, *The School of Peter Abelard* (1969) contains the best account available of the issues involved in the quarrel between Abelard and St. Bernard, as well as a great deal of useful material about Abelard's immediate influence. Abelard studies are still flourishing, and it may well be that many uncertainties concerning details of Abelard's career, the chronology of his works, and the significance of his specific teachings will soon be resolved.

Index

Medieval people are listed under their first names. Thus "Alberic of Rheims" appears under "Alberic" and not under "Rheims." At times medieval names are known to English readers in various forms—in Latin, in the original vernacular, or in Anglicized versions. I have tried to use the most common or obvious Anglicized forms, although at times other forms are commonplace and are hence used instead. For example, "Jean de Meun" is almost never called "John of Meun."

The saints are here placed together, so that, for example, Bernard of Clairvaux is listed under "St. Bernard," not under "Bernard."

INDEX